Language and Literacy Series

Dorothy S. Strickland and Celia Genishi, series editors

Beginning Reading and Writing
DOROTHY S. STRICKLAND and
LESLEY MANDEL MORROW, Editors

What Counts as Literacy: Challenging the School Standard
MARGARET GALLEGO and SANDRA HOLLINGSWORTH, Editors

Critical Encounters in High School English:
Teaching Literary Theory to Adolescents
DEBORAH APPLEMAN

Reading for Meaning:
Fostering Comprehension in the Middle Grades
BARBARA M. TAYLOR, MICHAEL F. GRAVES,
PAUL van den BROEK, Editors

Writing in the Real World:
Making the Transition from School to Work
ANNE BEAUFORT

Young Adult Literature and the New Literary Theories:
Developing Critical Readers in Middle School
ANNA O. SOTER

Literacy Matters: Writing and Reading the Social Self
ROBERT P. YAGELSKI

Building Family Literacy in an Urban Community
RUTH D. HANDEL

Children's Inquiry:
Using Language to Make Sense of the World
JUDITH WELLS LINDFORS

Engaged Reading:
Processes, Practices, and Policy Implications
JOHN T. GUTHRIE and DONNA E. ALVERMANN, Editors

Learning to Read: Beyond Phonics and Whole Language
G. BRIAN THOMPSON and TOM NICHOLSON, Editors

So Much to Say: Adolescents, Bilingualism, and ESL in the Secondary School
CHRISTIAN J. FALTIS and PAULA WOLFE, Editors

Close to Home: Oral and Literate Practices in a Transnational Mexicano Community
JUAN C. GUERRA

Authorizing Readers: Resistance and Respect in the Teaching of Literature
PETER J. RABINOWITZ and MICHAEL W. SMITH

On the Brink:
Negotiating Literature and Life with Adolescents
SUSAN HYNDS

Life at the Margins:
Literacy, Language, and Technology in Everyday Life
JULIET MERRIFIELD, MARY BETH BINGMAN,
DAVID HEMPHILL, and KATHLEEN P. BENNETT DeMARRAIS

One Child, Many Worlds:
Early Learning in Multicultural Communities
EVE GREGORY, Editor

Literacy for Life: Adult Learners, New Practices
HANNA ARLENE FINGERET and CASSANDRA DRENNON

Children's Literature and the Politics of Equality
PAT PINSENT

The Book Club Connection:
Literacy Learning and Classroom Talk
SUSAN I. MCMAHON and TAFFY E. RAPHAEL, Editors,
with VIRGINIA J. GOATLEY and LAURA S. PARDO

Until We Are Strong Together:
Women Writers in the Tenderloin
CAROLINE E. HELLER

Restructuring Schools for Linguistic Diversity:
Linking Decision Making to Effective Programs
OFELIA B. MIRAMONTES, ADEL NADEAU,
and NANCY L. COMMINS

Writing Superheroes: Contemporary Childhood, Popular Culture, and Classroom Literacy
ANNE HAAS DYSON

Opening Dialogue: Understanding the Dynamics of Language andLearning in the English Classroom
MARTIN NYSTRAND with ADAM GAMORAN, ROBERT KACHUR,
and CATHERINE PRENDERGAST

Reading Across Cultures:
Teaching Literature in a Diverse Society
THERESA ROGERS and ANNA O. SOTER, Editors

"You Gotta Be the Book": Teaching Engaged and Reflective Reading with Adolescents
JEFFREY D. WILHELM

Just Girls: Hidden Literacies and Life in Junior High
MARGARET J. FINDERS

The First R: Every Child's Right to Read
MICHAEL F. GRAVES, PAUL van den BROEK, and
BARBARA M. TAYLOR, Editors

Exploring Blue Highways: Literacy Reform, School Change, and the Creation of Learning Communities
JOBETH ALLEN, MARILYNN CARY, and
LISA DELGADO, Coordinators

Envisioning Literature: Literary Understanding and Literature Instruction
JUDITH A. LANGER

Teaching Writing as Reflective Practice
GEORGE HILLOCKS, JR.

Talking Their Way into Science: Hearing Children's Questions and Theories, Responding with Curricula
KAREN GALLAS

Whole Language Across the Curriculum: Grades 1, 2, 3
SHIRLEY C. RAINES, Editor

The Administration and Supervision of Reading Programs, Second Edition
SHELLEY B. WEPNER, JOAN T. FEELEY, and
DOROTHY S. STRICKLAND, Editors

No Quick Fix: Rethinking Literacy Programs in America's Elementary Schools
RICHARD L. ALLINGTON and SEAN A. WALMSLEY, Editors

Unequal Opportunity: Learning to Read in the U.S.A.
JILL SUNDAY BARTOLI

(continued)

Nonfiction for the Classroom: Milton Meltzer on Writing, History, and Social Responsibility
Edited and with an Introduction by E. WENDY SAUL

When Children Write: Critical Re-Visions of the Writing Workshop
TIMOTHY LENSMIRE

Dramatizing Literature in Whole Language Classrooms, Second Edition
JOHN WARREN STEWIG and CAROL BUEGE

The Languages of Learning: How Children Talk, Write, Dance, Draw, and Sing Their Understanding of the World
KAREN GALLAS

Partners in Learning: Teachers and Children in Reading Recovery
CAROL A. LYONS, GAY SU PINNELL, and DIANE E. DEFORD

Social Worlds of Children Learning to Write in an Urban Primary School
ANNE HAAS DYSON

The Politics of Workplace Literacy: A Case Study
SHERYL GREENWOOD GOWEN

Inside/Outside: Teacher Research and Knowledge
MARILYN COCHRAN-SMITH and SUSAN L. LYTLE

Literacy Events in a Community of Young Writers
YETTA M. GOODMAN and SANDRA WILDE, Editors

Whole Language Plus: Essays on Literacy in the United States and New Zealand
COURTNEY B. CAZDEN

Process Reading and Writing: A Literature-Based Approach
JOAN T. FEELEY, DOROTHY S. STRICKLAND, and SHELLEY B. WEPNER, Editors

The Child as Critic: Teaching Literature in Elementary and Middle Schools, Third Edition
GLENNA DAVIS SLOAN

The Triumph of Literature/The Fate of Literacy: English in the Secondary School Curriculum
JOHN WILLINSKY

The Child's Developing Sense of Theme: Responses to Literature
SUSAN S. LEHR

Literacy for a Diverse Society: Perspectives, Practices, and Policies
ELFRIEDA H. HIEBERT, Editor

The Complete Theory-to-Practice Handbook of Adult Literacy: Curriculum Design and Teaching Approaches
RENA SOIFER, MARTHA IRWIN, BARBARA CRUMRINE, EMO HONZAKI, BLAIR SIMMONS, and DEBORAH YOUNG

Beginning Reading and Writing

EDITED BY

Dorothy S. Strickland

AND

Lesley Mandel Morrow

FOREWORD BY Alan Farstrup

Teachers College, Columbia University
New York and London

Published by Teachers College Press, 1234 Amsterdam Avenue, New York, NY 10027

Library of Congress Cataloging-in-Publication Data

Beginning reading and writing / edited by Dorothy S. Strickland and Lesley M. Morrow.
p. cm. — (Language and literacy series)
Includes bibliographical references and index.
ISBN 0-8077-3976-6 (alk. paper) — ISBN 0-8077-3977-4 (alk. paper)
1. Language arts (Early childhood). I. Strickland, Dorothy S. II. Morrow, Lesley Mandel. III. Series.

LB1139.5.L35 B44 2000
372.6—dc21 00-044335

ISBN 0-8077-3976-6 (paper)
ISBN 0-8077-3977-4 (cloth)

Printed on acid-free paper

Manufactured in the United States of America

07 06 05 04 03 02 01 00 8 7 6 5 4 3 2 1

CONTENTS

PART TWO

Instructional Strategies for Beginning Readers and Writers

FOREWORD

Early reading is receiving intense public and professional attention owing to its critical importance in laying a foundation for lifelong reading success. This volume, *Beginning Reading and Writing,* builds on the solid foundation of an earlier volume by the same authors, *Emerging Literacy: Young Children Learn to Read and Write* (International Reading Association, 1989). In this new volume the authors focus on instruction and research topics of key concern. The editors, Dorothy Strickland and Lesley Morrow, have recruited superb authors whose experience and expertise in reading research and instruction are brought to bear on key topics in the field.

The book provides a comprehensive treatment of subjects ranging from historical perspectives on emerging literacy to developmentally appropriate practices, inclusion and diversity issues, and home-school connections. In addition, *Beginning Reading and Writing* includes an extensive treatment of child development and language development issues. It is an excellent resource for beginning as well as experienced teachers as they strive to provide well-organized and appropriately selected instruction to support the individual needs of children.

Consistent with current research findings, the discussions pay particular attention to the elements of language essential to reading success. Strategies to support such traditional approaches as phonemic awareness, however, are but a part of a much larger range of instructional strategies appropriate for beginning readers and writers. Also addressed are techniques to foster comprehension and writing in the early years; some fairly simple ways to use computers and other technology to aid writing and, more generally, representation and communication; and the value of including high-quality literature in the curriculum.

Beginning Reading and Writing is an invaluable resource for teacher educators working with preservice students and for experienced teachers working in advanced professional development programs throughout their career. This book should be on the shelf of every reading professional, and it should be placed in the hands of teachers in every community and school district. It is a fine contribution both to the discipline's knowledge base and to classroom practices promoting effective early reading and writing instruction.

Alan Farstrup
Executive Director of IRA

INTRODUCTION

More than a decade ago, we collaborated with some of the top researchers and scholars in the field of early literacy to produce *Emerging Literacy: Young Children Learn to Read and Write.* The impetus for that book was an abundance of new research on how young children attain literacy and what teachers can do to stimulate and support their learning. The influence of the early years, before formal schooling is begun, had emerged as an important and intriguing topic for teachers, administrators, and parents. The book was an immediate success and continues to be used for pre-service and in-service professional development throughout the United States and beyond.

Now, more than 10 years later, we return to the topic of early literacy with the goal of extending our earlier work to acknowledge the new research carried out during the past decade. With the help of many of the best scholars in the field, this new volume updates our readers on advances and refinements in the area of emerging literacy. It also provides current, research-based information regarding policy and practice for beginning formal instruction.

We expect *Beginning Reading and Writing* to be useful at the pre-service and in-service levels of professional development. We also believe it will be a resource for policy makers, administrators, and supervisors as they plan and implement state and local early literacy initiatives. Such initiatives often set goals for every child to become a reader by third or fourth grade, suggesting a need for continuity in philosophy, policy, and practice from the prekindergarten years through the primary grades. This book provides the framework for that to happen.

Beginning Reading and Writing is divided into two parts. Part One, Foundations for the Early Literacy Curriculum, covers topics that arc across all aspects of the early literacy curriculum. William Teale and Junko Yokota (Chapter 1) begin this section with a historical review and an update on early literacy, thus providing an excellent frame for all that follows. In Chapter 2, Susan Neuman and Sue Bredekamp craft vignettes that afford insight into working with the very young child, before formal instruction is begun. They emphasize the need to consider what is both effective and developmentally appropriate.

Other topics affecting all aspects of the curriculum are those of diversity, home-school linkages, the role of play in the literacy curriculum, and oral language development. In Chapter 3, Kathryn Au offers critical understandings along with many recommendations related to the challenging issues that emerge as our school-age population becomes more and more diverse.

Few topics are as well established in the literature as the need for supportive home environments and strong home-school partnerships to support young children's literacy learning. These issues of family literacy are addressed by Diane Tracey in Chapter 4.

The ever greater pressure to produce readers and writers at the earliest levels possible has raised concern over conflict with children's natural inclinations toward joy and playfulness while learning. In Chapter 5, Anthony Pelligrini and Lee Galda address the role of play as basic to children's well-being and as a mechanism through which literacy is achieved.

Concluding Part One, Celia Genishi, Donna Yung-Chan, and Susan Stires in Chapter 6 offer strategies to support oral language development, with a focus on English language learners. They describe sound classroom practices to help beginning readers and writers whose first language is other than English.

Part Two, Instructional Strategies for Beginning Readers and Writers, addresses specific curricular issues related to learning and teaching. Lesley Morrow launches this section with a chapter outlining the research evidence for and practical implications of providing a print-rich environment for learning (Chapter 7). An abundance of specific suggestions for organizing and managing the classroom are provided. In Chapter 8, Dorothy Strickland urges teachers to use what is known about successful intervention programs to focus more effectively on the struggling reader and writer in the regular classroom.

Karen Bromley in Chapter 9 addresses factors related to young children's writing development, a topic that received extraordinary attention in the 1990s and is still unfolding as a relatively new area of research. One topic that is highly linked to young children's writing development is phonics. A perspective on the controversial and sometimes confusing issues surrounding phonemic awareness and phonics is given by Margaret Moustafa in Chapter 10, with many vivid examples from the classroom included. In Chapter 11, Lee Galda and Bernice Cullinan address the use of literature in the curriculum. They place particular emphasis on including multicultural literature and on the importance of reading aloud to children. Understanding the literature that is read to one and the materials one reads independently is the essence of being a reader. Linda Gambrell and Ann Dromsky in Chapter 12 describe appropriate methods for assisting children to think with and reflect on the texts they encounter to help enhance their comprehension.

The final chapters in Part Two deal with assessment, technology, and the kinds of strategies that tie everything together in a successful literacy learning environment. Bill Harp and Jo Ann Brewer in Chapter 13 offer numerous strategies for assessing children's reading and writing development to inform instruction. The ideas offered in this chapter are integral to instruction and provide a sense of accountability for both student and teacher. The ever expanding and changing world of technology is addressed by Shelley Wepner and Lucinda Ray in Chapter 14. The 15th and final chapter is a gold mine of useful ideas. Diane Lapp, James Flood, and Nancy Roser offer a rich collection of strategies that truly exemplify the goal of this book: putting into action what is known about how young children learn literacy and how we can best teach them.

In addition to the thoughtful discussions prepared by the contributors to this book, we have offered a series of "good ideas" straight from practitioners in schools. These teacher-generated, classroom-tested ideas make the material presented even more concrete and useful to our readers.

We are extremely proud of this new volume. We know that it deals with a topic that is widely discussed among educators, parents, and policy makers, and we are confident it will make an important contribution to the conversation.

Publication of this book would not have been possible without the help of many individuals. We thank the respective chapter authors for their lively contributions to the ongoing discipline-wide discussion of early literacy development. In addition, we are grateful to the teachers who contributed the wonderful classroom ideas that appear at the end of each chapter, and we thank Melissa Marley for editing these sections. Carol Collins, our editor at Teachers College Press, provided guidance and supervised production of this book with meticulous concern for quality at every step. Danielle Lynch, Stephanie Adams, Mary Jane Kurabinski, and Deborah Hanna graciously allowed us to photograph children in their classrooms, and very kindly put at our disposal photographs they themselves had taken. We could not have done without the editorial help of Rebecca Brittain, Cristina Ferrone, and Tieka Harris and the secretarial assistance of Veena Shastri. To each of these individuals, and to many others, we are indebted.

Dorothy S. Strickland
Lesley Mandel Morrow

PART ONE

Foundations for the Early Literacy Curriculum

Part One deals with foundational understandings related to the context in which learning and teaching take place. The contents of the chapters in this section should be viewed as interrelated and interdependent. Each chapter deals with teaching and learning as dynamic processes. Children are viewed as active learners and their teachers as active, informed decision makers. Because children are multifaceted learners, their teachers must consider the social, emotional, intellectual, and physical environment so that successful learning can take place.

We believe that all learners, including adults, learn best when they are actively engaged in the process. With that in mind, we suggest that you support your reading and thinking by keeping a response log in which you react to various ideas as they are presented. No doubt there will be many times when you heartily agree with the information set forth, so much so that you feel compelled to comment on it. Now and then you may disagree with a particular point, or at least feel the need for some clarification. You may find an idea to be somewhat perplexing or confusing in terms of your own experience. Some information may simply be surprising or new to you, and you may want to note your thoughts on that as well. Written responses of this type make excellent points for discussion with others. The notes represent your personal interactions with the text. They also provide the basis for interactions with others by acting as a catalyst for clarifying and extending your own understandings and the understandings of others.

CHAPTER ONE

Beginning Reading and Writing: Perspectives on Instruction

William H. Teale and Junko Yokota

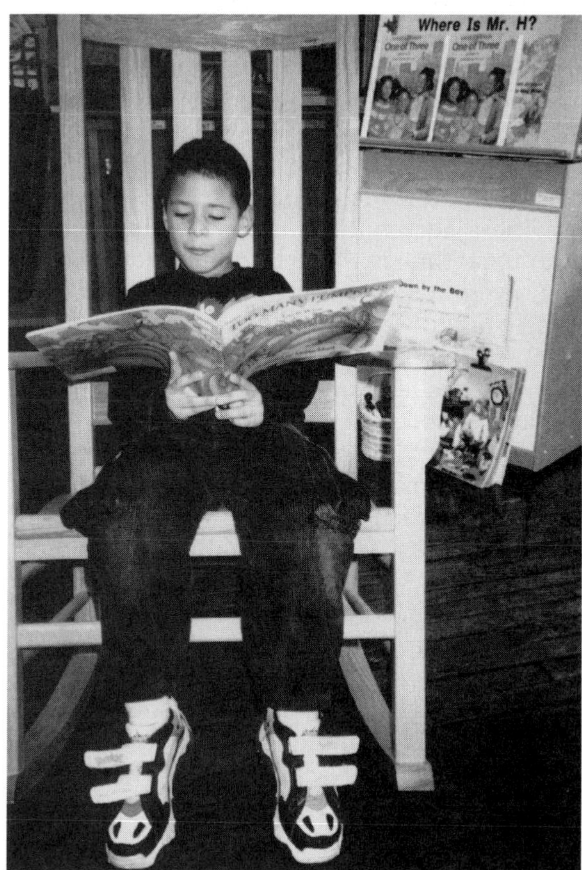

William Teale and Junko Yokota provide a historical overview and update of the research and practice related to beginning reading and writing.

For Reflection and Action: Consider the changes and the complexities involved in the way beginning reading instruction is discussed here. How does it fit with your personal experiences and observations of classrooms familiar to you? Describe and analyze the differences you find.

Likely no area of American education has been as fraught with controversy, confusion, fads, and politics as the teaching of beginning reading and writing. And, as our work in schools and teacher education also shows us, likely no other area has generated such passionate and creative teaching, as well as so many substantive instructional innovations, as early literacy instruction. Perhaps this is because there is no more exciting or more important educational endeavor than helping child learn to read and write. In this chapter, which offers a big-picture look at literacy in the first years of school, we have attempted to capture the excitement, the frustrations, the wrangling, the intellectual energy, and the wonders that envelop the teaching of beginning literacy. The discussion is divided into three topics:

- *Contentions:* A short historical look at the issues and controversies that have existed with respect to early literacy instruction over the past 25 years.

- *Conclusions from Research:* General agreements about what constitutes effective early literacy instruction, drawn from a thorough review of research literature and observations of the urban, suburban, and rural classrooms in which we have worked over the past two decades.
- *Continuing Challenges:* A discussion of unresolved issues and questions that represent the major challenges facing early literacy teachers and researchers today.

Our intention is to help readers become familiar with critical concerns in the area and to identify what we know and what we still need to find out about the job of ushering primary grade children into the community of readers and writers.

Contentions

Theoretical and pedagogical discussions related to school literacy instruction for 5- to 8-year-olds in the United States have gone on for centuries. We have chosen to report on these discussions in terms of *contentions,* not because the field is failing to move forward but because so much about it can be characterized as a debate among competing perspectives.

A detailed historical treatment of discussions about early literacy instruction as they unfolded in the course of the twentieth century in the United States can be found in Teale (1995). Here we provide an abbreviated version of that history, focusing specifically on developments in the past 25 years and examining three issues of continuing concern in early literacy:

1. How to provide the best foundation for beginning literacy instruction
2. When to begin formal literacy instruction
3. The nature of beginning literacy instruction

The Foundation for Beginning Literacy Instruction

For virtually all of the twentieth century in the United States, formal (i.e., deliberate) instruction in reading began in first grade (at about age 6). Kindergarten historically had the role of providing a period of preparation for the rest of schooling. Until the late 1980s, *reading readiness* was the approach used by most kindergartens to provide the foundation for formal reading instruction.

But during the reading readiness era, the issue of how children became prepared mentally for reading was pursued along two different paths. Down one path went educators who were convinced that reading readiness was essentially the result of maturation, or "neural ripeness." Down the other went those who believed that appropriate experiences created readiness or could accelerate it.

The implications of the maturation perspective for kindergarten instruction were straightforward: children who had sufficient "neural ripening" (as measured by their mental age on a cognitive or IQ test) were ready for reading instruction; others were not. Therefore, the kindergarten teacher was to let the first-grade teacher know which children had "passed" the readiness threshold and which would need additional time in the first-grade reading readiness program. The first-grade teacher in turn closely monitored the children's mental growth until the requisite stage of development had been reached, and only then began actual reading instruction.

Educators who held the alternative view—namely, that reading readiness was a product of experience—focused on getting children ready to read as soon as possible rather than merely sitting back and waiting. They implemented reading readiness programs in which children participated in activities (especially workbook activities) designed to foster visual and auditory discrimination skills, adequate speaking and listening skills, recognition of the letters of the alphabet, and the association of some letters with sounds. However, children were not taught to read or write until they had completed such a readiness program.

By the late 1980s the view that reading readiness was requisite to beginning literacy instruction was seriously challenged. Researchers and teachers moved toward the concept of *emergent literacy* (Strickland & Morrow, 1989; Teale & Sulzby, 1986), a revolution in thinking about early written language development that rejected both the maturation theory and the experiential readiness view. Emergent literacy turned many of the tenets of reading readiness around, proposing instead that

- Learning to read and write begins very early in life for virtually all children in a literate society, rather than at age 5 or 6.
- *Literacy* development is the more appropriate way to describe what was called *reading* readiness: the child develops not merely in reading but as a *writer/reader.* Reading, writing, and oral language develop concurrently and interrelatedly rather than sequentially.
- Literacy develops within the framework of real-life activities in order to "get things done." Therefore, the meaningful or purposeful bases of early literacy are a critical part of learning to read and write and must be emphasized in the curriculum.
- Children learn written language through active engagement with their world, not merely by completing workbook activities or other types of academic exercises.
- A much broader range of knowledge, dispositions, and strategies is involved in young children's becoming literate than is emphasized in reading readiness programs.
- Although children's acquisition of literacy can be described in general stages, children become literate at different rates and take a variety of paths to conventional reading and writing. Attempts to "scope and sequence" instruction, such as those typical of reading readiness programs, do not take this developmental variation into account.

Emergent literacy is the lens through which the majority of current teacher educators, researchers, educational policy makers, and major publishers of curriculum materials prefer to view prekindergarten and kindergarten literacy development. Also, many early childhood classrooms have moved to an emergent literacy perspective. However, the overall degree to which one would find more traditional reading readiness approaches or an emergent literacy approach predominating were one to visit kindergarten classrooms around the country remains unclear.

When to Begin Formal Literacy Instruction

The age at which children should begin formal reading and writing instruction was hotly debated in early childhood education and literacy education for many, many years. Educators cautioned that starting reading instruction too early could have negative effects. As a result, during the first three-quarters of the twentieth century, first grade—age 6—was generally accepted as the year to begin teaching reading.

In the 1970s, however, kindergartens increasingly incorporated reading instruction into their programs by including certain concepts and skills that previously had been covered in first grade. Many early childhood educators decried the "pushing down" of the first-grade curriculum into the kindergarten, but by the 1980s most kindergartens were providing reading instruction to 5-year-olds.

With the advent of an emergent literacy paradigm in kindergartens, the issue of when to begin formal instruction has become moot, because emergent literacy holds that reading and writing development begins long before children even reach kindergarten. Certainly an emergent literacy kindergarten would make reading and writing part of the curriculum. The difference, however, lies with how one defines *instruction.* A traditional beginning reading program consists largely of formal instruction in reading and decoding, reading in groups, and the use of basal readers. An emergent literacy kindergarten is not characterized by such activities. Instead, reading and writing instruction are embedded in the daily activities of the classroom, in shared reading and teacher read-alouds, in children's play, and in learning center activities (Labbo & Teale, 1997). Thus, with virtually all kindergartens professing that instruction in reading and writing is part of their mission, there is little argument about when to begin. The question now is *how.*

The Nature of Beginning Literacy Instruction

How to teach beginning reading is the flash point of all the contentions related to early literacy instruction. Perhaps the reason for the vehemence of the controversy is that so much of school success hinges on reading. In any case, the battles have been extended and hard fought, and the voices have been loud. For the past three decades these discussions have been termed the "great debate" (Chall, 1967, 1996).

Shortly after Rudolph Flesch published *Why Johnny Can't Read,* in 1955, there was widespread concern about the state of education in the United States, because the Soviets had been the first to put a satellite in space. The problem with reading, Flesch stated in unequivocal terms (using suspicious logic and distorted statistics), was that first- and second-grade teachers were not teaching phonics. The public popularity of Flesch's book was enormous, and many people asked why phonics was not emphasized more in school. During the following decade, a nationwide study of the best way to teach beginning reading was funded by the federal government (Bond & Dykstra, 1967). In 1967 Chall's scholarly review, *Learning to Read: The Great Debate,* appeared, and its findings paralleled those of the nationwide study: "code-emphasis" approaches to beginning reading were more effective than "meaning-emphasis" approaches. As a result, basal reading programs that stressed phonics in the primary grades became popular instructional materials.

Phonics remained the predominant approach to beginning reading until the 1980s, when whole language emerged as a grass-roots movement. A whole language perspective holds that reading and writing are learned best by actually engaging in reading and writing (not through reading and writing exercises), that literacy instruction should be rich in content, and that children's interests and purposes are paramount in learning to read and write. As a result, the whole language approach focuses on comprehension, uses "real" children's literature rather than texts designed to reflect phonics patterns, and teaches skills in context rather than in isolation. Primary grade whole language teachers teach phonics, but they do so as the need arises for individuals or small groups of children and in the context of more holistic lessons rather than as isolated, systematic phonics instruction for the entire class.

Through whole language, teachers had initiated a way of moving themselves forward as professionals. Whole language got a big boost in California in the late 1980s when a statewide "literature-based" framework was adopted for all of its elementary schools. This state-level action supplemented the work of teacher groups to get the attention of other states and publishers. The popularity of the whole language approach reached its zenith in the mid-1980s, when a new wave of "literature-based" basal readers made its way into elementary schools across the country. But even as whole language appeared to be widely accepted, a reaction against whole language approaches that had begun in the early 1990s was gathering steam. This reaction was spurred in part by the observation that although experienced, knowledgeable teachers were empowered to create strong programs by applying whole language concepts, many other teachers misinterpreted its principles and practices and had little direction in their classrooms. It was also prompted by factors such as the publication Marilyn Adams's *Beginning to Read: Thinking and Learning About Print* (1990), a book written in response to congressional inquiries about phonics that made a case for systematically teaching young children about phonemic awareness and decoding; the publication of a series of research studies conducted by the National Institute of Child Health and Human Development arguing that scientific research established the need for systematic instruction in phonological awareness and phonics in beginning reading (Lyon, 1998); and publication of the results from the 1994 National Assessment of Educational Progress that showed California students to be second to last in reading achievement in the country, a finding that politicians, the public, and even the former state superintendent of education (who was responsible for implementing California's literature-based curriculum a decade earlier) argued was the fault of whole language approaches.

It has been disconcerting to watch the politicizing of the whole language versus phonics controversy, but perhaps the most troubling aspect of the past decade of the great debate is that schools, states, and reading educators have lurched back and forth between paradigms and practices, searching for a single program that will solve the beginning reading puzzle. A major reason for these wild swings is that phonics approaches and meaning-based approaches are often characterized as two diametrically opposed ways of teaching reading. This perception is fueled by the popular press—newspapers, magazines such as *Time* and *Newsweek,* and television news shows—and sometimes even by education journals, which talk about the issue in terms of "reading wars" (see, e.g., Lemann, 1997; Rubin, 1997). Such stories take a strictly argumentative slant, depicting phonics and whole language as polar opposites, either/or choices for schools, teachers, and parents.

It is fortunate that primary grade literacy instruction has received unprecedented attention over the past decade, and unfortunate that many state reading initiatives and local policy decisions seem to have been sucked into the A-versus-B approach to beginning reading instruction. Others have called for a "balanced approach" that would incorporate systematic attention to phonics while also maintaining a focus on good literature and comprehension instruction from the start. Perhaps the most influential report from this perspective is the work of the National Academy of Education, which issued the research report *Preventing Reading Difficulties in Young Children* (Snow, Burns, & Griffin, 1998) and an accompanying volume aimed at parents, entitled *Starting Out Right: A Guide to Promoting Children's Reading Success* (Burns, Griffin, & Snow, 1999).

Because the reaction to whole language has been so severe in states such as California and Texas, it is unclear just what message local schools are actually implementing at the classroom level. Current patterns suggest there may be a "knee-jerk reaction" in which instruction becomes overly focused on phonemic awareness and phonics activities as *the* long-missing solution. As we write this chapter, approaches that stress systematic instruction in phonemic awareness and phonics have clearly captured the attention of educational policy makers and school boards in most parts of the country, to the extent that they are being promoted and even legislated as the way to conduct beginning literacy instruction, perhaps because they seem to offer a way of teaching that is formulated and tangible rather than one that depends on teacher decision making and must be constructed in the day-to-day interaction in the classroom.

Conclusions from Research

Although contentions and controversies have been a notable characteristic of the field of beginning literacy instruction for the past quarter century, and although political squabbles continue, research has produced a number of substantial advances in knowledge about early literacy learning and teaching. These studies, combined with classic reading research from the earlier decades of the twentieth century, have not provided *the* answer, but they have yielded unprecedented insight into how young children learn to read and write and what a good instructional program needs to contain. Sometimes—because of politics or ignorance, or because no one unifying vision of how we can best develop young children's literacy has emerged—this knowledge is not well used by school districts or states for making policy and curriculum decisions. Nevertheless, strong evidence exists. We have identified seven points that, according to our reading of the research evidence and our experience in classrooms, are robust enough to be considered conclusions about what is needed to have a successful early literacy program:

1. An emergent literacy approach provides the foundation.
2. Comprehension instruction is a core feature.
3. A multifaceted word study program is essential.
4. Writing—integrated and separated—is central.
5. Reading fluency must be developed.
6. Children need to practice by reading connected text.
7. The early literacy program is conceptualized as developmental.

An Emergent Literacy Approach Provides the Foundation

This first point applies mainly to kindergarten programs but also has relevance for intervention programs for first graders who are experiencing literacy difficulties. An emergent literacy program provides literacy learning opportunities that accommodate the wide range of knowledge and experiences children bring with them as they enter school. Some 5-year-olds have had little interaction with written language; others are on the verge of or actually reading and writing conventionally. Because emergent literacy classrooms embed literacy in children's everyday activities, view children as active constructors of their own literacy knowledge and strategies, support different developmental paths into literacy, and offer integrated language arts experiences, it is possible for all children, no matter what their literacy needs, to benefit from an emergent literacy program as they begin school. Labbo and Teale (1997) provide a portrait of the principles and instructional practices of an emergent literacy kindergarten. This discussion is not the place to detail the ins and outs of an emergent literacy classroom, but we encourage readers to examine emergent literacy as the model for prekindergarten and kindergarten programs. As Stahl and colleagues (Stahl, McKenna, & Pagnucco, 1994; Stahl & Miller, 1989) concluded from their quantitative reviews of literacy instruction in kindergarten and first grade, and as the recent joint position statement from the International Reading Association and the National Association for the Education of Young Children (1998) entitled "Learning to Read and Write: Developmentally Appropriate Practices for Young Children" suggests, an emergent literacy approach provides the broad range of literacy concepts and strategies that young children need to get off to the right start in reading and writing.

Comprehension Instruction Is a Core Feature

Comprehension—understanding what one reads—is the essence of reading. Comprehension instruction should be a central part of teaching young children how to read from the beginning, not something emphasized in the curriculum only after young children have learned how to decode.

At first—typically in kindergarten—before children can read conventionally from print, comprehension instruction actually revolves around children's understanding of written language that is read to them. Children experience stories, informational texts, and poems that are read aloud by the teacher. In conjunction with hearing such materials, children also tap their prior knowledge and discuss the texts, respond to them through art, music, or dramatic activities, and learn from lessons about comprehension strategies such as predicting or inferencing that are embedded as part of read-alouds. In these ways, children become more skilled at processing written language and learning from it, becoming familiar with its syntactic patterns and vocabulary, with talking about information, with different informational text structures (listing, cause-effect, comparison-contrast, and so on), and with responding to literary texts. By the end of kindergarten, children should be able to retell stories on their own, write or create art work that shows comprehension of a text that has been read to them, and make sensible predictions as a story is being read aloud.

Once a child becomes able to read on his or her own, typically in first grade, comprehension strategies can also be taught in the context of reading. With such instruction, we can expect that by the end of first grade, children will demonstrate their understanding of books they read independently or with a partner, be able to summarize a book, and be able to describe in their own words what they learned from a text. Comprehension goals for second graders include being able to summarize what has been read; answering pertinent comprehension questions; inferring cause-effect relationships; discussing how, why, and what-if questions about informational texts; responding to thematic issues in literature; and following characters, plot connections, and cause-effect relationships across earlier and later parts of stories. Fostering comprehension abilities like these in grades 1 and 2 takes place by having children read and discuss texts, and through comprehension strategy lessons.

It is also important to note that teachers should still read aloud to children during first and second grades because this practice fosters vocabulary learning and comprehension skills. At these ages, children typically are able to understand more complex concepts and language from texts that are read aloud than from what they can read themselves. Thus, the higher-level comprehension skills and word meanings can profitably be developed through read-aloud experiences throughout the primary grades.

Comprehension is not something to be left to chance or relegated to secondary importance just because children are young. It is critically important that early instruction systematically focus on helping children learn to process the content of the written language they hear and read.

A Multifaceted Word Study Program Is Essential

To become capable, mature readers and writers, students need to have a well-developed reading vocabulary (know the meanings of lots of words), be able to decode or figure out through structural analysis (analysis of words parts) words they have not seen before, recognize "by sight" a large number of words, and spell correctly most of the words they write. The early years are the time when children acquire the foundational knowledge and habits that allow all of these areas—vocabulary, decoding, sight word recognition, and spelling—to develop fully. Thus, a quality early literacy program establishes benchmarks for achievement in all of these facets of word study.

Decoding is the most talked-about part of word learning for primary-grade children. Understanding the alphabetic principle—how letters, letter combinations, and sounds relate to each other in a systematic way—is indispensable to becoming literate in an alphabetic language. Some children seem to pick up the alphabetic principle and decoding strategies almost on their own, with only minimal instruction in phonics, and with these children the teacher should concentrate on other important aspects of literacy. However, most young children need systematic attention to learning about words. This does not mean they must contend with mindless drill and endless worksheets, and grunt and groan out sounds. On the contrary, it means that they should learn about words within the realm of literacy as a goal-directed activity. There is a need for specific attention to letter-sound relations, but such instruction should be couched in a meaning-based curriculum. Recently, several fine publications have detailed ideas for teaching phonics and other aspects of word study to primary grade children in thoughtful and meaningful ways. Good suggestions can be found in Cunningham (1995), Bear, Invernizzi, Templeton, and Johnston (1995), Gaskins (1996), and various chapters in Part Two of this book.

It should be kept in mind that an important part of learning to decode actually begins before children can master letter-sound relationships, with what is called phonemic awareness. Phonemic awareness refers to the ability to hear the constituent sounds (phonemes) that make up words. It is abundantly clear from research that phonemic awareness is essential for learning to decode as a reader (Snow et al., 1998). Phonemic awareness instruction has become a hot issue in early literacy teaching. We believe that paying specific attention to children's phonemic awareness is a key aspect of word study in kindergarten and grade 1. However, as we discuss in more detail later in this chapter, how to teach phonemic awareness is one of the major challenges educators face, because not enough research has been conducted in classrooms to indicate how phonemic awareness instruction is best integrated into a developmentally appropriate kindergarten or grade 1 program.

Because vocabulary development is the single biggest factor in a child's reading comprehension skill (Blachowicz & Fisher, 1996), primary grade reading programs also seek to develop children's knowledge of word meanings through rich oral language activities, such as class discussions and read-alouds, as well as through written language experiences. Classrooms that immerse children in words by using words in meaningful, varied ways and through word play succeed best in building rich vocabularies. Wide reading by children (as well as reading to children) is important because when children encounter words in context, they can increase their vocabularies significantly. But deliberate vocabulary instruction is also an essential part of a word study program for beginning literacy. Activities that help children learn important words from stories, content vocabulary from science and social studies, and vocabulary-broadening words in a variety of contexts have a much more lasting impact than merely having children write definitions for 10 to 20 new words each week and then take a test at the end of the week.

Thus, primary grade classrooms need to be "word-rich" places. The aim is to establish an environment that builds rich and varied connections among words for children. The more words children understand and the deeper their knowledge of those words, the bigger the payoff as they go through both elementary and secondary school.

Writing—Integrated and Separated—Is Central

Fifteen years ago, the idea of having prekindergarten, kindergarten, or first-grade children write was positively radical. Today, in the vast majority of primary grade classrooms, children write on a daily basis. Why the change? Everyone—teachers, researchers, parents—saw the positive results of inviting kindergarten children to write in their own ways. We also saw that first and second graders were capable of great things when they were encouraged and expected to write on a daily basis.

In kindergarten, the approach is to provide a variety of writing materials (often in a writing center and in the dramatic play area), model writing, stimulate writing in conjunction with dramatic play, make writing part of everyday classroom activities (by creating room signs, making invitations to classroom events, and so forth), and devise many opportunities for children to write in conjunction with read-alouds, science and social studies activities, and other instructional experiences. Noticing, celebrating, and sharing kindergartners' writing with a variety of audiences in and out of school is also beneficial. Teachers accept the various forms of writing that kindergartners typically use (scribble, random letters, invented spelling) and, as appropriate for individual children, scaffold their writing attempts, thereby moving them toward more conventional writing systems.

The most widely accepted way of approaching writing instruction for first and second graders is known as process writing (see, e.g., Graves, 1983). Through writing workshop (Calkins, 1994), children are taught all phases of the writing process, and their creations are supported at each step along the way. They are involved in prewriting (brainstorming, free writing), drafting, revising (first and second graders typically make minimal revisions, but the concept is introduced to them), editing and proofreading, and, finally, publishing—either informally, by sharing writing during author's chair (Graves & Hansen, 1983) or posting pieces in the room, or more formally, by creating a bound book for the classroom or school library or putting a piece in the grade-level's or school's literary magazine.

Writing facilitates young children's literacy development in two broad ways. On the one hand, teaching writing develops composing knowledge and strategies that are critical for success in school and life. Composing involves creating stories, descriptions, and various types of expository text, thereby giving children experience with putting ideas together in a variety of ways. On the other hand, research into reading-writing relationships indicates that there are good reasons to integrate the teaching of writing with the teaching of reading because of their strong connections. Shanahan (1984), for example, found that for second graders, reading and writing mutually interacted with each other, with a particularly high relationship between phonics knowledge in reading and spelling knowledge. Thus, there are also good reasons to integrate writing instruction and reading instruction in the primary grades. As we encourage young children to write using invented spelling, to "write the sounds you can hear" or "write the way you think it's spelled," we are helping them build a concept of word and learn about sound-symbol relations. In other words, if teachers really want to provide high-quality phonics instruction for primary grade children, they will include a great deal of writing in their school experiences.

During the early years, then, we integrate reading and writing instruction because we know that having children write makes it easier for them to learn to read. But we also pay specific attention to writing, giving it its own identity and time in the classroom so that the unique aspects of writing are addressed separately. In short, making writing part of the primary grade curriculum is both an end in itself and a means of supporting the development of other literacy skills.

Reading Fluency Must Be Developed

Rate, accuracy, phrasing, and prosody (melody and expression) are all parts of fluent reading (Strecker, Roser, & Martinez, 1998). The ability to read fluently is a critically important part of becoming a capable reader (LaBerge & Samuels, 1974; Reutzel & Hollingsworth, 1993), and a significant fluency-comprehension link was found in analysis of data from the National Assessment of Educational Progress, which monitors nationwide literacy achievement in the United States (Pinnell et al., 1995). The research suggests that fluency and reading comprehension have a reciprocal relationship, with each fostering the other.

Although fostering fluency is significant throughout the elementary and secondary years, the beginnings of fluency occur during the primary grades, once children are reading conventionally on their own. For most children, grade 2 is an especially important year for reading fluency development.

Recently, attention to fluency instruction has picked up significantly. The National Reading Panel established by the U.S. Congress considered fluency as a primary learning area in reading as it examines research-based knowledge that can lead to improved reading instruction and greater learning (National Reading Panel, 2000), and a number of publications have detailed promising ways of teaching fluency (see, e.g., Opitz, Rasinski, & Bird, 1998; Rasinski, 1996).

Fluency instruction should be an integral part of a beginning literacy program. Methods found to be helpful for enhancing fluency include the following:

- Teacher modeling (through read-alouds and in the context of instructional techniques such as guided reading that, among other things, help build fluency)
- Ensuring that children have many chances to "practice" with texts they can read with ease
- Repeated readings (Rasinski, 1996; Samuels, 1979/1997)
- Other instructional formats designed to increase fluency, such as Hoffman's (1987) oral recitation lesson

In general, it is best to employ a variety of activities so that children will not end up bored with a repetitive format that becomes drill-like. It is particularly important to create situations in which young children can see legitimate purposes, or motivation, for reading texts over and over to increase accuracy and speed and to read with more expression. We have found it especially helpful to have children practice in preparation to read to real audiences, which may consist of peers (e.g., buddy reading or readers' theatre [Wolf, 1993]), younger or older children (e.g., cross-age reading [Labbo & Teale, 1990]), parents, other adults, stuffed animals (a Read-to-Me Bear), or any other listeners who motivate them to develop a fluent rendering of the text. Additional details on incorporating reading fluency instruction into the curriculum can be found in the references cited above.

Children Need to Practice by Reading Connected Text

One more activity is necessary for children to become readers during the primary grades: getting enough experience reading. There is a positive correlation between children's reading competency and the time they spend reading connected text, extended fiction or nonfiction passages such as selections from novels, biographies, informational books, magazines, newspaper articles, and so forth (Anderson, Wilson, & Fielding, 1988; Applebee, Langer, & Mullis, 1988). In fact, data from Anderson et al. (1988) suggest that if children spend at least 15 minutes a day reading, it makes a significant difference in their reading ability.

A quality early literacy program places priority on involving children in reading plenty of stories, informational books, magazines, and a variety of other appropriate texts. Teachers help children make reading a regular part of their out-of-school time by promoting reading as a fun and interesting way to spend time and by reaching out to parents to involve them in supporting their children's at-home reading habits.

There is no magic formula or program for getting young children into the habit of reading. Some teachers and schools have tried reading incentive programs connected to community businesses (e.g., Book-It), creating a "caterpillar" that grows around the walls of the classroom as children add a segment for each book they complete reading, or responding to a challenge from the principal, who agrees to eat fried worms or sit on the roof of the school overnight if the children read a certain number of books. Others have implemented sustained silent reading (DEAR, SQUIRT, and so forth), in which 15 to 30 minutes a day is set aside for both students and teacher to read self-selected material. Such programs may appear to offer a good solution to getting children to read, but they are not without controversy. The idea of promoting reading through extrinsic rewards such as pizza or the principal's suffering dire consequences has been questioned, and research on traditional sustained silent reading programs shows that they do not have a significant positive impact on reading achievement or attitudes toward reading (Teale & Bean, submitted for publication).

We encourage teachers to think broadly about how to design an early literacy program that will get children enthusiastic about reading for pleasure. Good materials are essential; classroom and school libraries stocked with interesting books that cover a full range of genres, varying levels of readability, and the many diverse cultures of our world make a difference. The importance of the teacher as a model is also critical. Teachers seen by their children as readers are much more likely to foster readers in their classrooms. But teachers also need to do more than provide good reading materials and be good models. There is no particular list of activities to be implemented. Rather, it is better to think of ways in which reading can be made "a way of being" in the classroom.

To make this happen, teachers develop a good background in knowing children and children's literature. They read widely, knowing whom and what to consult when they want to identify particular titles for children to read. Teachers also observe carefully what individual children in the class are reading and suggest specific titles that match or extend their current reading interests. Many teachers encourage children to do book talks about what they are reading or to develop other responses to share with classmates. They promote conversations among the children about what they are reading not only during reading lessons, but also at lunchtime, after school, during social studies, at recess, and at other times. In these and other ways, teachers go well beyond the traditional concept of sustained silent reading by embedding reading in a variety of school and home contexts and activities, thus creating plenty of opportunities for children to respond actively to what they are reading. As a result, reading becomes such a habit of mind that children feel the day is incomplete unless they have had an opportunity to read for pleasure.

The Early Literacy Program Is Conceptualized as Developmental

The preceding six points have offered conclusions about content matters in early literacy instruction. Our final conclusion addresses the more general issue of the theoretical perspective that best befits successful literacy programs. *Developmental* is an idea that is at the heart of early childhood education, and conceptualizing literacy learning and literacy instruction as developmental helps ensure that all children benefit maximally from their school literacy experiences.

It should also be noted, however, that *developmental* is a dangerous word to apply to any discussion of early literacy instruction. It is dangerous because the term has been used in so many ways that it means significantly different things to different educators. By using *developmental* in conjunction with early literacy learning and teaching, we imply the following:

- The changes that occur across years as children grow toward literacy occur in generally predictable ways.
- Children's concepts of, and strategies for, reading and writing are qualitatively different from those of adults, yet they grow toward adult modes.
- Children become better at reading and writing as a result of internal developments and learning opportunities.
- Different children have different patterns and timing in their literacy learning. Such a range in the rate and manner in which children learn to read and write is to be expected and therefore is considered normal development.

With such a developmental perspective, literacy instruction is enhanced because teachers (1) have a framework and associated benchmarks for progress, which helps with both assessment and instruction, (2) are able to note patterns in young children's literacy learning but also maintain a "set for diversity" (they see a continuum but no rigid "assembly line" sequence), (3) seek to understand children's changing concepts and strategies from the children's perspective (rather than seeing them as miniature adults), and (4) understand that not all children will attain literacy benchmarks at same time or in the same way. In all, teachers seek to provide developmentally appropriate literacy instruction, standards, and benchmarks that, as the IRA/NAEYC's 1998 joint position statement notes, should be "challenging but achievable."

This perspective also implies that the literacy program is seen as developmental not only for each grade level but also across the preschool through grade 2 years. Teachers and administrators create a program that monitors and supports growth across the age levels and also provides alternative routes by which children from different backgrounds and patterns of experience can realize the goal of being able to read and write.

Finally, a developmental perspective on literacy learning clearly implies that reading and writing instruction do not end with second or third grade. We are troubled by a popular saying that during the primary grades, children learn to read, and after that, they read to learn. We have tried to make a case for conceptualizing the early literacy curriculum as developmental, but we also want it to be understood that, in the larger picture, literacy instruction should be seen as developmental *from kindergarten through grade 12.* At no grade level should reading or writing instruction stop; rather, literacy learning and literacy teaching should be seen as lifelong processes.

About the Research Conclusions

Taken together, the seven conclusions just discussed represent the broad brush strokes of a successful beginning literacy program in a school, district, or state. We offer such a framework rather than identify specific teaching techniques because we believe that decisions about instructional activities are best made by the individual teacher. The key to building successful early literacy programs lies in formulating clear notions about the components necessary to facilitate young children's learning—an emergent literacy approach for kindergarten, developing their word knowledge, systematic attention to comprehension and decoding strategies, fostering reading habits, teaching writing, and building reading fluency, all within a developmental perspective. Being thoughtful about the various dimensions of literacy knowledge and literacy strategies children need is the foundation for success, and it is this foundation that we have attempted to elucidate.

Continuing Challenges

The seven conclusions strongly suggest directions indicated as promising by research and excellent practice in early literacy. But by no means are there answers to all the important questions about how to teach reading and writing in the early grades. We have identified five issues as especially important challenges for educators to address through research and practice and thereby gain greater insight into how to conduct classroom instruction. We urge educators to think carefully about them.

1. The how of phonemic awareness instruction
2. The role of reading aloud in the curriculum
3. The texts primary grade children should be reading
4. Student diversity
5. Use of computers

The How of Phonemic Awareness Instruction

Research has clearly established phonemic awareness as significant in early reading development (e.g., Adams, 1990) and in literacy achievement throughout the elementary school years (e.g., Juel, Griffith, & Gough, 1986). Researchers have also determined that it is possible to teach phonemic awareness to children as young as 5 and thereby positively affect their early reading development (e.g., Ball & Blachman, 1991; Lundberg, Frost, & Petersen, 1988; Torgeson, Morgan, & Davis, 1992). As a result, phonemic awareness instruction is now widely touted as necessary for kindergarten and first-grade programs.

As was indicated earlier in this chapter, we also advocate including phonemic awareness instruction as an essential part of early literacy programs. But, by the same token, we recognize that how to do so is far from clear. This is because the research on phonemic awareness instruction has been conducted under controlled conditions (as it should be for research purposes) rather than in regular classrooms (as it also needs to be to draw instructional implications). These controlled conditions included the use of scripted or semiscripted lessons that were almost exclusively whole-group instruction and programs that were "stand alone" or "add-ons," completely divorced from the regular curriculum (Teale, Patterson, Lieb, & Bean, 1999). Such an approach is not in keeping with the developmentally appropriate instruction model that most early childhood teachers are attempting to implement.

Thus, much remains to be determined about how phonemic awareness instruction can effectively be conducted within the context of a quality primary grade literacy program. As Labbo and Teale (1997) pointed out, the teacher's objective "is not to involve children in isolated skill-and-drill phonemic awareness activities, but to create activities that allow children to explore sounds in meaningful and playful ways" (p. 257).

Many teachers and classroom-based researchers are concerned about providing phonemic awareness instruction within the larger realm of literacy as a goal-directed activity. Such work on this topic promises to help us see a variety of ways in which phonemic awareness can be deliberately and systematically integrated into the context of a good kindergarten or first-grade program.

The Role of Reading Aloud in the Curriculum

We, like many other early childhood educators, have touted the importance of reading aloud to children as an instructional activity in kindergarten and first-grade classrooms (e.g., Sulzby & Teale, 1991). But we have also expressed reservations about the overuse and misuse of reading aloud (Teale, 1998). Abuses connected with reading aloud stem from what appears to be a belief among some educators that reading to primary grade children is a silver bullet, a singularly powerful key in teaching children to read. Find high-quality literature, read it in engaging ways, get children's active participation, and the results will be significant, they contend. But this is attributing too much to reading aloud. In fact, one study found negative correlations between achievement and the amount of time adults spent reading to children in kindergarten classes, and no significant relationship in first-grade classrooms (Meyer, Wardrop, Stahl, & Linn, 1994).

We continue to believe that reading aloud in primary grade classrooms is a key instructional activity for helping children learn important literacy concepts and skills. To ensure that reading aloud is an effective element in instruction, however, we recommend paying attention both to what is being read and to how the reading is done.

- **What Is Being Read:** There are many high-quality books appropriate for young children; to include anything less than excellent selections in what is read aloud lowers the quality of literacy instruction. Teachers can keep aware of high-quality children's literature by reading reviews of children's book in professional journals like *Book Links, Language Arts, The Reading Teacher,* and *Horn Book.* In addition, it is extremely important to make multicultural literature integral to read-alouds. Children need to see themselves and others in our diverse society reflected in the selections read by the teacher. Furthermore, we highly recommend reading a variety of text types. Stories, informational books, poetry, alphabet and counting books, and books that feature word play all are important as read-alouds for primary grade children. Finally, connecting read-alouds to the classroom units of study benefits both children's literacy learning and their subject area understandings.
- **How the Reading Is Done:** There are significant variations in the ways teachers read to children. Martinez and Teale (1993) found that even though a group of six teachers all read the same stories, what they had the children discuss during the readings and how it was discussed varied considerably. Furthermore, variations in storybook-reading style affect how children approach books as well as how much they comprehend and learn from being read to (Dickinson, Hao, & He, 1993; Dickinson & Smith, 1994; Ninio, 1980; Teale & Martinez, 1997). This is not to say that there is one best way to read aloud to children, but these studies suggest that the way the teacher conducts read-alouds significantly affects children's literacy learning. Hoffman, Roser, and Battle (1993) have offered suggestions for how to read to primary grade children in lively, engaging, and thought-provoking ways. Additional teacher research and reflection in this area will help us understand better how read-alouds can be as beneficial as possible an instructional activity for young children.

Thus, the practice of reading aloud to children offers important challenges to consider. We know that reading to primary grade children can be a powerful force in their literacy learning. But it can also end up being little more than a time filler. There is even such a thing as reading to children too much, if it takes the place of other important activities. Done thoughtfully, however, reading to children becomes a critically important means of teaching background knowledge, vocabulary, comprehension strategies, and knowledge of written language so crucial to becoming skilled and willing readers during the primary years and beyond.

The Texts Primary Grade Children Should Be Reading

One of the most discussed topics in early literacy instruction during the initial years of the twenty-first century promises to be what kinds of texts primary grade children should be reading in order to make learning to read most effective. The 1990s saw considerable use of authentic children's literature in kindergarten and first grade for reading instruction, in part owing to dissatisfaction with the "primerese" (e.g., "Look at me, Dick. Look at me. Oh, Dick. Come here. Run, Dick, run," or "A man had a ham. A man had a fat ham. A man had a gas can. Sad man!") previously used widely in beginning reading materials. Although authentic literature includes rich vocabulary, it is often "undecodable." "Predictable" books like *Brown Bear, Brown Bear, What Do You See?* (Martin, 1967), *Mrs. Wishy-Washy* (Cowley & Melser, 1980), or *The Chick and the Duckling* (Ginsburg, 1972) became popular reading material. Characterized by rhyme, rhythm, a close picture-text match, and repetitive words and phrases, such books enabled all children to participate successfully in meaningful "reading" experiences from the beginning. It was assumed that having children interact with such texts would foster the development of their word recognition skills. But with a steady diet of predictable texts, many children relied too much on memory and picture cues and, as a result, did not pay enough attention to the words they were supposed to be reading to develop much of a reading vocabulary.

Recently, a number of educators have proposed that children be given "decodable text" instead of literary text or predictable books because decodable text allows practice in applying the consistent letter-sound patterns taught in phonics lessons. What is meant by decodable text varies: some say that 70% to 80% of the words in what children read should be common letter-sound patterns, while others contend that decodable texts should consist of the particular letter-sound patterns taught in the curriculum up to that point. But all definitions focus on the central feature of phonetically regular texts.

Probably neither of these perspectives is adequate. Instead, children need a varied diet of texts to learn to read most successfully. Any one type of text has features that can prove useful in a child's literacy development, and it also has inherent limitations. *Predictable texts* do make it more likely that children will successfully complete the book; however, children often focus little of their attention on individual words or sound-symbol cues when reading such books. *Decodable texts* (controlled vocabulary texts) dispose children to use and practice what they know about sound-symbol relations, but they have two disadvantages. Many are so uninteresting that children choose not to read them, and therefore their potential benefits are lost; and their language is frequently so stilted that it undermines semantic and syntactic processing and thereby distorts the reading process. *Literary texts* appeal to children who have a well-developed understanding of story structure that can propel their reading; however, the rich and varied vocabulary in such books may be very difficult for beginners to recognize or decode. Of course, high interest and high motivation lead some children to persevere in making sense of very difficult stories or informational books, yet such challenges do not serve the purpose of providing children with material they can use to practice their reading on an everyday basis. In addition, there are texts based on *high-frequency words*. They offer beginning readers the opportunity to learn a relatively small number of words that make up a high percentage of all the texts that exist in the language, but these words also represent the most irregular spelling patterns and therefore impede a child's use of letter-sound knowledge. We can even think of *environmental print* (signs, labels, and so forth found in the home and community) as a type of text to be read by young children. Such print should be part of prekindergarten through first-grade classrooms because it helps children understand the functions and uses of the written language surrounding them every day, but its overall usefulness for learning to read is constrained by the real-life context in which it appears.

Thus, each type of text has features that recommend it as well as shortcomings. There is no magic formula for the mix of what types of texts a teacher should use with beginning readers. The next few years will almost certainly see a number of research studies examining this topic, and the results should help us understand the issue better. Yet the challenge for teachers will always be to keep in mind the individual child's prior experiences, needs, interests, and abilities in determining appropriate texts for given situations.

Student Diversity

Student diversity of all kinds is on the increase in our schools, but the teaching force as a whole is not very diverse. In addition, our record of helping children from nonmainstream cultural, ethnic, linguistic, or socioeconomic backgrounds learn to read and write is not particularly good; African-American and Latino students are significantly behind their Caucasian peers (Donahue, Voekl, Campbell, & Mazzeo, 1999).

To help improve early literacy instruction for diverse students, it is useful to keep in mind three characteristics of successful programs in schools and school districts with high percentages of such students. In these programs, teachers (1) become informed about issues faced by students of diversity, (2) recognize that differences are not necessarily a roadblock to literacy success, and (3) provide support and instruction relevant and appropriate to children of diversity as well as to mainstream populations.

Informed Teachers: A first step is committing oneself to becoming informed about issues that face diverse students. This means recognizing and validating the language and literacy experiences that children bring to school from their homes and communities, experiences often different from those of mainstream children in the classroom and even from those of the teacher. It also necessitates assessing students' strengths and weaknesses in ways that are culturally sensitive.

Differences, Not Deficits: Differences become a roadblock when we regard them as deficits to be overcome. But when variations in background experiences and in language and literacy use are sensitively considered as natural differences and prejudiced attitudes toward such differences are eliminated, it becomes much more likely that children will see themselves as readers and writers. In other words, being a student of diverse background does not necessarily imply difficulty in acquiring literacy. But because diversity is often part of a profile of students experiencing difficulty in literacy learning, the challenge is to find out how to eliminate the roadblocks that currently exist.

Relevant and Appropriate Instruction: What can teachers do to have the greatest chance of succeeding with diverse students? The practices already outlined in this chapter are important for all children. In being culturally sensitive, teachers can also follow the guidelines adapted from those offered by Yokota (1995):

- Create a culturally responsive language and literacy environment in the classroom and connect literacy instruction to students' backgrounds.
- Ensure that children see themselves and their families in the literacy curriculum. A good way is to include multicultural literature as reading material in classroom libraries and lessons and use the literature as a catalyst for discussions of diversity.
- Establish strong home-school-community connections. Parents from diverse backgrounds have much to contribute to the education of all children in the classroom. They also need to feel included in the entire spectrum of classroom activities, not just as contributors of cultural information. It may take extra effort and support for parents to understand the expectations of the school if those expectations differ from their own school experiences.
- Participate in staff development and seek support from others on issues related to ethnic, cultural, and linguistic diversity.

There has been comparatively little research into the issues related to teaching culturally or linguistically diverse primary grade children to read and write, and certainly no proven models for instruction have been developed. Thus, one of the biggest challenges facing early childhood teachers today is achieving greater success with literacy instruction for diverse students.

Use of Computers

Computers have become an essential aspect of daily life in our society. As a result, making such technology part of young children's education has received great attention. Because of this, many early childhood teachers are interested in integrating computers into reading and writing instruction in developmentally appropriate ways. Computers have the potential to enhance early literacy instruction. For example, some CD-ROMs offer books in interactive format that enable children to participate in innovative choral reading and echo reading activities (Labbo, Reinking, & McKenna, 1999) or provide supported practice that would not be possible without the expense of teacher aides or a highly developed volunteer program. Or, as another example, some teachers use a large-screen computer display to conduct morning message (Crowell, Kawakami, & Wong, 1986) and thereby enhance a well-established instructional activity.

Computers also are creating new kinds of texts for reading and writing and perhaps new "reading" and "writing" processes as well. Such

AN IDEA FROM A TEACHER

Using a Message Board to Encourage Reading, Writing, and Oral Language

I decided to try keeping a message board in the classroom for the children to communicate with one another in writing. I placed the corkboard in a prominent spot where the children can see it as they enter the room in the morning, and I put each child's name as well as mine on the board so that there is a place to leave and get messages. The children helped me decorate the board with self-portraits to accompany their names. Every day I leave a new message on the corkboard for the entire class. This note may be about holidays, themes we are studying, special events at school, or interesting current events. In addition, I leave a note for one or more individual children. I make sure that in a two-week period, I have left everyone one note. Notes can be about a special event in their lives, some good work they have done, or just a happy greeting. All messages are written so that they require a reply. A morning activity for my students is to check the message board and leave a message for someone. The children eagerly approach the message board each day and can be heard talking about messages and collaboratively reading messages to and with each other. They also leave messages they write themselves that are sparked by the message to everyone, their individual message, or something they just want to say. The message board is surrounded by children talking to each other, reading, and writing on a daily basis.

Bonnie Smith, First/Second-Grade Combination Class Teacher

"electronic literacy" (Reinking, 1995), or "digital literacy" (Labbo et al., 1999), is leading creative early childhood teachers and their students to explore frontiers in this area, discovering possibilities for activities like multimedia composing, shared viewings, sociodramatic play enhanced with technology, and so forth. Computers have also shown considerable promise for helping children who have great difficulty learning to read through regular instruction. These innovative uses of computers are called assistive technology; they help special-needs children who require alternative or multimodal/multisensory ways of processing to become literate.

Finding appropriate uses of technology for developing literacy is a great challenge. Many of the reading and writing computer applications aimed at young children are little more than electronic worksheets. They may be effective for keeping records of the answers children get right and wrong, and they may amuse and engage children, but they teach little of what children need to become capable readers and writers. What is needed instead are computer-related activities that (1) provide authentic and meaningful literacy experiences and (2) are woven into the fabric of the curriculum, connected to thematic units and to the curriculum areas outlined above.

From the work of Sulzby and her colleagues come two additional important points to keep in mind as we think about how to integrate computers into the early literacy program. First, computer uses for reading and writing are only as strong as the off-computer reading and writing environment in the classroom (Sulzby, 1996). In other words, computer technology cannot substitute for a good early literacy program, it can only complement it. Second, computers contribute most to children's literacy development when children are able to create with them, rather than just "use" or "consume" ready-made programs. (Nicholson, Lomangino, Young, & Sulzby, 1998). Open-ended programs such as child-friendly word processors and databases offer more learning opportunities than programs with predetermined ends.

In summary, the intersection of technology and early literacy is ripe with possibilities and challenges, but it is also fraught with hype and abuses. There is perhaps as much misinformation about computers in early literacy instruction as there is information, and for that reason we should all have reservations about them. In addition, we should always remember that the issue is not computer use but literacy. The computer is a tool that can help children achieve literacy, but it is not the end in itself. The primary grades are certainly the time for children to begin their journey into the literacy of the twenty-first century. It remains for us as teachers to understand better how computers and computer-related technology can be integrated into early literacy learning and teaching.

The Future of Early Literacy Instruction: Some Challenges

We have presented five significant challenges in the area of early literacy instruction, but it would not be difficult to discuss others. We have too little insight, for example, into what happens as children shift from emergent to conventional ways of reading and writing and how teachers can best support this shift. These days, writing instruction is more frequently a part of primary grade classrooms, but we could benefit from a closer look at a process approach to writing instruction to guard against its being implemented in superficial ways. We still know too little about spelling instruction in primary grade classrooms. And what of literature study? Should primary grade children be taking part in literature circles or book clubs, or is that something better left to students in grade 3 and above? Finally, many unresolved questions remain about appropriate phonics instruction for young children.

In short, this chapter could go on and on with issues that deserve attention. But we also should reflect on our successes in early literacy instruction. We discussed six conclusions that provided strong direction for building quality early literacy programs. In addition, the most recent international study of reading literacy (Elley, 1994) found that, among the 32 countries studied, U.S. 9-year-olds ranked second in the world in overall reading achievement. This figure suggests that we are doing a great deal right in primary grade literacy instruction.

It is an exciting time for the field of early literacy. Amid the controversies, literacy in kindergarten through grade 2 is receiving significant attention and funding. Curriculum development and research activities are abundant. There are more high-quality books being published for young children than ever before. Teachers are committed and enthusiastic in their teaching. But we have room to improve, and that is what is exciting about this area of education and this book on early literacy. We are not afraid to challenge ourselves to get better at beginning literacy instruction, and that means even better days are ahead for young children, their families, and their teachers.

References

Adams, M. J. (1990). *Beginning to read: Thinking and learning about print.* Cambridge, MA: MIT Press.

Anderson, R. C., Wilson, P., & Fielding, L. G. (1988). Growth in reading and how children spend their time outside of school. *Reading Research Quarterly, 23,* 285–303.

Applebee, A. N., Langer, J. A., & Mullis, I. V. S. (1988). *Who reads best? Factors related to reading achievement in grades 3, 7, and 11.* Princeton, NJ: Educational Testing Service.

Ball, E. W., & Blachman, B. A. (1991). Does phoneme awareness training in kindergarten make a difference in early word recognition and developmental spelling? *Reading Research Quarterly, 26,* 49–66.

Bear, D., Invernizzi, M., Templeton, S., & Johnston, F. (1995). *Words their way: Word study for phonics, vocabulary, and spelling.* Englewood Cliffs, NJ: Merrill.

Blachowicz, C., & Fisher, P. (1996). *Teaching vocabulary in all classrooms.* Englewood Cliffs, NJ: Merrill.

Bond, G. L., & Dykstra, R. (1967). The Cooperative Research Program in first-grade reading instruction. *Reading Research Quarterly, 2,* 5–141.

Burns, M. S., Griffin, P., & Snow, C. E. (1999). *Starting out right: A guide to promoting children's reading success.* Washington, DC: National Academy Press.

Calkins, L. M. (1994). *The art of teaching writing* (rev. ed.). Portsmouth, NH: Heinemann.

Chall, J. S. (1967). *Learning to read: The great debate.* New York: McGraw-Hill.

Chall, J. S. (1996). *Learning to read: The great debate* (3rd ed.). Fort Worth, TX: Harcourt Brace.

Cowley, J., & Melser, J. (1980). *Mrs. Wishy-Washy* (illus. by E. Fuller). Auckland, New Zealand: Shortland Publications.

Crowell, D., Kawakami, A., & Wong, J. (1986). Emerging literacy: Reading-writing experiences in a kindergarten classroom. *The Reading Teacher, 40,* 144–149.

Cunningham, P. M. (1995). *Phonics they use* (2nd ed.). New York: HarperCollins.

Dickinson, D. K., Hao, Z., & He, W. (1993, November). *Book reading: It makes a difference how you do it!* Paper presented at the 83rd Annual Convention of the National Council of the Teachers of English, Pittsburgh, PA.

Dickinson, D. K., & Smith, M. W. (1994). Long-term effects of preschool teachers' book readings on low-income children's vocabulary and story comprehension. *Reading Research Quarterly, 29,* 104–123.

Donahue, P. L., Voekl, K. E., Campbell, J. R., & Mazzeo, J. (1999). *NAEP 1998 reading report card for the nation.* Washington, DC: U.S. Department of Education, Office of Educational Research and Improvement, National Center for Educational Statistics.

Elley, W. B. (Ed.). (1994). *The IEA study of reading literacy: Achievement and instruction in thirty-two school systems.* Tarrytown, NY: Pergamon Press.

Flesch, R. (1955). *Why Johnny can't read.* New York: Harper & Row.

Gaskins, I. W. (1996). *Word detectives: Benchmark extended word identification program for beginning readers.* Media, PA: Benchmark Press.

Ginsburg, M. (1972). *The chick and the duckling* (illus. by J. Aruego & A. Dewey). New York: Macmillan.

Graves, D. H. (1983). *Writing: Teachers and children at work.* Exeter, NH: Heinemann.

Graves, D. H., & Hansen, J. (1983). The author's chair. *Language Arts, 60,* 176–183.

Hoffman, J. V. (1987). Rethinking the role of oral reading in basal instruction. *The Elementary School Journal, 87,* 367–374.

Hoffman, J. V., Roser, N. L., & Battle, J. (1993). Reading aloud in classrooms: From the modal toward a "model." *The Reading Teacher, 46,* 496–503.

[International Reading Association and National Association for the Education of Young Children]. (1998). Learning to read and write: Developmentally appropriate practices for young children. *Young Children, 53,* 30–46.

Juel, C., Griffith, P. L., & Gough, P. B. (1986). Acquisition of literacy: A longitudinal study of children in first and second grade. *Journal of Educational Psychology, 78,* 243–255.

Labbo, L. D., Reinking, D., & McKenna, M. C. (1999). The use of technology in literacy programs. In L. Gambrell, L. M. Morrow, S. B. Neuman, & M. Pressley (Eds.), *Best practices in literacy instruction* (pp. 311–327). New York: Guilford Press.

Labbo, L. D., & Teale, W. H. (1990). Cross-age reading: A strategy for helping poor readers. *The Reading Teacher, 43,* 362–369.

Labbo, L. D., & Teale, W. H. (1997). Emergent literacy as a model of reading instruction. In S. A. Stahl & D. A. Hayes (Eds.), *Instructional models in reading* (pp. 249–281). Mahwah, NJ: Erlbaum.

LaBerge, D., & Samuels, S. J. (1974). Toward a theory of automatic processing in reading. *Cognitive Psychology, 6,* 193–323.

Lemann, N. (1997, November). The reading wars. *Atlantic, 280,* 128–132.

Lundberg, I., Frost, J., & Petersen, O. P. (1988). Effects of an extensive program for stimulating phonological awareness in preschool children. *Reading Research Quarterly, 23,* 263–284.

Lyon, G. R. (1998). Why reading is not a natural process. *Educational Leadership, 55*(6), 14–18.

Martin, B. (1967). *Brown bear, brown bear, what do you see?* (illus. by E. Carle). New York: Holt.

Martinez, M., & Teale, W. (1993). Teacher storybook reading style: A comparison of six teachers. *Research in the Teaching of English, 27,* 175–199.

Meyer, L. A., Wardrop, J. L., Stahl, S. A., & Linn, R. L. (1994). Effects of reading storybooks aloud to children. *Journal of Educational Research, 88,* 69–85.

National Reading Panel. (2000). *Teaching children to read: An evidence-based assessment of the scientific research literature on reading and its implications for reading instruction.* Washington, DC: National Reading Panel. Available: http://www.nichd.nih.gov/publications/nrp/smallbook/pdf.

Nicholson, J., Lomangino, A. G., Young, S., & Sulzby, E. (1998). Influences of gender and open-ended software on first graders' collaborative composing activities on computer. *Journal of Computing in Childhood Education, 9*(1), 3–42.

Ninio, A. (1980). Picture-book reading in mother-infant dyads belonging to two subgroups in Israel. *Child Development, 51,* 587–590.

Opitz, M. F., Rasinski, T. V., & Bird, L. B. (1998). *Good-bye round robin: Twenty-five effective oral reading strategies.* Portsmouth, NH: Heinemann.

Pinnell, G. S., Pikulski, J. J., Wixson, K. K., Campbell, J. R., Gough, P. B., & Beatty, A. S. (1995). *Listening to children read aloud: Oral fluency.* Washington, DC: U.S. Department of Education, National Center for Educational Statistics.

Rasinski, T. V. (1996). *Holistic reading strategies: Teaching children who find reading difficult.* Englewood Cliffs, NJ: Prentice-Hall.

Reinking, D. (1995). Reading and writing with computers: Literacy research in a post-typographic world. *National Reading Conference Yearbook, 44,* 17–33.

Reutzel, D. R., & Hollingsworth, P. M. (1993). Effects of fluency training on second graders' reading comprehension. *Journal of Educational Research, 86,* 325–331.

Rubin, B. M. (1997, March 2). Reading wars: Endless squabbles keep kids from getting the help they need. *Chicago Tribune.* Perspective section, p. 1.

Samuels, S. J. (1979/1997). The method of repeated reading. *The Reading Teacher, 32/50,* 403–408/376–381.

Shanahan, T. (1984). Nature of the reading-writing relation: An exploratory multivariate analysis. *Journal of Educational Psychology, 76,* 466–477.

Snow, C. E., Burns, M. S., & Griffin, P. (Eds.). (1998). *Preventing reading difficulties in young children.* Washington, DC: National Academy Press.

Stahl, S. A., McKenna, M. C., & Pagnucco, J. R. (1994). The effects of whole language instruction: An update and a reappraisal. *Educational Psychologist, 9,* 178–186.

Stahl, S. A., & Miller, P. D. (1989). Whole language and language experience approaches for beginning reading: A qualitative research synthesis. *Review of Educational Research, 59,* 87–119.

Strecker, S. K., Roser, N. L., & Martinez, M. G. (1998). Toward understanding oral reading fluency. *National Reading Conference Yearbook, 47,* 295–310.

Strickland, D. S., & Morrow. L. M. (Eds.). (1989). *Emerging literacy: Young children learn to read and write.* Newark, DE: International Reading Association.

Sulzby, E. (1996, May). *Multimedia and multiple literacies in elementary and middle school classrooms.* Paper presented at the Preconference for the National Reading Research Center, International Reading Association, Anaheim, CA.

Sulzby, E., & Teale, W. H. (1991). Emergent literacy. In R. Barr, M. Kamil, P. Mosenthal, & P. D. Pearson (Eds.), *Handbook of Reading Research* (Vol. 2, pp. 727–757). New York: Longman.

Teale, W. H. (1995). Young children and reading: Trends across the 20th century. *Journal of Education, 177,* 95–125.

Teale, W. H. (1998, February). *Early literacy instruction: Rights, wrongs, and continuing challenges.* Paper presented at the 30th Annual Colorado Council of the International Reading Association Conference on Literacy, Denver, CO.

Teale, W. H., & Bean, K. (2000). SSR: What's a teacher to think—And do? Manuscript submitted for publication.

Teale, W. H., & Martinez, M. G. (1997). *Teachers' storybook reading styles and kindergartners' story comprehension.* Unpublished manuscript.

Teale, W. H., Patterson, J., & Lieb, E., & Bean, K. (1999, April). *Phonemic awareness instruction: From research findings to classroom practice.* Paper presented at the American Educational Research Association 1999 Annual Meeting, Montreal, Canada.

Teale, W. H., & Sulzby, E. (Eds.). (1986). *Emergent literacy: Writing and reading.* Norwood, NJ: Ablex.

Torgeson, J., Morgan, S., & Davis, C. (1992). The effects of two types of phonological awareness training on word learning in kindergarten children. *Journal of Educational Psychology, 84,* 364–370.

Wolf, S. A. (1993). What's in a name? Labels and literacy in readers theatre. *The Reading Teacher, 46,* 540–545.

Yokota, J. (1995). Literacy development for students of diverse populations. In S. B. Wepner, J. T. Feeley, & D. S. Strickland (Eds.), *The administration and supervision of reading programs* (2nd ed.). New York and Newark, DE: Teachers College Press and International Reading Association.

CHAPTER TWO

Becoming a Reader: A Developmentally Appropriate Approach

Susan B. Neuman and Sue Bredekamp

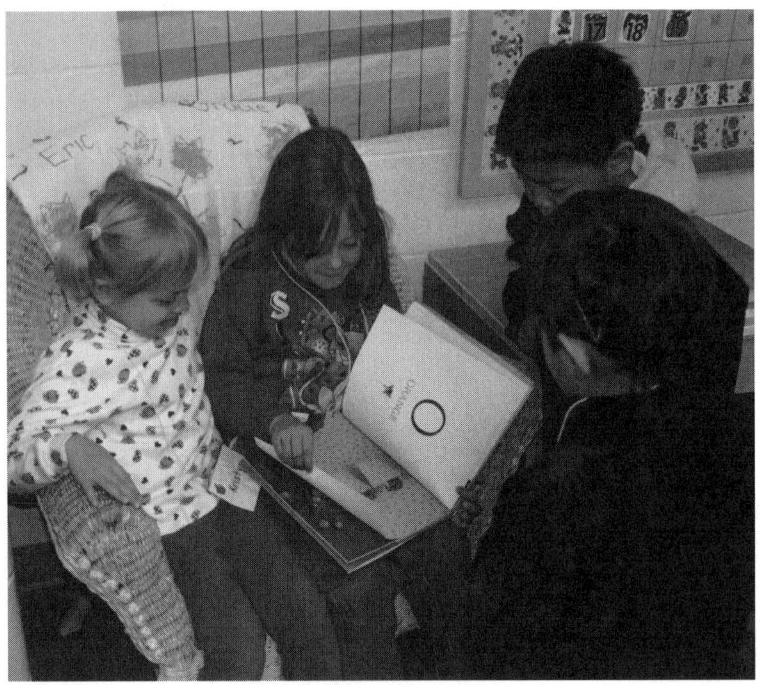

For Reflection and Action: Review your own early literacy development before first grade and consider how your experience might have been regarded and supported by today's educators. Compare and contrast your historical experience with contemporary classroom methods of supporting early literacy.

Susan Neuman and Sue Bredekamp describe strategies of literacy instruction in early childhood classrooms that support developmentally appropriate practice.

Although many activities contribute to early reading and writing development, none is more powerful than young children's interactions with books. Close observations of young children learning to read suggest that they thrive on the richness and diversity of reading materials and on being read to aloud. In fact, these early experiences feature prominently in the histories of successful readers, those children who not only know *how* to read but *choose* to read for learning and pleasure.

Children do not learn to read by magic. Rather, they learn by engaging with other, more accomplished readers around print. Caregivers and teachers play a critical role in promoting children's participation with books. They explain important concepts, encourage children's attention to meaningful events in stories, and involve them in using the information they are learning in dynamic ways that build connections beyond the printed page. Through assisted instruction, caregivers and teachers *teach* children that written words have meaning and power, keeping in mind the goal of creating independent readers and lifelong learners.

In 1998 the International Reading Association and the National Association for the Education of Young Children developed a joint position paper on developmentally appropriate practices for helping young children learn to read and write (IRA/NAEYC, 1998). This paper highlighted the importance of carefully mediated instruction that is sensitive to the social and cultural context of learning, the developmental patterns that may be universal to all children, and children's unique interests and needs. In this chapter we illustrate the importance of developmentally appropriate instruction, describe interactions that support children's experiences with books, and highlight some effective teaching strategies that enhance aloud and independent reading. The major topics discussed are:

- Age-appropriate engagement with print
- Strategies for reading aloud to young children
- Story-stretching projects for young learners
- Assisted instruction techniques
- The content and physical structure of a classroom library
- Scaffolding toward independent reading

Storybook Reading in the Beginning Years (Birth Through Preschool)

At age $2^1/_2$, Christopher can't read yet, and he hasn't shown much interest in letters. But he is always eager to listen to books. When he and his two friends at his child care center listen to *The Three Little Pigs*, they shout, "And I'll huff and I'll puff and I'll blow your house in." As Ms. Helen reads on, they wait for the next episode, only to repeat the lines even louder this time. While they are enjoying the story, they are probably not aware that the little black squiggles on the page are telling a story and that the words in the book are always the same. Nevertheless, they are learning important features of written knowledge, its rhythms and cadences, and displaying their knowledge of language structure. They are learning to participate in book-reading activities and to "talk like a book," which will have important consequences in successful reading later on (Snow, Tabors, Nicholson, & Kurland, 1995).

Even though their attention spans may be short, babies and toddlers benefit from hearing stories and being read to (Senechal, LeFevre, Thomas, & Daley, 1998; Whitehurst et al., 1988). They learn to focus their attention on the words and the pictures. Storybook reading by caregivers for very young children is highly social; interactions remain playful or gamelike, while instructional. Many caregivers do not just show the pictures to children but instead talk about them, asking questions like "What's that?" or making comments like "That's a lion. Remember when we went to the zoo?" Ms. Darlene, for example, finds that the clear photographs of everyday objects and animals in Tana Hoban's board book series, such as *Black on White, White on Black* (Hoban, 1993), fascinate 10-month-old Devon for about 5 minutes as he focuses all of his attention on one particular page. Later she finds him intently looking at the pictures by himself, holding the book and turning the pages.

Certain types of books are especially intriguing to babies and toddlers. Books with photographs or drawings of animals, people, and single, brightly colored objects draw children's attention and interest. Easy-to-hold board books that can stand hard wear enable toddlers to "read" by themselves. Interactive books, like Spot's lift-the-flap stories (also available in Spanish), playfully reinforce children's efforts to master the basics of book handling (even though the books are not likely to last long in the hands of toddlers). Books that take children though familiar routines or through a recitation of repeated questions and answers, such as Dr. Seuss's *Marvin K. Mooney, Will You Please Go Now!* (Gesell, 1972), help the young child become part of the story because of their predictable patterns and repetitive language. Teachers find that children tend to chime in, saying the last words of the phrase, "will you please go now." Such chiming in is a positive feature of early engagement: it provides for all sorts of language play, allowing the young child to say and use words that might be new and unfamiliar, and it keeps the child's attention from wandering. Nursery rhymes are well loved at this age as well, with children wanting to hear the same stories over and over again.

Story times for young children work best when they are relatively brief (about 5 to 10 minutes) and conversational. With the reader sitting with one or two children on each side, the children are able to follow the text and pictures closely, ask questions, and point to their favorite characters. It really doesn't matter whether the story is completed or not. Rather, the point of story time for very young listeners is for the interaction to be enjoyable and to be filled with language. Caregivers can choose "readable moments" throughout the day—time between activities, quiet times, or moments when stories can bring the day to a fulfilling close.

Assisted Instruction

It is the end of the day at Tiny Tots, a busy time when parents are picking up their children and gathering their many things. The attention of 3½-year-old Edward and his 4-year-old cousin Kalief is riveted, however, not on the door but on the short book, *Peek-a-Boo* (Ahlberg & Ahlberg, 1981), about houses, being read by Ms. Kimberly:

Ms. Kimberly: Do you see the plumber, Kalief?

Edward: I see the plumber.

Kalief: He's working on the pipes. I be working on the pipes.

Edward: Here go the ladder.

Kalief: There go the lights.

Edward: Who's in the house?

Kalief: A worker man?

Ms. Kimberly: The workers are painting and putting up the doors and the windows.

Edward: Turn it back [the page], turn it back, turn it back! I want to see the worker man.

(*Ms. Kimberly turns back the page.*)

Ms. Kimberly: Here's the workers. The workers leave. That means they go home. You know, like when you leave here with your mommy. They go home.

No doubt, Ms. Kimberly would consider this informal conversation rather typical and uneventful. But there are a number of striking features in this book-reading activity. For one, Ms. Kimberly has selected a book that is challenging but understandable for the children (IRA/NAEYC, 1998; Lidz, 1991; Rogoff, Mosier, Mistry, & Goncu, 1993). Although the story contains many new words, the topic is a familiar one and interesting to the boys. Here the children are labeling words that are related to their everyday lives.

Notice that Ms. Kimberly begins by recruiting their attention, asking them to focus on a page. Once the children become involved, she steps back a bit as they give meaning to the pictures. She then helps the children define "workers" and extends the description beyond the printed page, bridging what is seen in the picture to what they can relate to in their own lives. In this respect, Ms. Kimberly provides metacognitive support, controlling and taking primary responsibility for higher-level goals while the children engage at a level they are capable of at the time (Diaz, Neal, & Vachio, 1991).

Within the context of a book-reading activity, caregivers may accentuate the relevance and meaningfulness of some features more than others. Through this process, children learn the names of common objects and the relationships among objects and events. Once the context and meaningfulness of an activity are conveyed, caregivers may extend children's understanding by linking the activity to something that is either within or beyond the children's own experiences. For example, Ms. Kimberly defines what it means for the workers to leave, then compares it with the children's own leaving for the day. This task—helping children make sense of present experiences by relating them to the past—is seen as essential for intellectual growth. It may also facilitate children's understanding of events that cannot actually be perceived, by encouraging them to employ their imaginations to anticipate further activities. Sigel and his colleagues, for example, have described this concept as "distancing" and have documented an association of distancing with the cognitive development of preschoolers (McGillicuddy-De Lisi, Sigel, & Johnson, 1979; Sigel & McGillicuddy-De Lisi, 1984).

Not seen in this particular interaction but a critical feature of assisted instruction is the transfer of responsibility from caregiver to child (Rogoff, 1990; Tharp & Gallimore, 1988). Teachers need to carefully gauge their support to see when children are able to move beyond their current levels of ability. They may encourage and prompt the child to turn the pages, to ask questions, and to predict what might come next, so that the child can work toward independence and self-regulation. For example, the next day Ms. Kimberly will place the now familiar and well-loved book about houses in the block area or the classroom library so that Edward and Kalief can "read it by themselves." They may sit in the corner and reread the story. Or they may use blocks in the block corner to construct a house, with ladders, pipes, and lights, and pretend to be "worker men." In so doing they will be making the book their own, retelling parts of the book in their own language. In the course of their pretend play, they will engage in "decontextualized language," or language used (accurately) apart from the actual context in which it was crafted, which is predictive of academic success.

We have defined these critical steps in assisted instruction as (1) get set, (2) give meaning, (3) build bridges, and (4) step back (Neuman, 1995). *Get set* focuses on the importance of attention getting, such as recruiting children's interest by asking predictive questions, as well as structuring the physical setting (providing comfortable chairs that allow the children to see and point to the pictures) so that children can effectively participate. *Give meaning* helps children understand the story by focusing on the illustrations, describing new words, adding affect to the voice ("*meeeow*") to make the words or pictures more understandable to the children, and talking about and elaborating on the actions in a story. *Build bridges* highlights the importance of extending children's understanding by linking what is read to something that is either within or beyond their own experiences. Teachers might build connections between what is going on now in the classroom and other experiences, either past or present, to move the story experience beyond the pages. Finally, *step back* encourages caregivers to give children increasing responsibility, letting the children take turns and ask questions, and providing elaborated feedback to encourage their strategic thinking.

Essentially, assisted instruction reminds all caregivers and teachers that good instruction is sensitive to children's development and that teaching plays an important role in helping children develop higher-order thinking. Edward and Kalief's conversational turns, for example, would not have been as rich had Ms. Kimberly simply placed the book in the play center without first reading and discussing it. It was her sensitivity to careful book selection and interaction that supported their language and thinking.

Reading Aloud to Groups of Preschoolers

Even though children might not seem ready for sustained listening, most teachers will begin to involve children in daily group storybook-reading activity when they are about 3 years old. Starting the day with a story is a powerful learning technique, for several reasons. It builds a sense of community among children as they create a common knowledge base together. In addition, storybook reading is a primary way to build new vocabulary. Children learn many new words by listening to stories (Elley, 1989; Leung & Pikulski, 1990). Reading books can also serve as a source of learning throughout the day. In one class, for example, Ms. Wright read *The Carrot Seed* (Krauss, 1945), a story about a rather tenacious young boy who believed (against all odds) that his carrot seed would grow. She first used the story in an inquiry lesson to set the stage for a unit on growing things. She encouraged the children to describe some of the things (water, sunlight) plants need to grow and some of the dispositions that young gardeners must have (hope and determination) to be successful. With its strong predictable element and positive message, the children loved hearing the story again and again and used its lessons throughout the unit.

Not all children will be equally prepared for group storybook reading. Children with few previous experiences with storybook reading will probably be restless. For such young listeners, teachers should not try to engage the whole group at once in reading a complete story. It will probably be more effective to build up children's attention spans and ability to listen over time. Teachers need to help children develop these skills because they are essential for literacy development. But these skills are not developed by forcing children to sit still for long periods of time, punishing or removing children who do not conform, or spending group time correcting children's behavior rather than actually reading.

Children, like adults, thrive on routines and expectations. To build children's attention spans, particularly in the beginning, it is important to ensure that all children are seated comfortably on a rug or carpet square and have the opportunity to hear, see, and listen to stories. Smaller groups will be more effective at first. Having a turn in the group can become a special treat.

For children not accustomed to hearing stories read aloud, it is especially important to make sure that the classroom is quiet and not bustling with other, competing activity. In some centers, all teachers in classrooms hold storybook reading at the same time in the morning to maximize children's learning. Inviting assistant teachers or volunteers to help allows everyone, teacher and children, to concentrate better on the story and not be disrupted. Very restless children should be given an alternative, while some children may need to hold a book in their hands to capture their attention.

It is best to start with simple, predictable stories, such as counting or alphabet books, to elicit children's attention for short periods of time. It is more important to have a pleasant 10-minute story time than a 20-minute struggle for children's attention. Many teachers use books with only a few lines on a page and lively, interesting pictures, since long books with lots of dialogue might be difficult for children to follow. After a few successful story times, children will be ready for richer stories and information books. In some cases teachers introduce these stories over several days. For example, on the first day of reading a new story, Ms. Michaels uses the book to take a "picture walk." She shows the children the pictures in *Jesse Bear, What Will You Wear?* (Carlstrom, 1986) and points out some things about Jesse Bear—what he is wearing and doing. The next day she shows the same pictures and reads more of the text (or tells the story in her own words) and asks the children to help her name some of the prominent colors, like the color of Jesse's shirt. On the third day she reads more of the text, naming some of the foods that Jesse eats for lunch. By the fourth day the 3- and 4-year-olds are sitting in rapt attention as she reads the full text and shows them the now familiar pictures.

Many experienced teachers and caregivers have developed a pattern for storybook-reading sessions. They hold the story session in a special space or corner that makes the children feel cozy and protected. The teacher might begin with a special opening song, setting the mood for the session, and bring the session to a close with a different song or an action poem. Depending on the books selected and the interesting conversations that evolve, many children after a while are able to sit through a 25- to 30-minute activity session. For those with shorter attention spans, however, some teachers hold two or three shorter sessions a day, each 10 to 15 minutes long.

A Read-Aloud Session: The 3- and 4-year-olds in the Building Blocks Child-Care Center are just beginning their year and are new to the storybook-reading routine. Ms. Fernanda begins the day by gathering the children around her and speaking in a very soft voice, which makes the children use softer voices too. "I want to give you a seat, that is your magic carpet. When you sit on it, you can ride to a special place called storyland."

Once the children are seated, Ms. Fernanda shows the children her bag. "This is my magic bag. Some of the things in this bag are for you to keep forever and some are just for you to enjoy today." She then pulls out of her bag *Goldilocks and the Three Bears* (Miles, 1998) and reads it to the children. She adds words to make it interesting and uses a number of different voices and facial expressions to make the story come alive for the children. The children are mesmerized.

Next, Ms. Fernanda takes a stuffed spider out of her bag. She recites the nursery rhyme "Little Miss Muffet" for the children, using the spider to help illustrate the motions. The children recite the nursery rhyme three times together while Ms. Fernanda acts it out. She walks around to every child, and each one has a turn at touching the spider as they recite "Itsy Bitsy Spider." "Remember we did this before. Don't forget the hand motions." The children recite the poem two times with hand motions.

Ms. Fernanda now takes out of her bag a big book, *The Little Red Hen.* She tells the children that she needs help with reading the story. "I am going to read you a story about a little red hen. This story was written by Paul Galdone." Some children repeat, "He's the author!" Ms. Fernanda responds, "That's right. You guys remembered that the person who writes the story is called the author. That's great." She reads the story, using her finger to point to the words and stopping the reading just before she gets to "Not I." The children quickly realize what Ms. Fernanda wants them to do even though she does not explicitly tell them to repeat "Not I." They participate with great enthusiasm. After she reads the story, Ms. Fernanda asks, "Why wouldn't the red hen share her bread? What did you like most about the story?" The children engage in a lively discussion.

"Now storybook reading is about over. But before we end, we're going to sing a song you can sing to your mommy before you leave your house in the morning." She teaches them a song about having a clean body and clean clothes. She then sings another song, "My Rhythm Sticks Go Click Click Click" (on another day she will have them use sticks and follow the beat). After the singing she thanks the children for being good listeners, and they get ready for activity time.

A number of features make Ms. Fernanda's storybook-reading sessions special. Ms. Fernanda is sensitive to children's developmental needs. She helps children "get set" by clearly defining her expectations for acceptable behavior. She provides a high level of interactivity (she engages children's voices, hands, and images) and moves seamlessly from one activity to another. Books, action poems, and songs are all included in this session in an engaging format, one that is especially helpful for children who may need to release excess energy. A routine is established, with a beginning, stories, and an ending, that will help children define story time's boundaries.

Ms. Fernanda is also providing excellent language and literacy instruction. Throughout the session, the children are learning basic concepts of print (e.g., that stories are written by authors), the sounds of language (poems and rhymes have similar sounds and are recited and repeated, which enhances their recall), and vocabulary (representations of objects like spiders are shown; this is particularly important for children with limited background knowledge). The children see demonstrations of what a word looks like as Ms. Fernanda uses her finger to follow the print (sometimes referred to as "tracking print"). They are developing a sense of story format (introduction, episodes, and resolution). Ms. Fernanda is leading children to identify the theme and to add their own interpretations to the story. (In this case she does not interrupt the flow of the story with questions but waits until the end before engaging children in conversation). Finally, they are learning, through Ms. Fernanda's actions and animation, the sheer joy of sharing stories.

Stretching Children's Understanding: Sometimes it is useful to explore certain aspects of the story with children. Activities for this purpose, often called "story stretchers," help create greater meaning for children by stretching their understanding of the story. Some teachers combine art, science, and math activities as a natural outgrowth of reading a book. For example, the book *Mouse Paint* (Walsh, 1989), with its beautifully vivid colors, lends itself to an art activity where children mix colors and see what their mixtures bring.

Story stretchers work best when they relate directly to the story. For example, activities that engage children in retelling a story using puppets or a flannel board (with visual representations of words) encourage children to use their language to recall the sequence and events of the story from their perspective. Puppets, whether made of sticks, paper bags, or socks, are particularly helpful for involving reticent children or those who feel they do not have the language skills needed to retell the story. Creative dramatics also allow children to interpret stories in their unique fashion. After providing some guidance, teachers can "step back," giving children increasing responsibility for retelling the stories their way.

These types of story stretchers can be compared with the ones more typical of teacher activity books. For example, one resource book recommended that after reading *The Gingerbread Boy* (Galdone, 1973), teachers and children could make gingerbread cookies or use colored glue for icing on a gingerbread boy pattern. Gingerbread cookies make wonderful snacks, and gingerbread boy patterns may liven up a classroom bulletin board. But these activities are not real story stretchers. Neither engages children in understanding the essential lesson that the gingerbread boy, unfortunately, learned too late. Story stretchers that involve children in asking questions, retelling, making predictions, and discussing the story, possibly connecting it to other experiences in their lives, are far more instructional and meaningful to young children.

Ms. Olna regularly uses story stretchers for her group of very active 2½- through 4-year-olds. Today she reads *Freight Train* (Crews, 1978), to the group's delight. After reading, she reviews the details of the story: "How many cars were there on the train? Let's count." Then she asks, "What color was each train? Let's check." They return to the beginning of the book and recall each color of the cars on the train. Next, to stretch children's ideas about the story, Ms. Olna asks, "What would you look like if you were a car on the train? What might you carry?" (Here she is building bridges and stepping back.) Children get in a line (sometimes winding, sometimes straight), placing the right hand on the right shoulder of the child in front. Slowly they begin to move, reciting "Chuga, chuga, chuga, chuga, toot, toot," first softly, then loudly; quickly, then slowly. The children love the activity and ask to do it again. Through this story-stretching activity, Ms. Olna has helped them visualize the motion and the words associated with freight trains.

Creating a Classroom Library

Classroom libraries complement and extend children's learning from books. The library need not be large or fancy but it should feel cozy, and it is best set apart from the main part of the room with bookshelves or semifixed structures. The library should include about five quality books per child (changed regularly), and the books should be attractive-looking, not tattered and worn. Familiar titles, such as books that have been recently read by the teacher, will draw children's attention; multiple copies of these favorite books will encourage children to read to one another. Some critical features of a classroom library are the following:

- An accessible arrangement of books (open-faced shelves allow children to look at the pictures and titles at their eye level)
- A variety of materials, including magazines and information, alphabet, counting, and picture books
- Stuffed animals and comfortable seating (bean-bag chairs, mattress and pillows)
- Good lighting
- Lively displays (book covers) and posters, to add color and dimension to the walls of the

library, and a catchy name, like "Cozy Corner Library"

Before encouraging wide use, however, teachers should help children learn how to handle and care for books in their library. In some centers, teachers use old books to talk about a book's delicate spine and the importance of not ripping pages. Ms. Fernanda gives children lessons on turning pages. Giving them each a book, she guides their hands in a group lesson to go "across the top, down to the corner, and flip over." Ms. Fernanda also makes sure that the library includes a "book hospital"—an old dairy box—"where books go to get better." The book hospital contains torn books and invisible tape, eraser, scissors, and glue. Ms. Fernanda regularly invites children to a fix-it lesson, during which they watch while she repairs a well-loved book.

The library is not the only area to place books, however. Some teachers decentralize the classroom library, by placing books about fishes near the fish tank, books about cooking in the kitchen, and books and magazines in the "doctor's office" dramatic play center. Teachers find that it is common to observe children referring to these materials in their play and in project activities. In addition, placing books in different activity centers sends the important message that books are useful sources of information that can be turned to on all sorts of occasions.

Equally as important as the classroom library design and placement of reading materials is the time apportioned for children to use these resources. Giving children time to use the classroom library before circle time, during naptime, and before dismissal is good for transition but not good enough for learning. Children need a solid block of time during the day to browse, read silently on their own, read one on one with a parent, teacher, or aide, or read with their friends or teddy bears. Sometimes children will pretend to read, such as Clarissa, who opens a book and says, "Once upon a time, once upon a time, once upon a time. There, I readed it." Clarissa is demonstrating her motivation and interest in reading, which might lead the thoughtful teacher to ask a key question: "Would you like me to read it to you?"

Storybook Reading in Kindergarten

Classrooms built around the instructional techniques developed for preschool children help children begin to read on their own in kindergarten. Many kindergarten teachers extend their language and literacy curriculum to include reading aloud, shared reading, and independent reading activities.

Studies suggest that reading probably accounts for about one-third of a child's annual vocabulary growth, and that regular wide reading may result in substantial and permanent learning and school achievement (Anderson, 1995; Nagy & Herman, 1987). Reading aloud is the primary means of enriching children's vocabulary in these early years. Even if children can read a bit on their own, their oral vocabulary still far exceeds their knowledge of written words. It is especially important, therefore, for teachers to read quality books that contain some words that are not necessarily familiar to the children.

Before reading the book, a brief discussion about a few new vocabulary words is particularly effective for kindergarten children. Some teachers, like Ms. Theresa, use physical props to help children focus on the specific vocabulary to be encountered in the story. One day, as a "get set" activity before reading *Snow White,* she holds up a mirror and says, "Mirror, mirror on the wall, who's the fairest of them all?" She asks the group, "What does this mirror help us to do?" Sarah answers, "It lets me look at myself." Hoping to extend the children's understanding of words, Ms. Theresa then asks, "Well, what do you think she means by 'fairest'?" Showing the picture of the wicked old queen, Jennifer answers, "She just wants to be pretty." "Aaah, so in this case, fairest means being the prettiest," says Ms. Theresa.

Of course, it is not necessary to use props for every story or information book. Some teachers might use a flannel board, others might engage in casual conversation about the topic. But regardless of the particular strategies used, some vocabulary discussion *before* reading helps children better understand and enjoy the story. It is also a far more enriching activity than simply asking children to regurgitate the title of the book and the author's name. *During* the reading, it may be beneficial to stop at various junctures, show the pictures in the book, and ask questions that help children guess what might happen next. (Asking too many questions, however, can be distracting, since children's answers often are not brief or to the point.) *After* the story is an opportune time to take another look at the vocabulary and illustrations and talk about the story in ways that personalize it for children, bridging the experience from the known to the unknown. Whitehurst and his colleagues have found that asking open-ended *what* and *why* questions fosters richer conversations (Whitehurst, Arnold, Epstein, Angell, Smith, & Fischel, 1994). Asking "Why do you think Eeyore is doing that?" instead of "Is Eeyore playing or not?" encourages children to take increasing responsibility for their own learning.

During the kindergarten year, children may begin to retell stories in their own words. This is an important skill, for several reasons. Retelling helps children put various details of the story together and sequence events. It also aids in developing a sense of story—the concept that stories have settings, characters, problems, events, and resolutions. This is an insight that will help children come to anticipate how stories work, how plot events relate to the overall structure of a story. In addition, the retelling itself becomes a metacognitive activity for children, allowing them to assess their understanding by using their own words to analyze and synthesize what they have learned from the story.

All of these insights are further developed when children have the opportunity to hear the story read again. Elley (1989), for example, found that 7- and 8-year-olds who heard the same story read three times in the classroom demonstrated some gain in identifying the correct meanings of words. Children with weaker vocabularies may benefit from one-on-one rereadings, with someone providing more explicit instruction in vocabulary. Teachers can also use multiple rereadings of good books to focus on different categories of words. For example, Ms. Theresa uses Eric Carle's *The Very Hungry Caterpillar* (1984) to focus on "food words" one day and "days of the week" another day. Quality children's literature provides opportunities to read the same book from multiple perspectives.

Shared reading often follows the read-aloud activity. For shared reading, teachers often use a big book that has limited text per page and a recurring theme. With *Mrs. Wishy-Washy* (Cowley, 1999), the children observe and participate as Ms. Peterman opens up the book and glides her hand under the words as she reads. She and the children repeat the refrain, "wishy-washy, wishy-washy" many times and recall, "in went the pig, in went the cow, in went the duck" as the animals are marched into the tub by Mrs. Wishy-Washy. As she reads, and without specifically stating to the kindergartners what she is doing, she demonstrates many concepts of print: that writing moves from left to right, that print (not the illustrations) carries the message, and that the black marks on the page have meaning. Generally, Ms. Peterman will first read a text rather quickly to give children a sense of the story, then reread it, pausing where commas occur, making a full stop for periods, and tracking the print. She is modeling the message that print is a reliable conveyor of the text's message.

Big books are useful for a number of purposes. With their lively illustrations and predictable text, they are easily remembered. After several rereadings, children will act as if they were readers, fluently "reading" the text. The very act of fluent reading helps children develop a sense of what good readers do. In addition, once children have memorized the text, teachers can isolate various words and help the children begin to develop a sight vocabulary of new words—words that are quickly recognized without having to be sounded out. For Ms. Peterman's class, for example, the word "wishy-washy" leads her to ask, "Does anyone know any other words that begin like 'wishy-washy'?" Together the children generate some new words, which Ms. Peterman will write down and use in developing a word wall. Knowing some words may help children learn new words, through rhyming patterns and word families. Later Ms. Peterman will use the predictable features of another story (*Brown Bear, Brown Bear, What Do You See?*) to involve children in making their own big book story ("Trash Truck, Trash Truck, What Do You Do?").

Although big books have an important place in helping children learn to read, they should not be used exclusively in the instructional program. These books are not great literature. They are simple texts, designed for instructional purposes. Moreover, giving too much attention to memorized text may lead children to rely too much on sight vocabulary and picture illustrations as they develop as readers, rather than on alternative cue systems such as graphophonemic, syntactical, or semantic cue systems. Big books are best used in conjunction with good narrative and expository books to achieve a balance of reading activities, word learning, and daily writing practice.

Last but certainly not least, teachers need to set aside a time every day to ensure that all children spend a minimum of 15 to 20 minutes in independent reading (somewhat more time may be allotted in a full-day kindergarten). During this time children can choose what to read on their own, use the library area, and share books that have been read aloud before. Some teachers include a listening center, specially enhanced with read-alouds from their favorite stories. (Parents can be asked to make these tapes for the teachers.) Reading independently or with friends gives children a chance to develop interests and self-direction. In one project, for example, we created a buddy system in which children read daily in pairs (Neuman & Soundy, 1991). Some of the children were beginning to actually read, while others were still talking about the pictures. But in almost all cases, children were talking about books!

It is also essential to include at least one literacy-related play center in the classroom (Neuman & Roskos, 1997). If space is at a premium, teachers can enhance an already popular area such as the housekeeping corner with literacy by including cookbooks, magazines, Post-it notes, a chef's hat, a telephone and telephone book, message pads, and environmental print. Unlike theme-based centers (e.g., an apple orchard or a shoe store), children are highly familiar with activities in this area and are likely to engage in lots of conversations around this topic. Some teachers find that this area becomes more popular as new literacy-related materials, such as take-out menus, recipes, and coupons, are added.

After independent reading time, a brief class meeting is a wonderful way to tie the reading events of the day together and to let children share with others what they have read. General conversations about books give life to new titles.

Storybook Reading in the Primary Grades

During independent reading time in Ms. Panetta's first-grade classroom, Christopher and his friends, Tyree and David, are in the science area working on a project about animal habitats. They are trying to figure out how some animals protect themselves throughout the winter. Each has a different book, but their focus is the same: they are scanning for pictures and words that might help them become experts on the topic. Words on animals and their homes are written on index cards to become part of a word wall as well as part of their increasing sight vocabulary. As they glance through the books, however, they are not reading every sentence; rather, their focus is on getting answers to some of the questions they have posed together with their teacher. Ms. Panetta held a discussion the day before to help them develop their ideas through a KWL chart: what do you know, what do you want to learn, and what have you learned).

Earlier in the day, these children participated in a much more structured and teacher-supported small-group instruction emphasizing guided reading. In the primary grades, guided reading is the foundation of the literacy curriculum. Guided reading focuses on children's instructional levels, the levels at which children can read with the teacher's assistance. Many teachers use a basal reading program that provides an anthology of selections for children to read on their own with guidance and teaching support.

The essentials of guided reading include the teacher's first engaging the children in talking about the topic, calling up relevant background knowledge, and predicting what might be in the story or selection. In most cases the teacher will focus on some new vocabulary. Then the children silently read part of the selection. (Silent reading in the primary grades often sounds like quiet oral reading, as children try to figure out new words.) At various stopping points the teacher involves the children in drawing conclusions and inferences about the reading, summarizing the story and listening to them read aloud. As they read, the teacher jots down information, recording the accuracy and fluency of each child's reading and his or her meaning-making strategies. These notes will help to inform further instruction and aid the teacher in ascertaining when some children may need additional small-group or one-on-one instruction.

Whether or not to use a basal series has become a source of controversy in the past decade. Basal readers have been severely criticized by whole language critics for their abridged and uninteresting stories and for "vocabulary control"—the practice of repeating certain words to establish a criterion of frequency (e.g., "'Look, look, look,' said Jane"). In response to these and other concerns, basal readers published in recent years have moved to more "authentic" text, including longer, unabridged stories and informational texts with richer vocabulary in the anthologies.

The fact is, however, longer texts with more interesting words are more difficult for children to read, especially first graders and struggling readers. A comparable situation would be to hand adults a copy of the *Iliad* in Greek and say, "Now read it." Young children lack the facility to decipher unknown words. Consequently, teachers and publishers have chosen different instructional routes. Some have created reading programs using "leveled books." In this approach, children's literature books are categorized according to a set of criteria (e.g., links across collection, content, length, format, amount of print on a page) and placed on a continuum of difficulty. With guided reading instruction, children move from one level of text to another.

Another approach is to use decodable text for at least 6 months but not more than 12 months of instruction. These books exemplify certain letter-sound patterns that the children have learned through instruction. Although the stories are less interesting, they are systematically designed to allow children to use their decoding skills (developed thus far) to read new stories. Some teachers hesitate to use these books, claiming that children will be unmotivated to read. Others argue that, on the contrary, decodable texts enable children to practice what they have learned and to develop independence in reading. Whatever approach is used, reading selections should be comprehensible (so that children will be able to understand them) and instructive (so that children will learn from them). The ultimate goal is to help them become independent readers.

Grouping for instruction is important in the primary grades because it allows teachers to focus on children's strengths and weaknesses. However, inflexible ability grouping can be detrimental to children's self-confidence and self-esteem. No matter what teachers might call these groups, children are not blind to ability distinctions. Just ask the children: they will quickly tell you the difference between the "bluebirds" and the "squirrels." Some teachers apply "dynamic grouping techniques" that allow them to focus on children's particular instructional needs, such as more help with vocabulary, with the groups reformed on the basis of ongoing evaluation. Still others convene groups around interests, establish book clubs, or use peer tutoring-learning pairs.

Guided reading is a critical part of the reading program in the primary grades. But it is not the whole program. In addition to independent reading, for example, during the rest of the day the children might participate in a lively read-aloud session. As Ms. Panetta reads from a chapter book, children draw pictures of their favorite characters. After a read-aloud she spends a few minutes holding a book chat, so that children can share their interpretations of the story. These chats enable her to see how the children have constructed meaning from the story and how well they are able to express their ideas verbally. Ms. Panetta will also spend some time on shared reading with big books, today emphasiz-

AN IDEA FROM A TEACHER

A Developmentally Appropriate Way to Extend Learning

The children in my classroom begin each day by sharing some personal items from their special treasure chest. At the beginning of the year I provide a shoe box for each child, and I encourage each of them to decorate the box in a way that will help others know him or her better. Children can place special objects—a rabbit's foot, a favorite stuffed animal—in the box. Throughout the year they are encouraged to add or take away objects, according to their interests, the reading and language arts themes we are studying, and special times of year. For example, after our visit to the zoo in the fall many children brought in a picture of their favorite animal to share with others. A special holiday greeting card or family memento placed in the box may be especially comforting and personally gratifying at different times throughout the year.

During our morning share time, children take turns talking about their items. They may tell a story or give a personal account of why they like the object. Or they may describe the object, using favorite adjectives and richly detailed language, or explain how it relates to what we have read or learned in class. In any case, they are able to make connections to themes we are studying, convey their personal feelings, and help the class and me get to know them a little bit better.

Tonya Beck, Kindergarten Teacher

ing how dialogue is written down. As the children's skills in guided reading are increasing, however, she is slowly reducing the amount of time spent on this portion of her instructional program.

Early reading instruction should feature a delicate balance of carefully scaffolded experiences. Reading aloud to children pushes their development as readers, moving them beyond their current vocabulary and experiences to other worlds. Shared reading provides explicit demonstrations of early reading strategies in enjoyable and purposeful ways. Guided reading challenges children to stretch their abilities to learn new skills and understandings. Independent reading gives children choice and helps guide them toward self-regulation. None of these experiences alone is adequate. All are necessary components in learning to read.

Children's Books Cited

Ahlberg, J., & Ahlberg, A. (1981). *Peek-a-boo.* New York: Viking.

Carle, E. (1984). *The very hungry caterpillar.* New York: Putnam.

Carlstrom, N. W. (1986). *Jesse Bear, what will you wear?* New York: Simon & Schuster.

Cowley, J. (1999). *Mrs. Wishy-Washy.* New York: Philomel.

Crews, D. (1978). *Freight train.* New York: Greenwillow.

Galdone, P. (1973). *The little red hen.* Boston: Houghton Mifflin.

Galdone, P. (1993). *The gingerbread boy.* Boston: Houghton Mifflin.

Gesell, T. (Dr. Seuss). (1972). *Marvin K. Mooney, will you please go now!* New York: Random House.

Hoban, T. (1993). *Black on white, white on black.* New York: Greenwillow.

Krauss, R. (1945). *The carrot seed.* New York: Harper & Row.

Martin, B. (1992). *Brown bear, brown bear, what do you see?* New York: Holt.

Miles, B. (1998). *Goldilocks and the three bears.* New York: Simon & Schuster.

Walsh, E. (1989). *Mouse paint.* New York: Harcourt, Brace.

References

Anderson, R. C. (1995). *Research foundations for wide reading.* Urbana, IL: Center for the Study of Reading.

Diaz, R., Neal, C., & Vachio, A. (1991). Maternal teaching in the zone of proximal development: A comparison of low- and high-risk dyads. *Merrill-Palmer Quarterly, 37,* 83–108.

Elley, W. (1989). Vocabulary acquisition from listening to stories. *Reading Research Quarterly, 24,* 174–187.

IRA/NAEYC. (1998). Learning to read and write: Developmentally appropriate practices for young children. *The Reading Teacher, 52,* 193–216.

Leung, C. B., & Pikulski, J. J. (1990). Incidental learning of word meanings by kindergarten and first grade children through repeated read aloud events. In J. Zutell & S. McCormick (Eds.), *Literacy theory and research: Analyses from multiple paradigms* (pp. 231–240). Chicago: National Reading Conference.

Lidz, C. (1991). *Practitioner's guide to dynamic assessment.* New York: Guilford Press.

McGillicuddy-De Lisi, A., Sigel, I., & Johnson, J. (1979). The family as a system of mutual influences: Parental beliefs, distancing behaviors, and children's representational thinking. In M. Lewis & L. A. Rosenblum (Eds.), *The child and its family* (pp. 91–106). New York: Plenum Press.

Nagy, W., & Herman, P. (1987). Breadth and depth of vocabulary knowledge: Implications for acquisition and instruction. In M. G. McKeown & M. E. Curtis (Eds.), *The nature of vocabulary acquisition.* Hillsdale, NJ: Erlbaum.

Neuman, S. B. (1995). Enhancing adolescent mothers' guided participation in literacy. In L. M. Morrow (Ed.), *Family literacy* (pp. 104–114). Newark, DE: International Reading Association.

Neuman, S. B., & Roskos, K. (1997). Literacy knowledge in practice: Contexts of participation for young writers and readers. *Reading Research Quarterly, 32,* 10–32.

Neuman, S. B., & Soundy, C. (1991). The effects of storybook partnerships on young children's conceptions of story. In J. Zutell & S. McCormick (Eds.), *Learner factors/teacher factors: Issues in literacy research and instruction* (pp. 141–148). Chicago: National Reading Conference.

Rogoff, B. (1990). *Apprenticeship in thinking: Cognitive development in social context.* New York: Oxford University Press.

Rogoff, B., Mosier, C., Mistry, J., & Goncu, A. (1993). Toddlers' guided participation with their caregivers in cultural activity. In E. Forman, N. Minick, & A. Stone (Eds.), *Contexts for learning: Sociocultural dynamics in children's development* (pp. 230–253). New York: Oxford University Press.

Senechal, M., LeFevre, J., Thomas, E., & Daley, K. (1998). Differential effects of home literacy experiences on the development of oral and written language. *Reading Research Quarterly, 33,* 96–116.

Sigel, I. E., & McGillicuddy-De Lisi, A. (1984). Parents as teachers of their children: A distancing behavior model. In A. Pellegrini & T. Yawkey (Eds.), *The development of oral and written language in social contexts* (pp. 71–92). Norwood, NJ: Ablex.

Snow, C., Tabors, P., Nicholson, P., & Kurland, B. (1995). SHELL: Oral language and early literacy skills in kindergarten and first-grade children. *Journal of Research in Childhood Education, 10,* 37–48.

Tharp, R., & Gallimore, R. (1988). *Rousing minds to life.* Cambridge: Cambridge University Press.

Whitehurst, G., Arnold, D., Epstein, J., Angell, A., Smith, M., & Fischel, J. (1994). A picture book reading intervention in day care and home for children from low-income families. *Developmental Psychology, 30,* 679–689.

Whitehurst, G. J., et al. (1988). Accelerating language development through picture book reading. *Developmental Psychology, 24,* 552–559.

CHAPTER THREE

Literacy Instruction for Young Children of Diverse Backgrounds

Kathryn H. Au

Kathryn Au provides a thoughtful look at the increasing diversity among our nation's schoolchildren and the implications for policy and practice.

For Reflection and Action: Discuss the changing student demographics in schools today in terms of increased linguistic and cultural diversity. Consider the challenges faced by educators with respect to policy and practice. Compare examples of successful practices you have read about or heard about elsewhere.

A Classroom in Hawaii

One morning when I was in Jill Sakai's kindergarten classroom, a child named Kaylee brought a letter she had written at home for Jill. Jill remarked to me that this was the first letter from home that she had received that year. When she opened the envelope, Jill found a page of notebook paper densely covered with letterlike forms resembling *O*s, *P*s, and *D*s. Kaylee's name was signed at the bottom.

"What does it say?" Jill asked Kaylee.

"It says I love you," Kaylee replied.

After she gathered the children on the carpet to begin morning business, Jill shared Kaylee's letter and expressed her delight in having received such a wonderful message. She told the class she hoped others would follow Kaylee's example, and she posted the letter in a prominent spot on the message board. Not surprisingly, Jill received many letters in the days that followed. "When they bring writing pieces from home, even just a word or a letter, I make a big deal out of it," Jill told me. She wants the children to understand that reading and writing have a place at home as well as at school.

Jill is a teacher in a school in a low-income area of Hawaii in which about two-thirds of the students are of Native Hawaiian ancestry. About 85% of the students at this school come from low-income families. Almost all students speak Hawaii Creole English, a nonmainstream variety of English, as their first language.

The increasing diversity of the population in the United States (and elsewhere) poses a great challenge to teachers such as Jill, who wish to help the young children in their classrooms find success as readers and writers. I will use the term children of diverse backgrounds, in the context of the United States, to refer to children who are African American, Hispanic, Asian American, and Native American in ethnicity; who come from poor families; and who speak home languages other than standard American English (Au, 1993). We have long known of a gap between the literacy achievement of these children and their mainstream peers. According to the grade 4 results of the 1998 National Assessment of Educational Progress (Donahue, Voekl, Campbell, & Mazzeo, 1999, p. 456), 27% of white students scored below a basic level of proficiency in reading. In contrast, 64% of African-American students, 60% of Hispanic students, and 53% of Native American students scored at this low level.

Addressing issues posed by the literacy achievement gap has become more urgent than ever before, because the number of children of diverse backgrounds in the United States is steadily increasing. Of the students enrolled in kindergarten through fifth grade, 38.8% are of diverse ethnic backgrounds: 16.4% are African American, 13.1% Hispanic, 3.4% Asian American, and 1.0% Native American (Nettles & Perna, 1997). Many of these children grow up in poverty. For example, over 40% of African-American preschoolers live in households with incomes under $10,000, at a time when $15,000 in income puts a family of four at the poverty line.

As educators, we must be aware of the larger social conditions, such as poverty, that jeopardize children's well-being. These social conditions can make the challenge of bringing children of diverse backgrounds to high levels of literacy seem overwhelming, particularly to the beginning teacher. At the same time, we can derive hope from the knowledge that there are classrooms in which children of diverse backgrounds are learning to read and write well.

In this chapter we visit Jill Sakai's kindergarten classroom, a setting in which children of diverse backgrounds are successfully learning to read and write. Each of the sections below begins with a description of some aspect of the classroom's environment or instruction, then moves into related literacy research and practical implications. The descriptions are based on videotaping conducted in Jill's classroom in March during her second year as a teacher.

The year before this videotape was made, Jill participated in a research project to assess the effects of instruction centered on writers' and readers' workshops on children's literacy achievement. The results of this study showed that the approach was effective in helping approximately two-thirds of the children in all classrooms meet grade-level benchmarks, especially in writing (Au & Carroll, 1997). Au, Carroll, and Scheu (1997) provide a full description of the curriculum and instructional practices used by Jill and other teachers in the project.

A Print-Rich Kindergarten Classroom

A visitor to Jill's kindergarten classroom cannot help but notice all the print around the room. At the front of the room is a pocket chart. It contains a card with each child's name printed in large black letters and also a card with each child's photograph. One of the children's favorite activities during centers time is to mix the cards up and then match the names with the photographs.

A nearby chart lists topics the children might want to write about, such as family, the park, the beach, and friends. A smaller chart shows words the children frequently use in their writing, including *is, and, the, it, I, go, because,* and ten other words. Action words, such as *planting, sleeping, raking, eating, swimming,* and *surfing,* appear on another chart. More charts hang from clotheslines strung across the room. The message "We Like To Read!" stands out in bold letters on the front of a large case displaying books. In the case are big books, class books, picture storybooks, and books published by individual children.

As this quick tour suggests, Jill's classroom is a print-rich environment designed to support children's reading and writing. Research suggests that such an environment, rich in print and opportunities for reading and writing, is important to the literacy development of children of diverse backgrounds (e.g., Neuman & Roskos, 1992). A few children, such as Donny, a white Appalachian child studied by Purcell-Gates (1995), grow up with little print in the environment and few opportunities to engage with print. However, many others, such as the young African-American children in urban families living in poverty studied by D. Taylor and Dorsey-Gaines (1988), grow up surrounded by print and see adults reading and writing on a daily basis. The point is that most young children have some experience with print that can be built on in a classroom with a print-rich environment.

Uses of Literacy at Home and at School

Almost all young children, including those of diverse backgrounds, develop many understandings of language and literacy before they enter kindergarten and first grade. However, communities differ in the ways in which they use reading and writing. For example, Heath (1983) studied two working-class communities in the Piedmont Carolinas—Trackton, a black community, and Roadville, a white community. She found that families in both communities used reading to gain information to meet the practical needs of everyday life (e.g., labels on products), to gain information about other people or distant events (e.g., the newspaper), to support beliefs already held (e.g., the Bible), and to keep up social connections (e.g., greeting cards). However, the Roadville families also used reading for recreational and educational purposes. Adults in the Roadville families often read storybooks to their young children at bedtime, a pattern not observed in Trackton (Heath, 1982). When they entered school, the Roadville children had prior knowledge of storybook reading that they could bring to bear when the teacher read books aloud to the class. The children in Trackton did not share this advantage, although they had knowledge of many other functions of literacy. Similarly, Guerra (1998) does not cite bedtime storybook reading as a common literacy practice in homes in the transnational Mexicano community he studied. Children in these families experienced literacy in other ways. For example, they could often observe adults reading and writing personal letters to relatives and friends.

Teachers should certainly provide opportunities for children to listen to and read storybooks, whether or not children have experienced bedtime storybook reading at home. Yet, as this research implies, teachers can go a step further to support children's progress as readers and writers by including lessons on the functions of literacy already likely to be familiar. These lessons help young children see that the literacy knowledge they have gained in the home and community has a place in school and can contribute to their becoming good readers. For example, teachers can create a classroom supermarket and have children read product labels (e.g., on cereal boxes) and write and draw labels of their own. Activities with environmental print, such as labels and signs, appear to be most effective when children have the opportunity not only to engage with print themselves but also to interact with adults around print (Neuman & Roskos, 1993). Children can also be encouraged to read and write brief messages or letters to classmates, family members, and the teacher. Jill introduces message writing early in the school year and has a bulletin board on which messages can be posted. As we saw in the example of Kaylee's letter, Jill supports message writing at home as well as at school.

Daily News

Jill starts the day with an activity called the daily news or morning message (Crowell, Kawakami,

& Wong, 1986). It is March, and the children know by now that the daily news will begin with the sentence, "Today is [day of the week]." Jill asks the children how to spell *today*, and Tiare goes to find the word on yesterday's daily news chart. The children know that the word starts with *T*, and Jill reminds them, "It's the very first word that we always write on our daily news." Tiare uses a yardstick to point to the letters in *today*. As the children call out the letters, Jill prints the word *today* on the chart. Jill models how she leaves a space after the word *today*. She asks the children where they can find the word *is*. "On the word chart, on the daily news!" the children say. To spell the word *Friday*, the children look on the calendar, and Tyrone comes up to point to each letter. Jill prints as the children call out the letters in *Friday*. She follows the same careful procedure, having the children find and say the letters in each word, to compose a sentence about the weather:

Today is a cloudy day.

As this description suggests, Jill teaches in what she describes as a "routine and ritualistic" manner. During the first semester, the daily news is used to teach the children what Clay (1991) calls concepts about print: for example, that you start writing in the upper left-hand corner of the page, that you write from left to right, that you put spaces between words, and that you put a period at the end of a sentence. Jill wants her students to understand that when you put letters together they make a word, when you put words together they make a sentence, and when you put sentences together they make a story. But there is more. "The purpose also is to have them see me model writing," she says. "Last year I would say, 'Okay, write. You know your sounds and your alphabet.' It never dawned on me as a first-year kindergarten teacher that I could not assume that they knew how to use the sounds."

Having gained this insight, Jill consistently demonstrates how the children can apply their knowledge of letter-sound correspondences and how they can use the resources around the room. She encourages children to use the word charts and even to look in books to pick out the words they need to write a story.

Today it is Tyrone's turn to tell the class a story. Jill reviews with the children the three things that Tyrone must think about:

- What is happening?
- Where is it happening?
- Who is in the story?

She selects volunteers to interview Tyrone by asking these questions. Then Jill writes down Tyrone's story:

> I am riding the roller-coaster at the carnival with Braden.

Jill has good reasons for making interviewing part of the daily news. She believes that the children's thoughts need to be extended, to be more complete. At the beginning of the year, the children might simply state a topic, such as "the bus." By having the children talk about who is in the story, where the story is taking place, and what is happening, she can help them verbalize a sentence to be written later, during the writers' workshop. Jill does not necessarily use the terms character, setting, and events, but she helps the children understand these story elements, not only for writing but for reading comprehension. When she reads storybooks to the children, she points out that the author had to think about the character, setting, and events in the story. The children learn that other authors think about these things, just as they do.

As the daily news lesson nears its end, Jill prepares the children to write on their own in the writers' workshop. She asks the children what Tyrone should think about when he goes back to his seat and wants to extend his story.

"What else happened when I was riding the roller-coaster with Braden," reply the children, on Tyrone's behalf.

"Very good," says Jill. "So when you go back to your seat, Tyrone, you can ask yourself that."

"It's a long story," observes one of the children.

"Do you know why it looks like a long story?" asks Jill, taking advantage of this teachable moment. She turns to the chart and calls the children's attention to two words: *carnival* and *roller-coaster*. She notes that these big words make the story look longer.

Jill tells the children it's time to think about what they will write. Several children point and say, "Look at the topic chart!" to remind others where they might get ideas. They sit quietly for a moment to think about their topics.

Jill says, "And I know today all of you are going to write—"

"Really good stories," say the children, finishing her sentence.

As these observations show, Jill follows the same routine, day in and day out, when writing the daily news with the children. She takes the time to spell out every letter in every word, to point out spaces between words, and to call the children's attention to punctuation. Going through this process day after day requires considerable discipline on the part of the teacher. Fortunately, at this point in the school year Jill can see that her hard work is being rewarded. The children have learned the routine and know how to spell words, using their knowledge of print, including letter sounds, as well as resources around the room.

Much research on literacy learning emphasizes what is called the gradual release of responsibility from teacher to child (Pearson & Gallagher, 1983). When children are first developing new literacy knowledge, strategies, and skills, the teacher does much of the work of reading and writing for them, as Jill does during the daily news. As children gain proficiency, they can do more of the work on their own and the teacher can do less. Finally, the children gain independence and need little teacher assistance. Au and Raphael (1998) describe the different forms of instruction that teachers can use to move children toward independence. Because she is teaching kindergarten, Jill devotes much of her time to the first three forms of instruction described by Au and Raphael: explicit instruction, modeling, and scaffolding. Jill provides explicit instruction in the form of mini-lessons, in which she transmits knowledge to the children. Early in the year, she teaches many mini-lessons on letter-sound relationships and shows the children how to form these letters. She models writing through the daily message, as described above. When the children do their own writing, she provides them with scaffolding, or the temporary support needed to complete a task. For example, if a child wants to spell the word *sleeping*, she might teach her how to say the word slowly, listening for the sounds, or how to find the word on the chart posted at the front of the room.

Studies conducted as early as the 1970s (e.g., Barr, 1972) showed that children learn what they are taught, making it clear that teachers must carefully consider the nature of the literacy instruction and experiences young children receive in the classroom. These considerations are especially important if we want children of diverse backgrounds actually to apply skills when they read and write. Dahl and Freppon (1995) followed a group of African-American and white Appalachian children from low-income families during their kindergarten and first-grade years. Some of the children were in classrooms with skills-based instruction, including a strong emphasis on letter-sound relationships and practice in workbooks. The other children were in classes with whole-language instruction, including extended periods of reading and writing and individual and small-group instruction. Children in both approaches received instruction in letter-sound relationships, but they learned to apply this knowledge in different ways. The children who received skills-based instruction applied their knowledge when completing workbook pages but not during actual reading and writing. In contrast, the children who received whole-language instruction applied their knowledge when they read and wrote, with coaching or scaffolding provided by the teacher. The point is that any approach can be strengthened if young children are encouraged, through scaffolding, not just to practice skills but also to put skills to work during real reading and writing.

Writers' Workshop

Each day, Jill follows the daily news with a writers' workshop, in keeping with the process approach to writing (Calkins, 1994; Graves, 1983). She uses this time to teach the children how to plan, draft, edit, and share their stories.

After the children have had a chance to think of their topics, Jill puts them in pairs to share the stories they plan to write. She reminds them that it is "really important to share because—"

"You can help each other make your story good," says one of the children.

The children gather in pairs on the carpet to tell each other their ideas. Sarah tells Kainoa her story: "I am popping firecrackers with my friends."

"Good job," says Kainoa, leaning forward to pat her on the shoulder. Jill has taught the children to praise and encourage one another, and this is what Kainoa is attempting to do.

As writing time begins, Jill calls two children to work with her at a table to the side of the room. These are the children who most need her help to get their ideas down on paper. The other children in the class begin writing on their own. Gradually, six children move to the front of the room, where they refer to the name chart, the daily news, and the list of action words. As children look for the words they want to spell, other children come to their assistance. Children who remain at their seats to write occasionally ask others for help in spelling words. A girl refers to her personal word chart, a small copy of the list of often used words posted at the front of the room. A boy sitting next to her points out *the,* the word she is looking for. A few children approach Jill with questions.

After about 15 minutes, children who have finished drafting go over to read their stories to Jill. Each child receives specific feedback. Jill tells one boy, "You forgot something at the end of your story, very important." He goes back to his seat to add a period.

A girl reads Jill her story: " I am playing with my toys."

"With who?" Jill asks.

"With my mom," the girl replies.

"So you need to write that," Jill notes.

After she completes a quick check of the whole class, Jill pairs the children up again to read their stories to one another. She reminds them to ask questions and then praise their partner. She asks, "When you're sharing, do you look away?"

"No," the children reply in chorus.

Jill reminds the children to look at their partners, so that their partners will know they are being considerate and paying attention.

Justin reads his story to Sarah: "I am playing with my brother at the park—period! We are playing on the swings—period!"

"Shake hands," Sarah instructs him.

As they shake hands, Justin reminds Sarah, "Ask questions!"

"Oh, yeah, yeah, yeah," says Sarah. She leans over to get a close look at Justin's paper and points to his drawing.

"Who's this? What is this?" Sarah asks.

"That's not nothing," Justin replies.

Meanwhile, Jill is coaching Lehua, Tyrone's partner. Tyrone has written two pages, not only about riding the roller-coaster but also about how he and Braden both won prizes at the carnival. Part of his text reads:

AFTR BRADEN GOT A PRIS I GOT A PRIS.

Lehua points to a figure in Tyrone's drawing and asks him who it is. "Me!" answers Tyrone. In the afternoon, Tyrone and his classmates will have time to revise and edit their drafts.

As you can see, Jill works with her students to build a sense of community in the classroom. She encourages the children to take every opportunity to help each other become better writers. They plan their writing with a partner, and they seek help from and offer help to one another while writing. When they have finished their drafts, they read them aloud to a partner and respond to questions.

Research suggests that building a sense of community in the classroom, creating a family-like atmosphere of mutual support, may be especially beneficial to the literacy learning of many children of diverse backgrounds. For example, in many Hawaiian families, children are taught to turn to sisters, brothers, and other peers for help, not just to rely on adults (Jordan, 1985). By the time they enter school, children are well prepared to learn from and assist one another. Jill says that she deliberately promotes "a lot of community building within the classroom, because, as you notice, they help each other out a lot. Sometimes children are intimidated about coming up to me for help, even at this point in the year. So I'll just ask them to ask somebody else to help them or I'll have another child help them." Jill sees that community building results in benefits to the children's literacy learning: "Ever since we started having peer sharing and peers helping each other, they've gone a lot faster in their writing; they've progressed much better."

Jill has her students write from the first day of school. In September, the children tell their stories by drawing pictures and make no attempt to form letters. She reads picture storybooks aloud to the children and asks them to discuss how the story made them feel. They draw pictures to show their feelings about the story. A few children in the class know some sounds and letters, but they have no idea how to use these sounds and letters to write a story. Jill works with a few children at a time, showing them how to use sounds and letters to write their stories. She teaches the children that they can't just start writing but must first think about what they want to write.

Most important to Jill are modeling and consistent, daily opportunities to write: "It's modeling every day, and it's faithfully every day writing. Even if we have an assembly in the morning, and all I have is an hour in the afternoon, all I would do is tell them to write. That's something that I did faithfully every day."

Readers' Workshop

The writers' workshop runs until morning recess. Between recess and lunch time, Jill conducts a readers' workshop using literature-based instruction (Raphael & Au, 1998; Roser & Martinez, 1995). During this time she has the children work with big books to develop their word identification and comprehension ability. She starts the workshop by having the children gather on the carpet for shared reading (Holdaway, 1979). Today the children are rereading *To Town,* by Joy Cowley (1990). "I like this book," comments one of the children. Because the children are quite familiar with the text, Jill points silently to the words and listens as the children read in chorus. She stops them only once, when they read *on* for *in.*

Jill tells the children they will look for the word *to* in the story. They begin by finding *to* in the title of the book and on the chart of often used words. Then Jill calls on volunteers to find *to* in the pages of the big book. When the children have finished, Jill sends them to their seats. The children are in the process of illustrating their own pop-up books showing the different forms of transportation in *To Town.* Today Jill models how to draw a helicopter. They discuss the parts of the helicopter, such as its gas tank, and the shapes and colors they are using. When the children have completed their drawings, they cut out the helicopters and paste them carefully in their books. They show pride in their work. When the books are finished, the children will be able to take them home to read.

Jill has different learning centers set up around the room, and often before lunch the children have a chance to go to these centers. Literacy activities available to the children include writing messages, reading a book alone or with a partner, or matching classmates' name cards with their photographs. These activities give children the chance to explore and experiment with reading and writing in ways they choose for themselves. A combination of adult teaching and scaffolding, along with opportunities for independent exploration, may give children of diverse backgrounds a good chance of becoming successful readers and writers (Neuman & Roskos, 1993).

During the readers' workshop, one of Jill's goals is to help her students enjoy reading and stories. Some of the children have experienced storybook reading at home or at preschool, but others have not had these opportunities. Jill reads picture storybooks aloud, as well as big books. Gradually, she builds her students' knowledge of books, including the parts of a book (such as its cover) and the language of books ("once upon a time"). She makes the connection to writing by making sure the children know what authors and illustrators do, and she points out that they themselves can be authors and illustrators.

Jill views tracking print (being able to point to each word as one pronounces it) as an important skill for kindergarten children. This is one of the reasons she emphasizes the shared reading of big books, especially during the first semester. "I faithfully point to each word when we do shared reading," says Jill. She engages the children in a great deal of language play, such as using the pattern of language in the big book and thinking of rhyming words. She calls the children's attention to sight words, such as *to*, because she knows the children need a basic sight vocabulary in order to read the many irregularly spelled, common words in the English language.

Supporting Emergent Literacy in Children of Diverse Backgrounds

After I give a talk or workshop, one of the comments I often hear goes something like this:

> Kathy, you've made a lot of points about effective literacy instruction for children of diverse backgrounds. But I think that everything you've said is just plain good teaching that would help all children.

This same thought may have entered your mind as you read this chapter. I do agree with this sentiment. I think it is fair to say that all the instructional practices described in this chapter would also be effective in many classrooms with mainstream students. The point I would like to emphasize is that these practices may be *critical* to the literacy development of children of diverse backgrounds, who often need more school support for learning to read and write in conventional ways than children of mainstream backgrounds. In fact, it may be the tendency of schools to provide children of diverse backgrounds with less rich, less complex forms of instruction that contributes to the literacy achievement gap. Sadly, practices such as those seen in Jill's classroom appear to be less available to children of diverse backgrounds than to children of mainstream backgrounds, for a number of reasons. There is often a tendency in schools with many children of diverse backgrounds to overemphasize basic skills rather than higher-level thinking with text (Darling-Hammond, 1995). Furthermore, children of diverse backgrounds generally attend schools in less affluent districts, which may not have the funds to provide teachers with professional development centered on newer forms of instruction. We must be vigilant, then, in seeing that children of diverse backgrounds receive opportunities both for systematic skill instruction and for higher-level thinking with text.

An important starting point, I believe, is to provide children with a print-rich literacy environment. Jill's classroom was filled with charts, books, and labels, so that the children were literally surrounded by print. We have good evidence that many children of diverse backgrounds live in environments with a great deal of print (D. Taylor & Dorsey-Gaines, 1988). However, we also know that some children have little access to print, few opportunities to interact with print, and little chance to observe reading and writing (Purcell-Gates, 1995). Once print is made available in the classroom environment, it needs to be called to children's attention, and children should be encouraged to interact with it. For example, in Jill's classroom, the children worked with the print on charts, referring to it when they helped Jill with the daily news and when they wrote their own stories.

We should faithfully provide young children with daily opportunities to read and write. Jill reported that she conducted a writers' workshop and had the children write, even on days when the schedule had to be adjusted for special events. A good number of Jill's students had not experienced family storybook reading or had many opportunities to draw and write before coming to school, and this may be the case with other young children of diverse backgrounds as well. In this situation, it is especially important that children build a rich background of reading and writing experiences in school every day. Allington's (1991) research suggests that schools serving large numbers of students of diverse backgrounds often allocate less time for reading instruction than other schools. Clearly, children are more likely to make consistent progress as readers and writers if they have ample time to read and write, each and every day. In classrooms in the research project in which Jill participated, teachers allocated a minimum of

AN IDEA FROM A TEACHER

Using a Puppet to Encourage Literacy for Diverse Learners

In a classroom of learners from diverse backgrounds, it is imperative to consider the individual needs of each child. In my classroom, I find a wide spectrum of diversity, in regard to both experience in using the English language for writing and speaking and exposure to literary materials. I have found that many students are afraid or ashamed to ask for help during reading and writing time or to request reading materials to take home. To encourage my class to make the most of the resources in our classroom and to assist them in developing confidence to question and clarify their learning, I use a puppet named Wolly Word.

Wolly is a life-size puppet who "is learning to read." Wolly is introduced as a fellow classmate, and as the year progresses, he discusses with the class the many ways in which words can be used to read and write. Wolly also models ways of seeking help from the teacher, expressing feelings, and asking for and giving help. At the beginning of the year, to initiate conversation about learning differences, seeking help, and borrowing books, Wolly tells the class a secret. His secret is that he has never read a book before and no one has ever read a story to him. He talks about not having any books at home, and hopes that in class he will learn how to read. In response to Wolly sharing his feelings, students are asked to suggest things that Wolly can do. I prompt suggestions such as "borrow books from our classroom library," " ask a classmate to read with you," "collect words and stories in a notebook and practice reading them," and "pay close attention to lessons and ask many questions." Wolly then responds to these suggestions by asking if other students will also ask for help and borrow books.

Wolly is a model for action that I use on many occasions. Any puppet can be selected for this purpose, but I suggest that the puppet be large and kept out of sight when not in use. Wolly is especially useful when I foresee or detect a problem or struggle for some of my students in any area of learning. I have Wolly express his concerns, and we help review a reading skill or confront a difficult issue. Many students are more comfortable asking questions during reading and writing instruction when Wolly is around, because they want to learn with confidence, "just like he does."

Melissa Marley, First-Grade Teacher

45 minutes a day for the writers' workshop and 60 minutes for the readers' workshop.

Another important practice is to emphasize children's engagement in literacy activities they find motivating and meaningful. I believe that ownership of literacy should be the overarching goal in the teaching of students of diverse backgrounds (Au, 1997). Students with ownership have a positive attitude toward literacy and use reading and writing for their own purposes, at home as well as at school. This view of the importance of ownership is consistent with research conducted from the engagement perspective, in which reading is viewed as "motivated mental activity" (Guthrie & Anderson, 1999, p. 18). It is vitally important during the primary grades for children to learn skills of word identification. However, instruction in phonics, sight vocabulary, and other word identification skills should always be placed within the larger context of purposeful literacy activity. Jill's students, for example, were taught letter-sound relationships through mini-lessons during the writers' workshop, and they applied this knowledge while writing stories on topics of their own choosing.

We need to provide young children of diverse backgrounds with systematic instruction, including a great deal of modeling and scaffolding. As we have seen, Jill found such modeling to be the key to her success. She told me, "If you want them to write, you have to show them how you want them to write." In addition, recent research suggests that coaching or scaffolding is highly related to young children's successful learning of word identification skills (B. M. Taylor, 1999). That is, teachers should provide help that enables young children to apply the word identification skills they have been taught during ongoing reading and writing activity. Jill spends a great deal of time providing such assistance during the writers' workshop, for example, by having children say words slowly and listen for sounds or by reminding them about punctuation. In other words, it is not enough simply to introduce children to skills and strategies. It is also essential to provide modeling and scaffolding that lead children to apply skills and strategies on their own and help them gain independence as readers and writers.

We must also seek a balance between teacher-directed and child-selected literacy learning opportunities. Literacy educators often find themselves caught in the battle between two camps: one advocating a code-emphasis approach, in which phonics is seen as the key to success in beginning reading (Chall, 1967), and the other advocating a meaning-emphasis approach, in which comprehension, meaning making, and motivation are seen as the keys to success (Weaver, 1990). The advocates of a code-emphasis approach tend to stress the importance of teacher-directed lessons, while the advocates of a meaning-emphasis approach tend to stress the importance of child-selected literacy learning opportunities. I believe that the answer lies somewhere in between, in achieving a balance, on the one hand, between systematic instruction through teacher-directed lessons, and on the other, motivating activities that allow children choice and promote their ownership of literacy (Au, 1998). As we have seen, Jill devotes a considerable amount of time to teacher-directed instruction, but this is followed by time for children to write on topics of their own choosing, and during centers time, children read books of their own choosing.

Finally, and perhaps most important, we should connect instruction to the child rather than expect the child to connect to instruction. I have discussed research pointing to differences in children's experiences with language and literacy prior to entering school. These differences should be recognized and accepted, and literacy lessons planned accordingly. Jill uses a repertoire of strategies when she teaches, sometimes providing systematic instruction to the whole class, at other times having children teach and learn from one another. She provides some children with more scaffolding, other children with less. Jill notes that she has to be "very positive and very, very supportive of all [the children's] efforts, and each effort is different because each child puts out a different type of effort." I believe that the success of children of diverse backgrounds in learning to read and write in school depends on classroom teachers such as Jill, who have the expertise to develop literacy curricula around and for their students and who can embrace the diversity among learners.

References

Allington, R. L. (1991). Children who find learning to read difficult: School responses to diversity. In E. H. Hiebert (Ed.), *Literacy for a diverse society: Perspectives, practices, and policies* (pp. 237–252). New York: Teachers College Press.

Au, K. H. (1993). *Literacy instruction in multicultural settings.* Fort Worth, TX: Harcourt Brace Jovanovich.

Au, K. H. (1997). Ownership, literacy achievement, and students of diverse cultural backgrounds. In J. T. Guthrie & A. Wigfield (Eds.), *Reading engagement: Motivating readers through integrated instruction* (pp. 168–182). Newark, DE: International Reading Association.

Au, K. H. (1998). Constructivist approaches, phonics, and the literacy learning of students of diverse backgrounds. In T. Shanahan & F. Rodriguez-Brown (Eds.), *Forty-seventh yearbook of the National Reading Conference* (pp. 1–21). Chicago: National Reading Conference.

Au, K. H., & Carroll, J. H. (1997). Improving literacy achievement through a constructivist approach: The KEEP Demonstration Classroom Project. *Elementary School Journal, 97*(3), 203-221.

Au, K. H., Carroll, J. H., & Scheu, J. A. (1997). *Balanced literacy instruction: A teacher's resource book.* Norwood, MA: Christopher-Gordon.

Au, K. H., & Raphael, T. E. (1998). Curriculum and teaching in literature-based programs. In T. E. Raphael & K. H. Au (Eds.), *Literature-based instruction: Reshaping the curriculum* (pp. 123–148). Norwood, MA: Christopher-Gordon.

Barr, R. (1972). The influence of instructional conditions on word recognition errors. *Reading Research Quarterly, 7,* 509–529.

Calkins, L. M. (1994). *The art of teaching writing* (2nd ed.). Portsmouth, NH: Heinemann.

Chall, J. (1967). *Learning to read: The great debate.* New York: McGraw-Hill.

Clay, M. M. (1991). *Becoming literate: The construction of inner control.* Portsmouth, NH: Heinemann.

Cowley, J. (1990). *To town.* Bothell, WA: Wright Group.

Crowell, D. C., Kawakami, A. J., & Wong, J. L. (1986). Emerging literacy: Reading-writing experiences in a kindergarten classroom. *The Reading Teacher, 40*(2), 144–149.

Dahl, K., & Freppon, P. (1995). A comparison of innercity children's interpretations of reading and writing instruction in the early grades in skills-based and whole language classrooms. *Reading Research Quarterly, 30,* 50–74.

Darling-Hammond, L. (1995). Inequality and access to knowledge. In J. A. Banks & C. A. M. Banks (Eds.), *Handbook of research on multicultural education* (pp. 465–483). New York: Macmillan.

Donahue, P. L., Voekl, K. E., Campbell, J. R., & Mazzeo, J. (1999). *NAEP 1998 reading report card for the nation.* Washington, DC: National Center for Educational Statistics.

Graves, D. (1983). *Writing: Teachers and children at work.* Exeter, NH: Heinemann.

Guerra, J. C. (1998). *Close to home: Oral and literate practices in a transnational Mexicano community.* New York: Teachers College Press.

Guthrie, J. T., & Anderson, E. (1999). Engagement in reading: Processes of motivated, strategic, knowledgeable, social readers. In J. T. Guthrie & D. E. Alvermann (Eds.), *Engaged reading: Processes, practices, and policy implications* (pp. 17–45). New York: Teachers College Press.

Heath, S. B. (1982). What no bedtime story means: Narrative skills at home and school. *Language in Society, 11*(2), 49–76.

Heath, S. B. (1983). *Ways with words: Language, life, and work in communities and classrooms.* Cambridge: Cambridge University Press.

Holdaway, D. (1979). *The foundations of literacy.* Sydney, Australia: Ashton Scholastic.

Jordan, C. (1985). Translating culture: From ethnographic information to educational program. *Anthropology and Education Quarterly, 16,* 105–123.

Nettles, M. T., & Perna, L. W. (1997). *The African American data book: Vol. 2. Preschool through high school education.* Fairfax, VA: Frederick D. Patterson Research Institute.

Neuman, S. B., & Roskos, K. (1992). Literacy objects as cultural tools: Effects on children's literacy behaviors in play. *Reading Research Quarterly, 27*(3), 203–225.

Neuman, S. B., & Roskos, K. (1993). Access to print for children of poverty: Differential effects of adult mediation and literacy-enriched play settings on environmental and functional print tasks. *American Educational Research Journal, 30*(1), 95–122.

Pearson, P. D., & Gallagher, M. C. (1983). The instruction of reading comprehension. *Contemporary Educational Psychology, 8,* 317-344.

Purcell-Gates, V. (1995). *Other people's words: The cycle of low literacy.* Cambridge: Harvard University Press.

Raphael, T. E., & Au, K. H. (Eds.). (1998). *Literature-based instruction: Reshaping the curriculum.* Norwood, MA: Christopher-Gordon.

Roser, N. L., & Martinez, M. G. (Eds.). (1995). *Book talk and beyond: Children and teachers respond to literature.* Newark, DE: International Reading Association.

Taylor, B. M. (1999). *The impact of instructional scaffolding on student achievement: An analysis of teachers in effective schools.* Paper presented at the annual meeting of the National Reading Conference, Orlando, FL.

Taylor, D., & Dorsey-Gaines, C. (1988). *Growing up literate: Learning from inner-city families.* Portsmouth, NH: Heinemann.

Weaver, C. (1990). *Understanding whole language: Principles and practices.* Portsmouth, NH: Heinemann.

CHAPTER FOUR

Enhancing Literacy Growth Through Home-School Connections

Diane H. Tracey

For Reflection and Action: Discuss the importance of congruent experiences across home and school environments and how such experiences affect a child's ability to take advantage of what the school has to offer. In your discussion, focus particular attention on the need for the school to respect the culture of the home while helping families adapt to the culture of the school.

Diane Tracey provides an overview of the issues related to a supportive literacy environment in the home and the need for strong and continuing alliances between school and home.

Katie, age 2½, is curled up on her living room couch. In her lap she is holding a book and "reading" it to her mother. "Ducklings love— What does this say, Mommy?" questions Katie. Her mom answers, reading slowly as she points to each word, "Ducklings love to play in the water." A few moments later Katie queries, "Why does the duckling call her mommy 'mama'?" Katie's mother responds, "Well, some children call their mothers 'mommy,' some call their mothers 'mom,' some call their mothers 'mother,' and some call their mothers 'mama.' This duckling calls her mother 'mama.'"

This scene of a young child and her mother sharing literature together looks like an ordinary, everyday event—a normal part of life with young children. To those who study children's literacy development, however, the scene illustrates the power of home literacy experiences and offers a glimpse into the ways in which children's at-home literacy experiences can potentially affect their literacy learning in school. This chapter looks at the relationship between children's home and school literacy experiences. It also provides ideas for strengthening these connections in order to facilitate children's literacy growth. The following topics are considered:

- Framing the home-school connection
- The importance of the home literacy environment
- Parents as funds of knowledge
- Parents in the classroom

A Framework for Examining Home-School Connections

The connections that are established between students' home and school environments can dramatically affect their literacy learning. As Morrow and Paratore (1993) state, "[I]t is clear that if we do not attend to the home when we discuss literacy development, whatever strategies we carry out in school will never be completely successful. Schools need to view family literacy as part of the curriculum" (p. 194).

The term *family literacy* has been applied to the study of the relationships between families and the development of literacy (Tracey, 1995). Family literacy, therefore, is an umbrella term under which are gathered numerous issues, ranging from the role of the family in the development of children's literacy to the design of structured programs to support this relationship. Educators interested in positively influencing the home-school relationship in the area of literacy can frame their initiatives in one of two ways (for a fuller description of these terms and related research, see Morrow, 1995; Morrow, Tracey, & Maxwell, 1995; Tracey, 1995). *Parental involvement programs* are those efforts that are narrowest in scope and easiest for classroom teachers to implement. These programs are designed to work with parents in an effort to positively influence their abilities to support their children's literacy development. For example, initiatives designed to improve the quality or frequency of parent-child book sharing would fall into this category. In contrast to parent involvement programs, *intergenerational family literacy programs* are much more ambitious undertakings in which direct literacy instruction is given to more than one generation of family members (e.g., a mother and her child both receive direct instruction to improve their literacy skills [Tracey, 1995]). Such initiatives are usually created by school administrators or specialized organizations in the community or government. The general term *family literacy program* denotes a program that recognizes the influences of the family on the literacy development of family members and tries to have a positive effect on those influences (Tracey, 1995). This term, therefore, is applicable to both parental involvement programs and intergenerational family literacy programs. Educators who are striving to progress in the area of home-school connections should be clear about the size and scope of any initiative they attempt. Sorting out parental involvement from intergenerational family literacy programs is the first step that educators who are considering initiatives in this area are recommended to take.

The second decision to be made is the style of communication for the initiative. The home-school connection has traditionally been viewed as a process through which the school transmits information to parents regarding how they can best help their children at home to progress academically (Auerbach, 1989, 1995). Examples of this type of communication are newsletters, workshops, and programs that dispense information about the importance of reading to children and regular study habits. Thus, in the past, home-school connections were grounded in one-way communications. Beginning in the 1980s, however, the importance of two-way communications in home-school connections has been recognized (Auerbach, 1989, 1995; Baumann & Thomas, 1997; Lazar & Weisberg, 1996; Moll & Greenberg, 1990; Paratore, Meliz, & Krol-Sinclair, 1999; Shockley, 1994). This position stresses the value of parents' knowledge about their own children—how their children learn best, the types of activities they engage in at home, their feelings about school and learning, and so on. As Neuman, Caperelli, and Kee (1998) note, "Parents come with rich histories and experiences that should be honored and used in program development. Programs that build on participants' already existing 'funds of knowledge' or cultural capital (Moll & Greenberg, 1990) are far more likely to yield effects than those that approach parents as tabula rasa—blank slates to be written upon with new knowledge" (p. 250). A perspective that views the home-school connection as a vehicle for two-way communication sets the foundation for an egalitarian and true partnership between families and schools. In this perspective, both families and schools can be viewed as collaborating partners, each bringing its own area of expertise to facilitate the child's development. This perspective may be particularly relevant for families from low socioeconomic backgrounds whose home literacy practices may be largely incongruent with school-based literacy activities but meaningful and significant to the child's literacy nonetheless (Auerbach, 1989, 1995; Taylor & Dorsey-Gaines, 1988).

The present chapter includes ideas based on both one-way communications (transmission model) and two-way communications between home and school. It is important to note that the one-way transmission model has been shown to be effective in improving many aspects of children's literacy development, but many educators currently working in the field find programs based on the two-way communication model to be even more powerful. Educators seeking to strengthen home-school literacy connections are urged to consider this important dimension of the program prior to designing their own initiative, and may also want to combine several strategies to maximize the effect of their efforts. Both parental involvement and intergenerational literacy initiatives can be based on either the transmission model or the two-way communication model. Thus, the structural decisions to be made are (1) parental involvement or intergenerational family literacy initiatives, and (2) one-way or two-way home-school communications. Any combination can improve a child's home literacy environment and increase parental involvement in the classroom.

The Importance of Children's Home Literacy Environments

Educators have become increasingly aware of the importance of children's home literacy environment to their school literacy performance. One of the most important areas of the home literacy environment is the physical environment.

The Physical Environment

In her landmark research, Durkin (1966, 1974–75) discovered that children who came to kindergarten already reading shared a common background, namely, all of their homes possessed rich literacy environments. In rich literacy home environments books are found everywhere throughout the house and even, if one peeks into the garage, in the family car. Often books are piled throughout the house—nightstand stacks grow, bookshelves overflow, coffee tables abound. In addition to the large number of reading materials present, rich home literacy environments have plentiful writing materials within easy access for children. Children, even very young ones, often have their own desks equipped with several kinds of paper and writing implements. Children without their own work space often have corners, storage boxes, or drawers that contain these items. Importantly, children can get to these writing materials easily and independently, and are allowed to use them frequently. Other items frequently found in literacy-rich home environments that support writing are computers, typewriters, chalkboards, and magnetic letters.

Teachers who wish to positively influence the physical environment of their students' homes need to find ways in which to communicate with parents about this important dimension of literacy acquisition. Newsletters, pamphlets, back-to-school nights, and workshops are all vehicles through which information about home literacy environments can be shared. What needs to be communicated is the importance of a print-rich environment. Children need to have books, writing materials, and, in general, extensive exposure to print in their lives. Children will greatly benefit from having their own collection of well-cared-for books and other reading materials that are developmentally appropriate and easily accessible. Some of these books should be permanently owned by the child or family; others can be borrowed from the classroom, school, or public library. Children's reading materials should have a special place where they are safely kept, and children should have at least one quiet place in the home where they can read.

Lending books from the classroom library is one way to strengthen children's physical home environments by increasing the number of books in the home. Morrow (1997) lists some guidelines for creating classroom libraries and literacy centers from which children can borrow books. Based on research showing that greater access to books corresponds positively with children's literacy development (Neuman, 1999), children are encouraged to borrow books from the classroom library using a structured but simple check-out system. Some ideas for borrowing books include copying the titles and dates onto index cards and filing the cards under the children's names in a box or on a bulletin board, or using a looseleaf notebook with a page for each child indicating books borrowed and returned (Morrow, 1997).

An alternative approach to increasing book reading in the home is being pioneered through the use of audiotapes (Koskinen, Blum, Tennant, Parker, Straub, & Curry, 1995). In this type of initiative teachers create backpacks containing tape recorders, books, and read-along audiotapes for students to borrow throughout the school year. In-class activities precede the borrowing of materials, and the books are previewed, read, and reread by the teacher. Thereafter the books and accompanying tapes are available for students to use in the classroom and to borrow to take home using a check-out system. Although the idea is appropriate for children from a wide variety of backgrounds, some educators find it especially meaningful for second-language learners, since it gives these students an opportunity to hear English daily in their home environments. A similar idea that has also been shown to be effective is to send home videotapes of teachers reading a storybook with a class or small group, along with the accompanying reading material (Enz & Searfoss, 1996).

Shared Book-Reading Experiences

One of the most informative areas of study in evaluating the effects of children's home environment on their literacy development is parent-child book reading. Investigations of *naturally occurring interactions* describe the types of interactions and types of learning that take place when parents read to their young children. Early work in this area suggests that parents play many roles during shared storybook reading, elicit children's participation, and try to make sure that the storybook-reading sessions are meaningful (Altwerger, Diehl-Faxon, & Dockstader-Anderson, 1985; Roser & Martinez, 1985). For example, Taylor and Strickland (1986) observed that parents helped children learn new words or concepts during reading, used their intimate knowledge of their children's background to connect what was in the text to real life, scaffolded the text for their children to avoid confusion, and expanded or extended the story being read. Additionally, Taylor and Strickland noted the genuine conversational aspect of the storybook experience and the pleasure with which most families read. Taylor and Strickland's observations are particularly noteworthy because they studied families from a wide cross section of socioeconomic and cultural backgrounds. Other researchers who have examined naturally occurring interactions during parent-child book reading have determined that parents focus children's attention, check their comprehension, and elicit labels for objects and descriptive attributes during reading (DeTemple & Beals, 1991).

While some investigations of parent-child book reading focus on describing naturally occurring interactions, as presented above, others try to relate the quality of the observed parent-child interactions to the level of the child's literacy development. For example, six factors have been found to be positively related to children's literacy development: (1) the total number of words spoken by the child during the storybook reading, (2) the total number of questions answered by the child, (3) the number of questions asked by the child, (4) the number of warm-up, preparatory questions asked by the parent, (5) the number of postreading evaluative questions asked by the parent, and (6) the amount of positive reinforcement provided by the parent (Flood, 1977). Studies such as this one show that the ways in which parents interact with their children during storybook reading are related to children's performance on tasks related to reading. Such work also emphasizes the importance of *children's active involvement* in parent-child storybook reading and children's literacy growth. More recently, high-level conversation during parent-child storybook reading has been found to be positively associated with children's performance on a test of early print skills (Beals, DeTemple, & Dickinson, 1994). Classroom educators can use these ideas to help their students' parents improve their shared storybook reading time at home.

Parent-Child Interactions

A third area of storybook reading research focuses on the relationship between parent-child interactions during storybook reading and *children's oral language development.* This type of research is based on the hypothesis that storybook reading, which leads to gains in children's oral language, will also ultimately lead to gains in children's reading ability. Studies in this area were pioneered by Snow (1983), who suggested that storybook reading might well be the ideal situation for facilitating children's oral language development. Subsequent research has shown that teaching parents specific strategies to use during storybook reading (see below) results in significant gains in children's language ability, compared to children in control groups. Importantly, these gains persisted in a follow-up assessment (Whitehurst et al., 1988). For example, mothers from a low socioeconomic status community were able to more than double their children's production of elicited speech during storybook reading after being trained in a 7-week program designed to stimulate children's oral language development (DeBaryshe, Daly, & Rodarmel, 1992). These studies demonstrate the powerful effect that storybook reading can have on children's oral language development.

The following guidelines for reading with children are based on the research presented above. These ideas can be given to parents to help them maximize the benefits of their shared literacy experiences with their children. Although they are written here with parents in mind, the principles are also applicable to teachers sharing literature with students in the school setting. Recommended literature to foster conversation during parent-child storybook reading is listed in Appendix A.

Ten Ideas Parents Can Use to Improve the Quality of Shared Literacy Experiences

1. *Get your children to talk!* Children learn by talking and asking questions. Encourage your children to talk about what you are reading. One way to get them to talk is to have them guess what will happen next in the story.
2. *Help your children understand the story.* Sometimes children don't understand what is happening in a book. Check regularly to see whether your children understand the story. If they do not, try to explain what is happening in your own words.
3. *Praise your children.* Children love to be told nice things by their parents. Let your children know that you are proud of them when they ask a good question, say something interesting about a book, or read well.
4. *Relate the book to your life.* Use the book as a jumping-off point to tell your children something interesting about your life or an event the book reminds you of that really hap-

pened. Ask your children to relate the book to their lives as well.

5. *Ask your children good questions during storybook reading.* Questions that will help your children the most are those that require them to talk a lot to answer. *Why* and *how* questions are especially useful, such as "Why do you think the Pokey Puppy was sad?" and "How else could the prince have found Cinderella?"
6. *Wait for answers.* After you ask a question, give your children time to answer. Most children need time to think of good answers to good questions.
7. *With younger children, point to words when you read.* Pointing to words when you read to young children will help them learn what the words are, that we read from left to right, and that we turn pages only after we have finished reading all the words on a page. These ideas will help young children learn how to read.
8. *With older children, take turns reading.* Your children may find reading aloud to be difficult. Support your children's efforts by taking turns when reading.
9. *Choose books carefully.* Many books are enjoyable, but to help your children the most it is important to choose books that are not too easy and not too difficult. If you are not sure about the difficulty level of certain books, librarians can help.
10. *Have fun!* Above all, try to keep the book-sharing experience enjoyable! As long as you and your children are having fun together with books, you will be helping them in a great many ways.

Despite the abundance of studies suggesting that storybook reading is positively related to children's language and literacy development, it is important to note that several studies on the topic have urged educators to be wary of overestimating the influence that storybook reading has on children's ultimate literacy performance. For example, after investigating many aspects of home literacy related to storybook reading, Leseman and DeJong (1998) reported that the quality of parental storybook reading instruction was largely determined by socioeconomic status. Despite these warnings, however, it appears that sufficient support for the value of storybook reading exists to warrant its continued advocacy. Overall, research suggests that engaging the child in verbal interaction during storybook reading is the most powerful key to facilitating his or her literacy growth (Arnold & Whitehurst, 1994).

Based on such research findings, many programs have been created to improve the quality with which parents read to children. The Parents as Partners reading program (Edwards, 1995) is specifically designed to help low-income parents improve the quality with which they share books with their children. Using both live modeling and videotapes, this program teaches parents how to preview a book and how to relate stories to children's lives, with the ultimate goal of improving the quality of parent-child conversations during storybook sharing. One especially valuable component of the program is that parent participants who successfully complete the course are eligible to become parent leaders in future sessions. A similar program has been created by France and Hager (1993). Their program is based on six 1-hour workshops in which low-income parents and their children learn how to optimize their interactions during the reading of predictable literature. Ideas presented during the sessions include echo reading, choral reading, paired reading, storytelling, readers' theatre, and chanting. Follow-up activities for home use are offered to the parents after each session.

Storymates (Fox & Wright, 1997) is a family literacy program that teaches school-age children, rather than parents, the nuances of high-quality shared storybook reading. The program is built on the modeling of high-quality read-alouds of books carefully chosen by teachers, followed by the modeling of comprehension activities such as completing semantic maps, Venn diagrams, and story frames. After teachers model the reading and follow-up activities, students participating in the program practice the activities they observed with each other in pairs in the classroom. Finally, students take home the books they studied in the classroom and share them with other children using the learned techniques.

During the course of the 9-week program students share at least 18 books with younger siblings, relatives, and friends at home. An analysis of program effectiveness showed positive outcomes for students' comprehension achievement as measured by a story retelling measure, and positive influences on the home literacy environment as measured by parent questionnaires. This program was piloted in a rural low socioeconomic status, southeastern community where one-third of the parents had less than a high school education; however, it can be adapted for use in a wide variety of community settings.

The Three for the Road program (Richgels & Wold, 1998) is another approach that teaches activities that can be used to extend storybook reading at home. The program is built on the use of carefully chosen children's literacy materials. Teachers weekly send home backpacks to each child in the class containing three high-quality pieces of literature at increasing levels of difficulty but all on a single theme or in the same genre. Additional materials for each backpack include a letter to parents with directions for using the materials, a response journal, writing and drawing materials, hand puppets, a lost-and-found tag, and a checklist of the backpack's contents. After the backpacks have been prepared, teachers demonstrate their use in an introductory session with the students during which books are previewed and ideas for using the response journal, writing and drawing materials, and puppets are discussed. Backpacks are then distributed and shared among class members, who are free to use whichever book from the pack they feel most comfortable with. In-class follow-up occurs after a predetermined amount of time has elapsed, during which students meet in literature discussion groups.

Parents as Funds of Knowledge

The programs and activities suggested so far have been grounded in the transmission model of communication: home and school are connected through a two-way flow of information from the school to the home. However, many educators involved in promoting home-school connections emphasize the importance of programs built on two-way communication. For example, Neuman (1995) writes, "We knew, as Delgado-Gaitan (1990) has suggested, that not only is the family influenced by the school, but the school is influenced by the family. Successful programs are ones that see children in the context of their families and the families in the context of their surroundings" (p. 121). Thus, each of the following descriptions highlights an initiative that stresses the value of acquiring information from parents in order to help teachers enhance children's school literacy experiences.

In her article, "Forming a Parent Reading-Writing Class: Connecting Cultures One Parent at a Time," elementary school principal Akroyd (1995) described her experiences with families from 35 countries who spoke a total of 21 different languages. With no formal translators on hand, parents met weekly for 10 weeks, with the simple goal of writing something to their children. Forms of writing included diaries, memory books, and photo journals. Parents wrote for about 20 minutes each week and then shared what they had written. At the end of the 10 weeks, parents wrote about their experiences in the program. One parent commented that although she had learned about writing, even more important, she had learned that "a parent's love is truly the same everywhere." Akroyd was equally moved by the parent writing project. She says, "I've thought about how often large sums of money are sought to create new programs to improve student achievement and to encourage parental involvement, and about how this powerful experience cost nothing but time willingly given" (p. 584). She concludes, "The parent-writing group turned out to be the most memorable experience of my career" (p. 582).

Buchoff (1995) also encourages parents' telling family stories as a way to enhance children's literacy development. Using literature related to the theme of families as a springboard, she has students and parents explore different formats for the sharing of family experiences, including oral retellings, audio- and videotaped recordings, and written family stories. She also suggests providing parents with story-starting prompts, such as "Tell your child about the neighborhood where you lived when you were a child," or "Tell about a favorite relative when you were a child." These activities build shared literacy experiences at home while at the same time providing the classroom teacher with greater knowledge of the students' backgrounds.

Lazar and Weisberg (1996) also recommend eliciting information from parents to strengthen students' literacy skills, but rather than focusing on family stories, their solicitations are aimed specifically at parents' perceptions of their children's literacy development. These authors note that not only can parents convey critical content through such communications, but "[h]ow parents structure, observe, and record family reading events tells much about their philosophies of learning, teaching, and literacy" (p. 230). In this approach teachers hold interviews with parents about their children's literacy development and then ask parents to keep a journal of home activities related to literacy. Teachers respond to parents' journal entries on a weekly basis so that a dialogue related to each student's literacy growth is established between parents and classroom teachers. In some cases students are also invited to make entries in the journals. The end-of-the-year evaluations by parents and teachers have indicated much support for the project. Other ideas for the use of parent-teacher journals to support children's literacy growth are described by Morningstar (1999) and Shockley (1994).

Inviting Parents Into the Classroom

A third form of connecting home and school literacy environments entails placing parents in the classroom. This form of parental involvement completes the home-school connection circle by inviting parents to participate in children's literacy learning at school.

Enz and Searfoss (1996) provide a variety of ideas for promoting parental involvement in the classroom. They suggest inviting parents to read stories to children, assist with children's reading and writing, take dictation, and provide supervision at classroom centers. Parents can also be invited to tell stories on topics ranging from childhood experiences to recent special occasions to the ways in which they use reading and writing in their jobs. Depending on the needs of the class, these suggestions can be implemented with the whole group, a small group, pairs, or individual children.

In contrast to these relatively simple suggestions for parental involvement, Neuman (1995) describes a large-scale program devoted to getting parents involved in their children's classrooms. Reading Together is a parental involvement literacy program that has been implemented in an impoverished urban community in the Northeast where many parents are not literate in their primary language. The central component of the program is the involvement of community leaders in the school-based literacy initiative. The program begins with training community leaders in the importance of children's early literacy development. The training includes high-quality storybook reading and instilling phonemic awareness. Community leaders are then introduced to *prop boxes* containing a variety of theme-related literacy items such as books, play objects, chants, jingles, fingerplays, and blank writing books. The community leaders are taught how to share prop boxes with small groups of children in the classroom. The community leaders then become the recruiters and trainers for the program, soliciting the participation of parents from their community base. Using this system of training and recruitment, Neuman has been able to substantially increase the number of parent volunteers who participate and remain active in the classroom involvement program. Using the boxes, parent volunteers work with the same few children (not their own) for 30 to 45 minutes twice a week. Some parent volunteers eventually become recruiters and trainers for the programs themselves. Neuman reports, "Two years of implementing Reading Together have demonstrated that, despite poor economic circumstances, families in these communities continue to hold strong beliefs about the power of literacy and its importance in their lives" (p. 128).

AN IDEA FROM A TEACHER

Word Cards for Home and School

At the beginning of the school year, I give each of my first graders 15 to 20 index cards. I ask them to think about people or things that are very important to them. When they have decided on these words, I write each word on a card for them with a black magic marker. I also give each student a plastic baggie to hold their cards. I have the children read their cards to each other, and they copy the words and write them in sentences. I also ask the students to look for letter patterns or word families we have been studying, such as the *an* family or the *at* family, and to make new words by adding another initial sound at the beginning. In addition, I send home an assignment for the family to extend this activity in the home. I indicate in my letter home that an important aspect of the child's learning to read is having "very own words" available both at school and at home. I ask that parents participate in helping children collect word cards at home as we do in school. Each night for many weeks, I send home five index cards. The child works with a family member, writing words on cards at home, reading the words, and writing them in sentences. I also suggest looking for word patterns to make new words. Each day the children are able to share the words they collected for their home with their family. We also talk about words children share in common, stories children have written with their words, and letter patterns they have discovered in their words.

Bernardine A. Scholz, First-Grade Teacher

In Conclusion

Children are profoundly affected by their literacy experiences at home. These experiences can be shaped in positive ways by educators who understand the role of the home literacy environment in children's literacy development and who strive to share valuable information about the home literacy environment with parents. For instance, children's literacy development can be significantly affected by the quality of at-home reading opportunities with parents. Informed educators can share information with parents about how best to optimize these shared literacy experiences.

The power of home-school relationships in facilitating children's literacy development is not limited to a transmission model in which information regarding children's literacy flows in one direction, from the school to the home. I have suggested in this chapter that home-school relationships will be most beneficial to children in cases in which schools recognize and use two-way models of communication. To this end, I have described some strategies that stress the value of acquiring information from parents that will help teachers enhance children's school literacy experiences. Parental involvement with their children's literacy learning in the classroom may be particularly helpful for families whose first language is not English or whose home literacy environment does not include much print.

In sum, many kinds of home-school connections can enhance children's literacy growth. All educators are encouraged to become more informed about these critical connections and strategies for implementing them. Finally, all are invited to choose whatever ideas may work best to strengthen the home-school connections as a part of the literacy program in their school district.

Appendix A

Selected Literature to Promote Conversation During Parent-Child Storybook Reading

Abercrombe, B. (1990). *Charlie Anderson.* New York: Simon & Schuster.
Girls of a divorced family have two homes. So does the cat they find on their doorstep.

Baylor, B. (1994). *The table where rich people sit.* New York: Simon & Schuster.
A look at family values through a child's eyes.

Brown, M. T., & Brown, L. K. (1988). *Dinosaurs divorce: A guide for changing families.* Boston: Little, Brown.
Understanding change and separation within families.

Bunting, E. *Smoky night.* (1994). New York: Harcourt Brace.
Because of danger, a young boy and his mother are forced to flee their home. A Caldecott Award winner.

Cameron, A. (1989). *The stories Julian tells.* New York: Knopf.
Julian is great at telling stories, but some get him into trouble.

Curtis, J. L. (1998). *Today I feel silly & other moods that make my day.* New York: HarperCollins.
A little girl experiences 13 different moods in a single day.

Eastman, P. D. (1988). *Are you my mother*? New York: Random House.
A little bird searches for his mother. A classic.

Herron, C. (1997). *Nappy hair.* New York: Knopf.
Written in the African call-and-response tradition. Issues of God, family, Africa, slavery, and, of course, hair are discussed among family members.

Hoban, R. (1995). *Bedtime for Frances* (new ed.). New York: Harper/Trophy.
Bedtime experiences familiar to many children and parents.

Milne, A. A. (1992). *When we were very young* (new ed.). New York: Puffin.
The life of a little boy growing up in the turn-of-the-century England, told through poetry. A classic.

Rathman, P. (1998). *Ten minutes till bedtime.* New York: Putnam.
Countdown of the last 10 minutes before bedtime, and all that can occur during that interval.

Rylant, C. (1985). *The relatives came.* New York: Simon & Schuster.
An extended family celebration grows large.

Rylant, C. (1995). *Dog heaven.* New York: Scholastic.
A comforting story for children or adults dealing with the loss of a pet.

Schlessinger, L. C. (1999). *Why do you love me?* New York: HarperCollins.
Understanding a mother's unconditional love for her child.

Selden, G. (1999). *The cricket in Times Square.* New York: Bantam.
A boy, his Italian family, and a cricket run a Times Square newsstand. A Newberry Award Honor Book.

Shannon, D. (1998). *No, David!* New York: Scholastic.
The antics of a relentless troublemaker and his mother's responses. A Caldecott Award Honor Book.

Shriver, M. (1999). *What's heaven?* New York: Golden Books.
Conversations regarding the death of a beloved great-grandmother.

Steptoe, J. (1997). *In Daddy's arms I am tall: African-Americans celebrating fathers.* New York: Lee & Low.
Poems about fathers and their children.

Stewart, S. (1997). *The gardener.* New York: Farrar, Strauss & Giroux.
When hard times hit a family, a child helps out by gardening. 1998 Caldecott Award winner.

Thompson, K. (1969). *Eloise.* New York: Simon & Schuster.
A little girl lives alone in the Plaza Hotel in New York. A classic.

Viorst, J. (1997). *Absolutely, positively Alexander: the complete stories.* New York: Simon & Schuster/Atheneum.
Three Alexander stories—"Alexander and the Terrible, Horrible, No Good, Very Bad Day" (1972), "Alexander Who Used to Be Rich Last Sunday" (1978), and "Alexander Who's Not (Do You Hear Me? I Mean It!) Going to Move" (1995)—bound in a single volume.

Yolen, J. (1988). *Owl moon.* New York: Philomel.
A father and daughter take a quiet walk in the snow on a moonlit evening. A Caldecott Award winner.

References

Akroyd, S. (1995). Forming a parent reading-writing class: Connecting cultures, one pen at a time. *The Reading Teacher, 48*(7), 580–586.

Altwerger, B., Diehl-Faxon, J., & Dockstader-Anderson, K. (1985). Read-aloud events as meaning construction. *Language Arts, 62*(5), 476–484.

Arnold, D. S., & Whitehurst, G. J. (1994). Accelerating language development through picture book reading: A summary of dialogic reading and its effects. In D. K. Dickinson (Ed.), *Bridges to literacy: Children, families, and schools* (pp. 103–128). Cambridge, England: Blackwell.

Auerbach, E. R. (1989). Toward a socio-contextual approach to family literacy. *Harvard Educational Review, 59,* 165–181.

Auerbach, E. R. (1995). Which way for family literacy: intervention or empowerment? In L. M. Morrow (Ed.), *Family literacy: Connections in schools and communities* (pp. 11–27). Newark, DE: International Reading Association.

Baumann, J. F., & Thomas, D. (1997). "If you can pass Momma's tests, then she knows you're getting your education": A case study of support for literacy learning within an African American family. *The Reading Teacher, 51*(2), 108–120.

Beals, D. E., DeTemple, J. M., & Dickinson, D. K. (1994). Talking and listening that support early literacy development of children from low-income families. In D. K. Dickinson (Ed.), *Bridges to literacy: Children, families, and schools* (pp. 19–40). Cambridge, England: Blackwell.

Buchoff, R. (1995). Family stories. *The Reading Teacher, 49*(3), 230–233.

DeBaryshe, B. D., Daly, B. A., & Rodarmel, S. L. (1992). Evaluation of a home read-aloud program for low SES mothers and children. Unpublished manuscript.

Delgado-Gaitan, C. (1990). *Literacy for empowerment.* New York: Falmer Press.

DeTemple, J. M., & Beals, D. E. (1991). Family talk: Sources of support for the development of decontextualized language skills. *Journal of Research in Childhood Education, 6*(1), 11–19.

Durkin, D. (1966). *Children who read early.* New York: Teachers College Press.

Durkin, D. (1974–75). A six year study of children who learned to read in school at the age of four. *Reading Research Quarterly, 10,* 9–61.

Edwards, P. A. (1995). Combining parents' and teachers' thoughts about storybook reading at home and school. In L. M. Morrow (Ed.), *Family literacy: Connections in schools and communities* (pp. 54–69). Newark, DE: International Reading Association.

Enz, B. J., & Searfoss, L. W. (1996). Expanding our views of family literacy. *The Reading Teacher, 49*(7), 576–579.

Flood, J. (1977). Parental styles in reading episodes with young children. *The Reading Teacher, 30,* 864–867.

Fox, B. J., & Wright, M. (1997). Connecting school and home literacy experiences through cross-age reading. *The Reading Teacher, 50*(5), 396–403.

France, M. G., & Hager, J. M. (1993). Recruit, respect, respond: A model for working with low-income families and their preschoolers. *The Reading Teacher, 46*(7), 568–572.

Koskinen, P. S., Blum, I. H., Tennant, N., Parker, E. M., Straub, M. W., & Curry, C. (1995). Have you heard any good books lately? Encouraging shared reading at home with books and audiotapes. In L. M. Morrow (Ed.), *Family literacy: Connections in schools and communities* (pp. 87–103). Newark, DE: International Reading Association.

Lazar, A. M., & Weisberg, R. (1996). Inviting parents' perspectives: Building home-school partnerships to support children who struggle with literacy. *The Reading Teacher, 50*(3), 228–237.

Leseman, P. P. M., & DeJong, P. F. (1998). Home literacy: Opportunity, instruction, cooperation, and social-emotional quality predicting early reading achievement. *Reading Research Quarterly, 33*(5), 294–318.

Moll, L., & Greenberg, J. (1990). Creating zones of possibilities: Combining social contexts for instruction. In L. C. Moll (Ed.), *Vygotsky and education* (pp. 319–348). New York: Cambridge University Press.

Morningstar, J. W. (1999). Home response journals: Parents as informed contributors in the understanding of their child's literacy development. *The Reading Teacher, 52*(7), 690–697.

Morrow, L. M. (Ed.). (1995). *Family literacy: Connections in schools and communities.* Newark, DE: International Reading Association.

Morrow, L. M. (1997). *Literacy development in the early years: helping children read and write* (3rd ed.). Boston: Allyn and Bacon.

Morrow, L. M., & Paratore, J. (1993). Family literacy: Perspective and practices. *The Reading Teacher, 47*(3), 194–200.

Morrow, L. M., Tracey, D. H., & Maxwell, C. M. (Eds.). (1995). *A survey of family literacy in the United States.* Newark, DE: International Reading Association.

Neuman, S. B. (1995). Reading together: A community-supported parent tutoring program. *The Reading Teacher, 49*(2), 120–129.

Neuman, S. B. (1999). Books make a difference: A study of access to literacy. *Reading Research Quarterly, 34*(3), 286–311.

Neuman, S. B., Caperelli, B. J., & Kee, C. (1998). Literacy learning, a family matter. *The Reading Teacher, 52*(3), 244–252.

Paratore, J. R., Meliz, G., & Krol-Sinclair, B. (1999). *What should we expect of family literacy? Experiences of Latino children whose parents participate in an intergenerational literacy project.* Newark, DE: International Reading Association.

Richgels, D. J., & Wold, L. S. (1998). Literacy on the road: Backpacking partnerships between school and home. *The Reading Teacher, 52*(1), 18–29.

Roser, N., & Martinez, M. (1985). Roles adults play in preschoolers' responses to literature. *Language Arts, 62*(5), 485–490.

Shockley, B. (1994). Extending the literate community: Home-to-school and school-to-home. *The Reading Teacher, 47*(6), 500–503.

Snow, C. E. (1983). Literacy and language: Relationships during the preschool years. *Harvard Educational Review, 53,* 165–189.

Taylor, D., & Dorsey-Gaines, C. (1988). *Growing up literate: Learning from inner-city families.* Portsmouth, NH: Heinemann.

Taylor, D., & Strickland, D. S. (1986). *Family storybook reading.* Exeter, NH: Heinemann.

Tracey, D. H. (1995). Family literacy: Overview and synthesis of an ERIC search. In K. A. Hinchman, D. J. Leu, & C. K. Kinzer (Eds.), *Perspectives on literacy research and practice: Forty-fourth yearbook of the National Reading Conference* (pp. 280–288). Chicago: National Reading Conference.

Whitehurst, G. J., Falco, F. L., Lonigan, C. J., Fischel, J. E., DeBaryshe, B. D., Valdez-Menchaca, M. C., & Caulfield, M. (1988). Accelerating language development through picture book reading. *Developmental Psychology, 24*(4), 552–559.

CHAPTER FIVE

Children's Pretend Play and Literacy

Anthony D. Pellegrini and Lee Galda

For Reflection and Action: Think about the increasing demands for higher standards of achievement in the schools. Deliberate on the tensions that can emerge as educators attempt to promote higher achievement while maintaining a developmentally appropriate environment in which play is valued as an important part of learning.

Anthony Pellegrini and Lee Galda address the importance of play in the child's literacy development and as a means of fostering well-balanced, engaged learners.

Play is an important part of children's schooling. It is a vital part of young children's lives and offers many opportunities to make classroom learning fun and relatively easy. One kind of play, pretend play, is observed most frequently during the preschool and early primary school years (Fein, 1981). Thus, pretend play can be used most effectively in teaching during the early years (Pellegrini & Galda, 1991).

This chapter considers some of the ways in which the classroom environment can be arranged to facilitate children's pretend play and "literate language." (Generally, literate language is a variant of language that is often used in school-based literacy events by teachers and literate students and is encountered in texts.) After briefly defining pretend play, we discuss its importance to the development of children's early literacy. We then outline ways in which physical and social aspects of the classroom environment influence play and literate language.

The following list summarizes the main ideas presented in this chapter:

- Pretend play begins in the second year of life, peaks in the preschool years, and then declines.
- The features of social pretend play important for early literacy include the use of explicit language, the use of metalanguage, and the use of narrative language.
- Most children are capable of sustaining play with their peers by age 3 years.
- Children's play is more sophisticated in the presence of peers than in the presence of adults, and more complex with friends than with acquaintances.
- Functionally ambiguous props (e.g., blocks) elicit children's use of explicit language, while explicit props (e.g., doctor props) elicit the construction of complex narratives.

What Is Pretend Play?

Pretend play is a form of play in which children use one thing to represent something else. Pretend play has also been labeled symbolic play, because the process of allowing one thing to represent another entails symbolization (Fein, 1981; Heath, 1983). For example, a child may pick up a banana, hold it like a telephone, and then start talking into it. In this case the child has "transformed" one object (a banana) into another object (a telephone). As the child holds the banana, he or she has a mental representation, or picture, of a telephone. Other, more abstract sorts of pretend play transformations are not dependent on objects. An example is role transformation, in which a child proclaims himself to be, say, Johnny Quest. With age and social and verbal facility, children weave individual transformations together into longer story-like episodes (Heath, 1983).

Pretend play is first observed in children around 2 years of age, peaks during the preschool and kindergarten years, and then declines rapidly during the primary school grades (Fein, 1981). Girls tend to engage in pretend play more than boys, and their pretend play also tends to be more sophisticated (Fein, 1982). Boys' pretend play is usually more physically vigorous than girls' pretend play and often has a "superhero" theme, whereas girls' play themes more frequently revolve around familiar social roles and constructs. For example, boys are more likely to pretend to be some kind of superhero, jumping off walls and play fighting, while girls are more likely to play school or doctor. It would be interesting, however, to examine the impact of television shows that portray female superheroes on girls' pretend play.

So, from a developmental perspective, we suggest that pretend play is an excellent and appropriate instructional medium for children in preschool and the early primary grades, when children's spontaneous interest in it is at its peak. As they get older, other strategies may be more appropriate (Pellegrini, 1984; Pellegrini & Galda, 1982). Beginning around 3 years of age, children from very diverse social circumstances are capable of initiating and maintaining social pretend play with minimal adult support (Fein, Moorin, & Enslein, 1982; McLoyd, 1982). What they need is a social environment that supports and encourages this type of play. As we will see, the presence of too many adults can inhibit children's pretend play.

Features of Social Pretend Play Important in Early Literacy Learning

When children are engaged in pretend play with a peer (as opposed to solitary pretend play), they must communicate clearly the meaning of their playful transformations (in which they change the meaning of one thing into its playful meaning) if they want their playmates to join in and sustain the play episode ("I'll be Johnny Quest," or "This will be the castle"). Without this sort of language, pretend play transformations can be ambiguous, as there is often little correspondence between the "real" meaning or function of an object, such as a banana, and its pretend meaning, a telephone. As a result, clarifications and definitions of play themes take a fair amount of negotiation between peers. In most cases, children stop the pretend mode and negotiate the meaning of the "play frame" (Sachs, Goldman, & Chaille, 1984). These negotiations occur whenever there is a "fracture" or ambiguity in the flow of play. And the fractures are frequent: it is probably the case that children spend more time negotiating the meaning of play than in the play frame per se (Garvey, 1990).

Explication of Meaning: As children learn to read and write they move away from reliance on context, such as pictures and gestures, to convey meaning and learn to use language as the primary vehicle for meaning conveyance. This is also what they are learning to do in social pretend play.

Children from the early preschool years onward routinely interrupt their play partners to ask for a clarification of meaning or to disagree with the course of the play theme (Pellegrini, 1982). For very young children, the interruption for clarification often takes the form of repeating a partner's ambiguous transformation, adding a questioning intonation: "A castle?" Older children might simply ask, "What castle?" These interruptions generally result in the play theme being clarified so that play can continue.

Negotiation of meaning in pretend play also occurs when children disagree with their peers' interpretations of roles and events being enacted. There are numerous observations of preschoolers telling their playmates that roles are being enacted inappropriately: "Doctors can't say that!" Interpretive negotiations typically involve reflecting on the nature of the language a character has used and making alternative suggestions. In other words, the process of negotiation during social pretend play results in children reflecting metacognitively on the social and linguistic processes of their interactions, as evidenced by their use of such meta-terms as *say, think, talk,* and *words.*

The process of meaning clarification and explication is very important in children's school performance generally and in school-based literacy specifically. In school, children are expected to use language that is clear and explicates meaning, not ambiguous and reliant on implicit meanings. They are expected to use and understand language that conveys meaning through words and syntax, not through gestures or shared information (Bernstein, 1971; Cook-Gumperz, 1982; Heath, 1993). Simply put, children are expected to say what they mean and not to rely on others gathering meaning from shared implicit assumptions. Children should be saying "I mean this," not "You know what I mean?"

Reflection on Meaning: When children clarify and renegotiate the meaning of their play themes and transformations, they introduce a metacognitive perspective into the language of their play. They think and talk about the language they are using. Children's talk about the language of their play is indicative of a more general metalinguistic awareness (Pellegrini, Galda, Shockley, & Stahl, 1995). The ability to use metalinguistic words predicts performance on traditional measures of school-based reading and writing (see, e.g., Pellegrini & Galda, 1991; Pellegrini, Galda, Bartini, & Charack, 1998), possibly because of the importance of both metalinguistic and metacognitive processing in learning to read. In short, children's talk about talk is an indicator of their metalinguistic awareness, and metalinguistic awareness in turn is a powerful predictor of success in school-based reading (Adams, Treiman, & Pressley, 1998).

Narrative Structure: During children's pretend play, individual transformations are often woven together into longer and more involved story-like narratives. For example, most pretend play themes have a clear beginning (e.g., "I'll be the dad and you be the mom") from which a narrative progresses temporally, with children adding to and changing the play themes.

Initially, young preschool children have an easier time integrating individual play transformation into an involved narrative when they have explicit play props, such as dolls, a doctor's kit, or kitchenware (Pellegrini, 1985). It takes a fair amount of cognitive work to make play themes understandable to peers. If the props are functionally ambiguous—such as a piece of polyfoam or a towel—children must redefine these props so that they are understandable to their peers and play can be sustained around the props. With more realistic props, that work is already done, and children can spend their cognitive resources weaving a narrative theme. As children approach kindergarten age, they are more capable of integrating functionally ambiguous props into a larger narrative frame.

Knowledge of narrative structures is particularly important in young children's learning school-based literacy, as most of the texts they are exposed to are stories (Galda, 1984). Developing a narrative structure, or schema, in pretend play, then, should enable children to generate narrative styles that are consistent with school-based literacy (Michaels, 1981) and should allow them to more easily comprehend texts read in class (Galda, 1984).

In summary, we specify three dimensions of social pretend play that are important for young children's school-based literacy: explication of meaning, reflection on meaning, and building narrative structure. These are important dimensions of a form of language we call literate language. Children as young as 3 years are capable of initiating and sustaining pretend play with their peers, if their environment affords those opportunities. What aspects of the classroom support social pretend play and the development of literate language?

Classroom Contextual Effects on Pretend Play and Literate Language

In this section we discuss some of the ways in which children's play and language vary according to two general sets of classrooms variables: (1) play props/interest centers and (2) social groupings. Before we delve into the details, we provide some principles that have guided our work in this area. First, we recognize that play props and social groupings can independently affect children's play. We also recognize, however, that children will play with some props in very different ways, depending on their playmates. Second, children's play with peers varies according to the relationship they have with each other (i.e., whether they are friends or acquaintances) and according to children's individual differences.

Effects of Props: The type of toys children interact with affects their play. Generally, the theme of the toy determines the theme of the play. For example, when preschool children are given doctor props, their play will relate to doctor themes. Similarly, housekeeping props elicit domestic themes (Pellegrini, 1986; Pellegrini & Perlmutter, 1989). Although they do use elements of the language of pretend play that we described above, the concreteness of theme toys minimizes ambiguity and so minimizes the need to use literate language. The thematic support provided by these toys does enable children to weave very involved play themes, however (Pellegrini, 1985), and so these explicit props tend to support complex play narratives.

When preschool children are exposed to low-structure props, or props that do not have an explicit theme, such as pieces of polyfoam or pipe cleaners, their play is less predictable and, because of the functional ambiguity, is also characterized by explicit language (Pellegrini, 1985). However, the cognitive demands associated with using explicit language tend to limit the richness of their narratives. When preschool children play with ambiguous props, they spend considerable effort verbally explicating the meaning of these props in play episodes. Consequently they do not have many cognitive resources to spend on embedding these individual transformations in longer, more involved themes.

We have also examined the way in which different types of play props affect the literate language of older children (first graders). In one series of settings, pairs of children were observed playing with a same-sex peer with replica play figures from popular narrative films, such as *Aladdin* and *The Lion King*. In another series of settings, children were read a narrative text and then given "literacy props," such as pens and paper, and asked to talk, play, and write about the stories.

We expected the play props to elicit more literate language than the literacy center props simply because in play, children disagree and negotiate the meaning of the play themes. This conceptual conflict would in turn, we thought, prompt greater use of literate language. To our surprise, this did not happen. Much more literate language was observed with the literacy props than with the play props. This observation may have resulted from the fact that the play props were in fact realistic and left little room for disagreement about theme. When interacting with literacy props children talked about their interactions with them, and this talk reflected the literate bias of the materials: *write, talk, story, word,* and so on. The use of literate language in turn related to children's performance on standardized measures of reading (Pellegrini, Galda, Bartini, et al., 1998).

To summarize thus far, we find that children's literate language can be encouraged in settings where they are asked to talk and write about stories. This type of language is linked to performance on traditional measures of reading and writing. Thus, an implication of our work is that children's talk about language is important for early literacy. We stress this basic finding, given the pressure in many classrooms to have children work alone and silently.

Effects of Different Peer Groupings

The field of early literacy is currently very much concerned with the role of social context in children's literacy learning. For the most part, work in this area has been concerned with adult-child interactions, following variants of Vygotsky's (1978) idea of the zone of proximal development. According to this theory, children learn specific skills by interacting in apprenticeship fashion with a more competent member of their community (see Reeder, Shapiro, Watson, & Goelman, 1996, for an example of this sort of approach to literacy learning). Here we examine the role of peer interactions in children's use of literate language (see Pellegrini & Galda, 1998, for an extended discussion). According to Piaget's (1983) equilibration theory, cognitive development begins from disequilibration, or when one set of ideas conflicts with another. Children reestablish cognitive balance, or equilibration, through a complementary process of assimilation and accommodation. The resolution of conflict in peer interactions, we found, was associated with a greater use of literate language.

Peers or Adults? According to Piaget, peer social groupings are reciprocal and maximize the possibility of conceptual conflict and resolution because peers are co-equals and are likely to disagree. Adult-child groupings, on the other hand, are complementary, and children have roles subordinate to adults' roles; consequently there is little likelihood of disagreement. At a global level, then, we would expect children to behave differently with adults than with age peers. Observations of preschool children in their classrooms conform to these theoretical expectations. In two studies (Pellegrini, 1984; Pellegrini & Perlmutter, 1989) we found that children's pretend play was inhibited as the number of adults in their presence increased but was stimulated as the number of peers increased. Further, we found that children used language in much more varied and sophisticated ways when interacting with peers than when interacting with adults (Pellegrini, 1984). It is likely that children took on more roles when interacting with peers than when adults were obviously present, and that the behavioral and linguistic variety associated with playing different roles was reflected in language use. When children are in the presence of adults, they often follow the lead of the adults. They are less likely to try new things, challenge the existing order, or take on different roles.

Some qualification of these results is needed. First, the results apply to child behaviors, such as pretend play, that require a fair amount of child initiative. In less open tasks, such as following a specific order of steps, adult guidance is probably more effective than peer interaction (e.g., Tudge & Rogoff, 1989). Additionally, the observations were made in children age 3½ to 5 years. In younger children (2-year-olds) the opposite was observed: social behavior and play

AN IDEA FROM A TEACHER

Using Prop Boxes to Encourage Literature-Based Play

I have limited space in my classroom, so it is difficult to have permanent centers set up to accommodate all the areas of learning I would like. To make best use of available space, I store materials in boxes that are easily accessed during the class day. During center time and free play time, I take out boxes of materials and place them in areas and on tables around the room.

To encourage dramatic play and literacy development, three of my stations are prop boxes. The first box has explicit props, such as dolls, doctor's kits, and costumes for occupations such as police officer and fire fighter. I include a short story for each prop in the box so that the children can look through the books and make connections between their play and the stories. The second box has puppets and a cardboard theater, so that children can retell stories and create their own stories to perform. The third box has suggestive props that accompany popular stories. For example, a hat, basket, and silk flowers are accompanied by *Little Red Riding Hood.*

Children in my class enjoy using the prop boxes during free time and center time. I see them engage in writing activities and reading as a result of the available props. Many students choose to add their favorite stories to the boxes and create props and puppets to assist them in retelling the stories.

Angela DeWitt, Kindergarten Teacher

were more sophisticated in the presence of adults than in the presence of peers.

Types of Peers: Just as not all adults are equally supportive of children's social, emotional, and cognitive growth, so not all peer groups are equally supportive. In general, boys and girls tend to play in same-sex dyads with specific and predictable types of toys (Pellegrini & Perlmutter, 1989). Preschool boys tend to play with blocks and large motor toys. They also enjoy physically vigorous outdoor play. Girls prefer to play with dramatic play props, such as those in the housekeeping corner, and their play is generally sedentary. When boys are forced to play with female-preferred props, like dolls or in housekeeping centers (as they sometimes are in some preschools), they suppress their exhibition of competence, especially if they are made to play with these props with girls. In such cases boys are often passive and nonresponsive to play initiatives from girls. Further, the abstractness of their play is often lowered in such circumstances. Girls, on the other hand, seem to be more willing to play with males and male-preferred props. This difference probably reflects the higher status of male roles relative to female roles among both boys and girls. In short, the level of sophistication of children's play is affected by both the props with which they play and the gender composition of the play group.

The quality of the social relationship of children interacting with each is also important. Children act differently with friends than with familiar peers who are not friends. Friendships are reciprocal relationships (in which each individual considers the other his or her friend) between two individuals that are typified by emotional investment and trust (Hartup, 1996). Given this trust and mutuality, friends are usually more willing than nonfriends to disagree with each other and then to resolve the disagreement (Hartup, 1996; Pellegrini, Galda, Flor, Bartini, & Charak, 1997). For these reasons, friendship groupings should, we thought, support the sorts of disequilibration cycles that, following Piaget, would be expected to support children's use of literate language. Conflicts and resolutions should give rise to reflection on the language and thought processes that occur in the interactive process.

This expectation was borne out in a series of experiments with first graders. We found that friends engaged in more conflict resolution than nonfriends and that these negotiations led to friends' use of literate language (Pellegrini, Galda, Bartini, et al., 1998). Especially interesting was the finding that "difficult" children, or children who were either highly active and emotional or withdrawn, did particularly well with friends compared to acquaintances. Active and emotional children, when paired with friends, tended to cool their emotions after conceptual conflicts by talking about the emotional events. At that point, they could then reflect on the language and thought process of the literacy events (Pellegrini, Galda, Flor, et al., 1997).

The instructional implications of these findings are quite important. Children's level of cognitive sophistication is increased when they interact with friends, compared to nonfriends. So, rather than separating friends in the classroom, it makes sense to put them together and encourage them to interact.

Summary

Social pretend play is important in children's early literacy instruction because the sorts of language used in social pretend play are also used in school-based literacy events. We have called this form of language literate language. Different social groupings and play props affect play and literate language, with friendly peers most likely to use the literate metalanguage that is related to early literacy. Providing children in specific social groupings with different types of props also influences the development of literate language. For example, giving first graders pens, papers, and books maximizes the use of literate language. Play as an instructional strategy seems particularly useful during the preschool and very early primary grades, a time when it is typically observed in children's spontaneous behavior with peers.

References

Adams, M. J., Treiman, R., & Pressley, G. M. (1998). Reading, writing, and literacy. In I. E. Sigel & K. A. Renninger (Eds.), *Handbook of child psychology: Vol. 4. Child psychology in practice* (pp. 275–356). New York: Wiley.

Bernstein, B. (1971). *Class, codes, and control* (Vol. 1). London: Routledge & Kegan Paul.

Cook-Gumperz, J. (1982). Situated instructions. In S. Ervin-Tripp & C. Mitchell-Kernan (Eds.), *Child discourse* (pp. 103–124), New York: Academic Press.

Fein, G. G. (1981). Pretend play: An integrative review. *Child Development, 52,* 1095–1118.

Fein, G. G., Moorin, E., & Enslein, J. (1982). Pretense and peer behavior. *Human Development, 25,* 392–406.

Galda, L. (1984). Play, story telling, and story comprehension: Narrative competence. In A. D. Pellegrini & T. D. Yawkey (Eds.), *The development of oral and written language in social context* (pp. 105–115). Norwood, NJ: Ablex.

Garvey, C. (1990). *Play.* Cambridge: Harvard University Press.

Hartup, W. W. (1996). The company they keep: Friendships and their developmental significance. *Child Development, 67,* 1–13.

Heath, S. B. (1983). *Ways with words.* New York: Cambridge University Press.

McLoyd, V. (1982). Social class differences in social dramatic play. *Developmental Review, 2,* 1–30.

Michaels, S. (1981). Sharing time: Children's styles and access to literacy. *Language in Society, 10,* 423–442.

Pellegrini, A. D. (1982). Explorations in preschoolers' construction of cohesive text. *Discourse Processes, 5,* 101–108.

Pellegrini, A. D. (1984). Identifying causal elements in the thematic fantasy play paradigm. *American Educational Research Journal, 21,* 691–703.

Pellegrini, A. D. (1985). The narrative organization of children's play. *Educational Psychology, 5,* 17–25.

Pellegrini, A. D. (1986). Play centers and the production of imaginative language. *Discourse Processes, 9,* 115–125.

Pellegrini, A. D., & Galda, L. (1982). The effects of thematic fantasy play training on the development of story comprehension. *American Educational Research Journal, 19,* 443–452.

Pellegrini, A. D., & Galda, L. (1991). Longitudinal relations among preschoolers' symbolic play, linguistic verbs, and emergent literacy. In J. Christie (Ed.), *Play and early literacy* (pp. 47–68). Albany, NY: SUNY Press.

Pellegrini, A. D., & Galda, L. (1998). *The development of school-based literacy: A social ecological approach.* London: Routledge.

Pellegrini, A. D., Galda, L., Bartini, M., & Charak, D. (1998). Oral language and literacy learning in context: The role of social relationships. *Merrill-Palmer Quarterly, 44,* 38–54,

Pellegrini, A. D., Galda, L., Flor, D., Bartini, M., & Charak, D. (1997). Close relationships, individual differences, and early literacy learning. *Journal of Experimental Child Psychology, 67,* 409–422.

Pellegrini, A. D., Galda, L., Shockley, B., & Stahl, S. (1995). The nexus of social and literacy experiences at home and at school: Implications for primary school oral language and literacy. *British Journal of Educational Psychology, 65,* 273–285.

Pellegrini, A. D., & Perlmutter, J. C. (1989). Classroom contextual effects on children's play. *Developmental Psychology, 25,* 289–296.

Piaget, J. (1983). Piaget's theory. In W. Kessen (Ed.), *Handbook of child psychology: Vol. 1* (pp. 103–128). New York: Wiley.

Reeder, K., Shapiro, J., Watson, R., & Goelman, H. (1996). *Literate apprenticeships: The emergence of language and literacy in the preschool years.* Norwood, NJ: Ablex.

Sachs, J., Goldman, J., & Chaille, C. (1984). Planning in pretend. In A. D. Pellegrini & T. D. Yawkey (Eds.), *The development of oral and written language in social context* (pp. 119–128). Norwood, NJ: Ablex.

Tudge, J. R. H., & Rogoff, B. (1989). Peer influences on cognitive development. In M. Bornstein & J. S. Bruner (Eds.), *Interactions in human development* (pp. 17–40). Hillsdale, NJ: Erlbaum.

Vygotsky, L. S. (1978). *Mind in society.* Cambridge: Harvard University Press.

CHAPTER SIX

Talking Their Way Into Print: English Language Learners in a Prekindergarten Classroom

Celia Genishi, Donna Yung-Chan, and Susan Stires

For Reflection and Action: Contemplate the particular challenges faced by teachers who work with children whose first language is other than English. In what ways do the approaches discussed in previous chapters need to be adapted for these children?

Celia Genishi, Donna Yung-Chan, and Susan Stires offer practical strategies for developing oral language and literacy among young learners whose first language is not English.

Newcomers in countries around the world face the challenges of learning a second language. Newcomers who are children in classrooms in North America feel the challenges most deeply as they discover that they lack a basic key to classroom learning: the ability to communicate in English. In this chapter, we look at young children as they enter the worlds of spoken and written English in a prekindergarten classroom. We include:

- A description of the collaborative study we are engaged in
- Descriptions of activities that were especially helpful to children as they learned English
- Teaching strategies that promote language and literacy learning, along with several teaching tips
- A review of recent research related to language and literacy learning

Although peers are crucial in both language-learning and socialization processes, our discussion focuses on the teacher's role in an early childhood classroom, for two reasons. First, looking at teacher-student interaction was a major, though not an exclusive, focus of our research. Second, we anticipate that many teachers want to know what they can do in their classrooms to assist English language learners in effective ways.

A Collaborative Look at Donna's Classroom

Example 1

Susan: Tommy, tell me about your picture.

Tommy: I am doing something night.

Susan: You're doing something light?

Tommy: It's black. I want to do something blue. Whoops, purple. (*He continues to draw: stars, moon, and the beginning of a house.*)

Donna: Good night, moon. It's nighttime. Oops! You forgot to close the marker. I do see the moon, the sky.

"Tell me about your picture" is a familiar request in early childhood classrooms, including Donna Yung-Chan's prekindergarten room in a New York City public school. Donna is a general education teacher, not officially designated as a bilingual teacher or a teacher of English as a second language (ESL). Susan Stires, a staff developer at Donna's school, has a dual role there. She supports teachers in their literacy programs, and in the fall of 1997 she became a co-researcher, with Donna and Celia Genishi, a teacher at Columbia University's Teachers College, as all three began a two-year study focusing on children learning English as a second language. Susan was a regular visitor in Donna's classroom, where she was comfortable asking children about their activities and listening as well when Donna clarified things children said. In our example, Donna subtly lets Susan know that Tommy was depicting something night, as in nighttime, from the picture book *Good Night, Moon* (Brown, 1947/1991), which she had recently read to the class.

We are able to study examples like this one as a result of Donna's formulation of her overall research question: How do children new to the English language learn vocabulary? In 10 years of teaching children, primarily of Chinese background,Donna had observed that word meanings are learned gradually. For example, like first-language learners (Clark, 1973), Donna's children might learn the word *shoe,* but not *slipper* or *sandal* until quite a bit later. Donna became curious about how word learning occurred, and this was a topic that interested Susan and Celia as well. In 1997–1998 the three of us collected and began to study many examples of language use by Donna's 16 children, through written notes, audiotapes, and videotapes. Some of those examples were language experience stories, based on experiences like class trips, and writing, most often writing dictated to Donna or to Rose Anne Cipriano, the assistant teacher. We are currently studying those examples, looking for which children learned what kinds of words and in what contexts. We are also learning at what point in the school year they accomplished the learning, and we are learning about the interactional configurations in which the learning occurred: adult-child, child-child, adult–small group, or adult–large group.

Learning English Through Experience

Donna believes strongly that children learn best in an environment in which they can explore, listen to, and experiment with the English language. Singing songs, listening to books, collaborating on projects, using the computer, and talking to each other and to the adults around them all contribute to language learning. It is important to Donna that children share their ideas about what they plan to do during work time and later review how they carried out their plans.

Most of the children start the school year as speakers of a Chinese language, Cantonese, which Donna also speaks. (Two of the children are English dominant, two speak Fujianese, and one speaks Mandarin but has learned Cantonese.) Visits to Donna's classroom demonstrate her belief that all these children are learners. Every morning the six girls and ten boys in her class begin the day by having a school-provided breakfast together, while some parents linger and talk with the teacher. A short transition time follows, which some children use to finish breakfast while others leaf through and talk about books, alone or in pairs or clusters, as they wait for the class to assemble. Often these are books that Donna has read to them multiple times, and the children role-play reading or discuss information that they know the text provides. They use either English or a Chinese language.

The beginning of group time is marked by singing "There Are Seven Days in the Week," to the tune of "My Darling Clementine." In song, Donna and the children repeat "There are seven days in the week" several times and name the days of the week, as a prelude to marking the date on the calendar. A description of the day's weather follows as Donna uses the class computer to ask and record whether it's sunny or cloudy, windy or not, and so on. (She uses the software program called Weather Machine.) As the year has progressed, the words that the children use during morning meeting and for other daily routines, such as eating and making requests, have become a core vocabulary that even the least sophisticated English speaker in the class understands and employs.

What happens next varies. Donna may read a book or describe an activity that children will engage in later, such as using plastic cubes to measure the length of their hands, or she may show the children a special choice activity for the morning. The curriculum for the prekindergartens in Donna's school generally follows guidelines for HighScope (Hohmann, Banet, & Weikart, 1979), especially in the overall structure of activities, which follow a plan-do-review format. Children all plan at the end of group time by choosing an activity for activity or work time. The choices are displayed on a board to which the child attaches his or her name (see Figures 6.1 and 6.2). In making the selections the children state their intentions, as in this exchange with Alice:

Example 2

Alice: Want to go to water table.

Donna: You want to go to the water table? Okay, what do you need to do first before you go to water?

Alice: I do water.

Donna: Okay, you go to the water table, but what do you need to do first? What do you need to put on?

Alice: Bubbles.

Donna: You're going to the water table and you're going to play with bubbles, but what do you need to wear? (Gently pulls Alice back as she starts to walk away.)

Tommy: Smock!

Donna: We don't want to get this beautiful dress wet. What do we need to wear? Do you need to wear something?

Tommy: Smock!

Alice: Jacket.

Donna: Okay, we call that a smock. Can you say smock?

Alice: Smock.

Donna: Okay, you need to sign your name, right? (*Alice nods.*)

Learning/Teaching Through Conferring

"Doing" includes completing the chosen morning activity, which in many cases is open-ended. During this time children work in twos and threes, and Donna circulates, conferring with the

Figure 6.1. The activity board, showing children's choices.

children about their activities. She can occasionally be heard teaching English vocabulary, as she did in Example 2. Some of the time she code-switches, or alternates between English and Cantonese, so that children will understand her. Unless she is setting up for something else, Rose Anne also circulates. This is in contrast to the afternoon small-group activities, during which teacher and assistant split the class into small groups and lead the children through an activity.

In the morning, the teachers are following the children's lead yet still finding opportunities to teach, as Rose Anne does when she talks with Alice about creating a flower, starting with a circle, to which she will attach colored feathers. After attempting unsuccessfully to cut a circle, Alice poses her problem to Rose Anne, who responds with specific help. She draws a circle that Alice can follow with her scissors. When Alice finishes, Rose Anne celebrates Alice's accomplishment. While engaging in a three-part conference with Alice, Rose Anne also engages in conversation at the art/writing area with Tiffany, who is also making a flower, and with Adam, who is writing about his father's work.

Donna's conferences range from a few inquiry sentences to full conversational engagement in the activity with the students. The conferences are often one to one, but they may also engage several children at the same area. Children generally request her attention when they have completed something; otherwise, Donna moves around the room interacting with the students during their selected activities. While Kevin and Kenneth are in the housekeeping area one morning, they switch from being doctors to domestic activities after talking about sticky ears and juice (saliva) in the mouth. Donna had joined them a few minutes earlier. With the mention of juice, Kenneth starts to cook, and Donna says, "We're not at the doctor's office anymore?" After a short time of cooking and serving, this sequence takes place:

Example 3

Kenneth: Drink it!

Donna: You hand me a cup and say, "Drink it!" What am I drinking?

Kenneth: Drink it, drinking this one!

Donna: I don't know what it is!

Kenneth: It's this—this one! (*shows her the box of butter*).

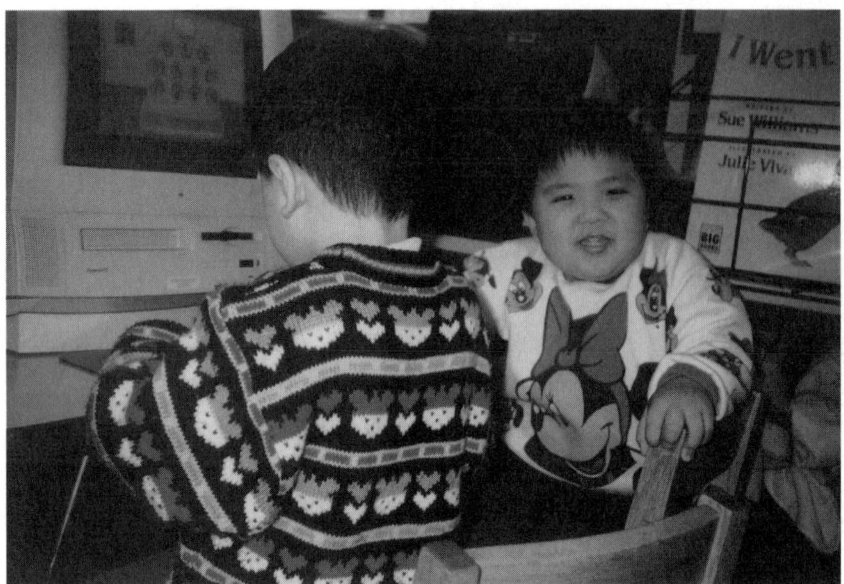

Figure 6.2. James (right) and Tommy choose at the computer.

Donna: I don't drink butter. It's too fattening.
Kevin: Orange, apple . . .
Kenneth: Squeezing out!
Donna: That tastes like a fruit punch, Kevin.
Kevin (*picking up a box of Jell-O*): Jelly—jelly, jelly.
Donna: Orange, apple?
Kenneth: I'm going to cook something. I don't think so. . . .
Kevin: Smells good.

On another occasion Kenneth and Ashley are drawing at the computer when Donna approaches them. She asks Ashley, who is seated before the screen with her hand on the computer's mouse, what she did. Referring to the screen, Ashley replies that she made two houses and a car that is parked. Donna prints out Ashley's drawing, asking Kenneth to alert her to the finished product, while she asks Ashley about what she used to make her drawing. Ashley replies that she used the mouse to make her drawing. Donna accepts her response and also encourages her to think about the computer itself as the instrument, then has her write the word *computer*.

Reviewing the "Doing"

Reviewing occurs mainly during group time following work time, when children volunteer or are asked to tell the class about what they did. Donna considers this review an important opportunity for remembering and articulating in English what was done. In other words, it is a key part of language learning.

The following two dialogues took place near the end of the year. Both children are Cantonese speakers, but Brian is now a beginning English speaker, whereas Tiffany is relatively advanced:

Example 4

Donna: I know that Brian did something very, very special today. What did you do today, Brian? (*translates into Cantonese and points at the art table*). Art.
Brian: Art. Made worms.
Donna: And you say you made worms? Why don't you show everybody your art collage? Go ahead. Look at Brian's art collage work. Isn't that nice? He used a lot of strips, glued them down, and he said he made them worms. What color worms? (*translates into Cantonese*). Red and yellow.

Brian: Red, yellow (*points to strips of paper*).
Donna: Okay! Now come back. Who else wants to share what they did today?

Example 5

Tiffany: Ms. Yung, I want to do my butterfly sharing.
Donna: You want to share your butterfly? Upstairs, we'll share [that] later [referring to the class's butterfly display upstairs in the gym]. What did you do today at the water table?
Tiffany: I made flowers with water and soup with Alice. Washed the bowl, made soup with it.
Donna: I remember. I saw you were growing flowers there and making soup.

Understanding the Physical World Through Language

During the year there are special things to observe in the center of Donna's room, from leaves and pumpkins in the fall to caterpillars turning into butterflies in the spring. One day the children were surrounding the box because all of the butterflies had emerged. When Rose Anne was about to check on one of the most recently hatched butterflies, she asked Donna how to open the butterfly box, which elicited this reaction from Andy and others:

Example 6

Andy: No! Don't open it. No open! Fly! (*He motions excitedly with his hands, waving them above his head.*)
Rose Anne: Where's it gonna go?
Andy (*shrugging his shoulders and throwing up his hands in question*): Don't know.
Ashley: Went out!
Kevin: Out the window!
Andy: Out the window!
Rose Anne: Out the window?
Everybody (*looking toward the window and pointing*): Yeah, yeah, yeah.

Experiential learning is combined with social learning during all parts of the day in Donna's classroom. While engaged in work activities at the centers, students often cooperate in the construction of something or respond to each other's constructions. There is similar interaction at the whole-group level. During Donna's reading-aloud sessions, the students offer their predictions and connections to texts as Donna pauses for them to do so, or she makes statements or asks questions such as "What do you think will happen?" to which they respond. Snack time and lunchtime, as well as play and even rest time, may be occasions for conversation that generate word learning in the most conversational ways. In the following examples, the specific naming of an item comes into play during lunch and again after a snack at the end of the day:

Example 7

Adam: Ms. Yung!
Donna: Yes, Adam?
Adam: One, one, one— One night when my mom was taking me to the doctor's office, it was raining so hard.
Donna: Yesterday?
Adam: Yeah.
Donna: You know what? When I was driving home yesterday, I felt something, like someone was throwing something hard onto my car—
Tommy: What?
Adam: Mine's too.
Donna: —but it wasn't someone throwing something hard.
Tiffany: It was a—
Donna: What? What did you see?
Tiffany (*making hand motions like the rain coming out of the sky, but hard and fast*): I see, I see like a rocks, like raining down—
Julie (*interrupts, pointing her finger at Tiffany and Donna and speaking fast in Cantonese, with Donna translating*): It's not rain, not water, it's—
Donna: If it's not water, what is it then? What was it then?
Tiffany: It's a ice!
Julie: Ice!
Tiffany: The white thing was the ice! Ice.
Donna: The white thing was the ice. You know what it's called?

Alice: I saw that too.
Donna: You saw that too?
Tommy: Me too, me too!!
Tiffany: I saw a giant go boom! (*She stamps her foot and motions.*)
Donna: Yeah, like a giant, it makes giant sounds.
Julie: [Cantonese]
Donna: And it hurt? You feel it—did it hurt?
Julie: Noooo.
Alice: [Cantonese]
Adam: It's cold.
Donna: You know what? When I saw the ice coming down, I thought someone was throwing something at my car, but it wasn't. It was hail. You know that? What we call ice coming down from the sky. Hail. We call that hail. Can you say that?
Everyone: Hail.
Adam: Mum and me stayed in the tunnel. It was too scary. We stayed in the tunnel because—
Ashley: Ms. Yung.
Donna: What happened, Ashley?
Ashley: Not dark. The tunnel's not dark.
Donna: What? The tunnel's not dark? Why isn't the tunnel dark?
Ashley: Because of the lights.
Donna: Lights!

Example 8

During snack time, Tiffany requests paper, and Donna at first directs her to the writing center, then realizes that isn't what Tiffany means.

Donna: You want a paper, Tiffany?
Tiffany: Yeah. I wipe my hand!
Donna: You want paper to wipe your hands? What do you need?
Tiffany: Tissue.
Donna: Okay. . . . There are tissues behind you. Or do you mean a napkin?
Tiffany: Napkin!
Susan: It's made of paper, though, isn't it, Tiffany?
Donna: Yes, it is. A different kind of paper.
Tiffany (*holding up her napkin*): Tissue.
Donna: The tissue's right behind you. . . .
Tiffany: That is, um, nose. This napkin is wipe hands and that is for bathroom wash hands (*points to the roll of paper towels in the corner*).
Donna: Paper towels! All different types of paper, right?
Tiffany: Yup.

Examples 7 and 8 illustrate well how Donna is able to engage children in talk about words and their properties. The extended conversation about hail is talk about science, which embeds a new vocabulary word and the qualities that define it (what it is made of, where it appears to come from, what sound it makes, and how it was experienced). Much narrower in focus is Donna's conversation with Tiffany about kinds of paper, defined by their functions. Donna makes visible and audible the thinking—categorizing—that learners must experience in order to understand and internalize the words they hear and repeat.

Tommy and Andy: Making the Transition to English

In September, when the school year began, Tommy was a monolingual speaker of Cantonese. He lives with his mother and grandmother, also both Cantonese speakers. By the end of the year Tommy speaks English almost all the time, and he speaks it eagerly as he participates in the full range of activities that Donna provides. The videotapes that we collected in the last three months of the year demonstrate that Tommy is a frequent contributor to group times, that he often initiates conversations with adults, and that he is enthusiastic about early literacy activities.

Two examples focusing on Tommy illustrate how he engages with the curriculum. Here he responds to Donna's questions and suggestions regarding a drawing of a building:

Example 9

Donna: That's a big building! Yeah, that is a big house—building. You live in an apartment, right?

Tommy: Nope.

Donna: That's called an apartment. When you live in a building like that, its called an apartment. . . . I like your building. Do you know your address?

Tommy: I know.

Donna: You know? What is your address?

Tommy: 9-D!

Donna: 9-D? You live in apartment 9-D? Can you write 9-D on your drawing somewhere, so we know that is your apartment? (*He writes it.*)

The conversation continues, and in the course of it, Donna asks Tommy what street he lives on. He says it's Madison Street, and knowing his interest in letters and sounds, she prompts him with the sounds that make up *Madison.* He writes the letters *M-R-D-S-N.* After writing the *N,* he exclaims, "N, that's easy!" Donna responds, "Very good." Tommy's interest is unusual in this class, but Donna is prepared to teach if the interest and ability are there. She is aware of Tommy's interest because of the responses he has shown whenever she includes phonemic awareness activities in her teaching.

At the end of the conference Donna asks what the number of his building is, and Tommy does not know. She tells him to go home today and look for it. The next day Tommy, without prompting from Donna, makes an elaborate construction in the block area, complete with written signs, that depicts his neighborhood:

Example 10

Donna: Why don't you talk about all the signs that you have?

Tommy: This one's 9-D.

Donna: Your house, yeah, and—

Tommy: This one's STOP, 100, and—

Donna: Ten miles an hour, and what about—

Tommy: It's 100!

Donna: One hundred miles! That's too fast for cars, don't you think, Tommy? And what do you have there?

Tommy: Um, Madison Street.

Donna: Oh, that's good. So when people go down the street, they know where they're going now. Down Madison Street

Tommy: Madison Street, New York.

In fact, Tommy does not mention the number of his building on Madison Street, but he recreates the drawing he made the day before with blocks, cutting, writing, and taping signs on different blocks to show 9-D, STOP, 100, and Madison Street, New York. He coordinates an informal lesson learned with Donna with a self-initiated activity. Woven through both the lesson and the block building are information about Tommy's experience of his neighborhood and his growing interest in and abilities with print (see Brian and Jenny having a similar experience in Figure 6.3).

Andy is learning English differently from the way Tommy is, but Andy too is strongly influenced by the curricular activities. Andy chooses the block area frequently, but unlike Tommy, he rarely chooses the writing center. It is more common to find him at the computer or water table. He is highly engaged in books about science concepts and is excited by transformations in science. And whereas Tommy is able to code switch easily, Andy often responds in Cantonese with attached English words for concepts known or newly acquired.

One day, before reading a book on the life cycle of the butterfly, Donna engages the class in a conversation about the caterpillars in the observation tank in the center of the classroom. Andy has just said the word *big* and gestured with his hands opening wide to show his concept of big when Donna says that the caterpillars will stay in the container. Referring to the caterpillars and the last observation charted, Donna asks, "Did they look like this on Thursday?" Andy, Kenneth, Alice, and James respond, mostly by saying no, that the caterpillars do not look like an egg.

As Donna begins to read *See How They Grow: Butterfly* (Ling, 1992), Andy calls out "Butterflies!" followed by some Cantonese. As she reads about the egg and the hatching of a tiny caterpillar, James and Andy both talked excitedly in Cantonese in response to Donna's translation into Cantonese. They both look intently at the

Figure 6.3. Brian and Jenny represent their experiences in the block area.

pictures Donna is showing the class. Once the caterpillar in the book hatched, Andy began predicting.

Example 11

Andy: [Cantonese] . . . Gonna turn butterfly!

Donna: Yes, it's going to turn into a butterfly.

Kenneth: You, you, you gonna open it gonna open and let the butterfly, school . . . out and fly!

Donna: Yeah, we are going to let the butterfly out!

Andy: [Cantonese] . . . Butterfly! Big butterfly!

Donna returns to the story and continues reading about the caterpillar getting bigger and bigger. After reading about the caterpillar shedding its skin over and over in order to grow in size, she points to the book and says, "See the new skin?" All the while Andy keeps up a running monologue in Cantonese. After reading a bit more Donna looks at him after she asks the class in English and then Cantonese about the growing caterpillar, "How many legs?" Andy answers in Cantonese, and Donna typically responds in English, "Ten legs, that's right." Andy repeats what she said, holding up ten fingers: "ten legs!" Then he repeats "ten legs" in Cantonese and engages James in a brief dialogue in Cantonese. Donna re-engages the class with the story by continuing to read about the caterpillar eating the plant. She tries to calm Andy's excitement in his discussion with James while allowing him to make meaning of the text.

Donna later reads about the chrysalis and the metamorphosis of the caterpillar to the butterfly (see Figure 6.4). Realizing the transformation, Tommy observes, "It is a butterfly. A butterfly turning! And it is pushing!" Andy also realizes what is happening and makes his own observation, "Big, big, big!" While Donna reads about the butterfly drying its wings and sipping nectar, Andy continues talking in Cantonese as he attends to the book and its closing:

Example 12

Donna: You become a wonderful butterfly.

Andy: The end.

Andy, who looks intently at the pictures of the featured book, keeps up a stream of Cantonese, usually quietly and to himself, during the read-

Figure 6.4. Donna reads to the class during morning meeting.

ing of the story. However, he also makes animated comments from time to time, and in addition makes 15 utterances in English, some in response to questions. Most of the English utterances are spontaneous observations, connections, or predictions—evidence of Andy's growing interest in and understanding of his world.

Integrating the Curriculum in Multiple Contexts

Donna's classroom is seldom quiet, as it is usually occupied by active and expressive children and adults. Although there are clearly separate spaces for such activities as art, block building, or tabletop activities, there is also movement between these areas as children seek out friends or the teacher or assistant. Activities similarly blend into each other. A math activity, for example, incorporates early reading after Jenny has estimated how long her hand is, as measured by plastic cubes, then measures her hand:

Example 13

Donna: Can you read this with me?
Jenny: (*nods yes*)
Donna: Or you want to read it yourself? Go ahead.
Jenny: (*nods yes*) My hand—
Donna: —hand is?
Jenny: Seven cubes tall.
Donna: Very good, let's try it again.
Jenny: My hand is 7 cubes tall. (*Donna says it with her, holding her finger under the words in the sentence.*)

Embedded within an activity involving estimation and measurement is an early literacy lesson.

Categorizing is another important skill that is learned and reinforced while literacy is also learned, and it takes many forms. One day while Tiffany, Kevin, and Kenneth are together in the block area, they begin to sort the rubber and plastic animals into zoo, farm, and sea animals. Since they have recently been on a field trip to the aquarium, Donna has read a book entitled *Sea Animals* (Royston, 1992). The companion text, *Zoo Animals* (Dowell, 1991), Donna has also read. When Donna asks Tiffany about a particular group of animals, she identifies them:

Example 14

Donna: Come here. You've got all the animals. Come here, sweetheart. Where is the title, *zoo animals*? Find *zoo animals*. (*Tiffany points to the word* animals *on the front cover.*) What's this? (*Donna points to the word* zoo.)

Tiffany: Z!

Donna: Z. What's this? (*Points to each letter in the word* zoo.)

Tiffany: Zoo! Zoo animals. . . .

Donna: Okay. Can you take this and write the words *zoo animals*? Take that and write *zoo animals*. Just like that. Go make a sign.

Kenneth: Found it.

Donna: You found a little zebra, right.

Tiffany: Tiger! Tiger! (*goes to make her sign, cuts, tapes, and returns later*).

Kevin: Find the shark. Shark. Where's the shark?

Donna: What did you write, Tiffany?

Tiffany: Zoo animals!

Donna: Oh, you wrote it nicely, too!

Tiffany: Look.

The sorting activity is based on what Tiffany has been learning about categorizing different kinds of animals. Donna expects Tiffany not only to label or name the category "zoo animals" orally in English but also to use her growing literacy skills to read it in the book title, then write it. Donna pushes Tiffany because she knows what Tiffany is capable of doing. For Jenny, the activity entails saying, writing, and reading the English words that represent the length of her hand. Jenny's participation in the mathematical activity is on a different conceptual level from Tiffany's more independent participation in the science-oriented activity. However, each is an example of the kind of student-teacher interaction that gives children greater and greater control over spoken and written language in particular content areas.

Investing in the Teaching and Learning of Language

By spring, many children, such as Tiffany, are speaking English most of the time, switching to Cantonese only occasionally. However, four children, including Brian and Jenny, are still more comfortable speaking Cantonese. Alice, Julie, and Andy mix Cantonese and English. Donna accepts the language they choose to speak, and she helps them by translating and paraphrasing so that all children can hear how their ideas sound in English. Even if children are not yet fluent in English, Donna supports their participation with her own explanations. She knows each child well and holds high expectations for each individual and for the group. Thus, although some would call the children "limited English proficient," Donna views them first as learners who are all capable of learning English and much more from a rich curriculum.

Donna expects her students to talk about their activities, whether those activities are group or individual. She believes that consistent routines and constant conferring help the children acquire vocabulary. Her children have definite routines, and they know what to expect in their well-structured classroom. They know where to find materials and have been taught how to take care of them. Donna expects them to explore and create with the materials she provides. She provides possible projects, but she also encourages inventiveness and elaboration on ideas that she sets forth. Donna believes in the "talking" teachable moment, and she pursues it mightily so that the children benefit.

In addition, Donna is a curriculum maker. Each year she finds a subject that the children show a sustained interest in and pursues it in an integrated manner. She writes,

> As a teacher, I strongly believe I need to be able to create and offer a curriculum that is alive for the children. There are certain units I do with them that are generally interesting to 4-year-olds—seasons, animals, food, holidays, etc.; but I also create a theme after observing and listening to children in their play. Last year it was cookies, this year it is insects. I listen to what they know and then build on that knowledge by reading books, finding materials to use, introducing art and other activities about the topic, setting up props in the centers for the children to use to role-play, and going on field trips associated with the topic.

Donna also finds that one group-generated topic will lead to another: a trip to a neighborhood bakery during the cookie theme generated intense interest in environmental print once the children started reading the signs. This year the study of insects led to an author study of Eric Carle, since so many of his books contain insects. Increasing children's knowledge leads to expanded vocabulary as well as a greater knowledge base that will help children as they move on in school.

Donna believes that her greatest resources for language teaching and learning are the other children who are English dominant or speak some English. She observes, "I find that some of the children speak English to each other more easily than to me. I think this is because they don't feel the pressure of an adult. A class as a whole learns to speak English faster when there are a couple of English-speaking children integrated with the Chinese-speaking children."

To summarize, the following are strategies that Donna and Rose Anne use to create the most favorable environment for learning language and learning through language:

- Accept children's own ways of expressing themselves, whether they speak English or another language or use nonverbal forms of communication.
- Approach every activity or interaction as a potential "teachable moment," whether children are role-playing reading or taking on roles in dramatic play.
- Think flexibly about the curriculum, within a predictable and repetitive structure. Although literacy was strongly emphasized in her school district and school, Donna implemented a broadly integrated curriculum. Her regularly scheduled activities with the children could at any moment transform themselves into "literacy events," mini-lessons in math or how to be a thoughtful student, or science explorations.
- Be unafraid to use yourself as the children's most important model for using English and for being an active learner and thinker. (Donna and Rose Anne both spoke in highly audible voices and were often heard repeating words or explanations, expanding what children said into more elaborate utterances or asking questions to which only the children knew the answers.)
- Be unafraid to translate for children if you are fortunate enough to speak their home language.
- Be unafraid to use children's interest in each other to encourage the use of language among peers; children can be both persistent learners and teachers.

Relating Our Classroom Research to Previous Work

In this section we ask how previous research on children's primary or second language is related to what we have found thus far in Donna's room. A number of principles come to light from research on language and literacy learning and the conditions that enhance it. We conclude by noting some commonalities among teachers whose students make the transition from apprentice to confident learner.

In her research on the development of language in children from birth to age 3 years, Lois Bloom (1998) sees expression and interpretation of language as the motivation for learning language. She proposes an "intentionality" model, stating, "All the functions of language including its personal, interpersonal, instrumental, regulatory, problem-solving, and other functions depend on the power of language for expression and interpretation" (p. 310). Specifically in relation to vocabulary, Bloom demonstrates that vocabulary growth is slow at first, then increases dramatically, but in a nonlinear, individual fashion.

Braided with language are cognition, affect, and social connectedness, which Bloom sees as developing together as transactions occur between children's internal intentional states and the external social and physical world. This view of development based on a child acting on his or her environment is the cornerstone of many early childhood teachers' conceptions of child-centered classrooms. Although Bloom proposes that all functions of language stem from basic expression, we cannot presume that they will necessarily be fostered in an early childhood

AN IDEA FROM A TEACHER

Donna's Teaching Tips

Introducing Reading with a Daily Agenda: In my classroom, an agenda is posted at the children's eye level. I use it to transition from one activity to another, and I also encourage them to become aware that a schedule can be read. During transition time, I ask them to "read" the activity that is ending and the activity that will be beginning. They find and point to the appropriate words and say them to me. For the most part, the schedule stays the same and is posted as Breakfast, Circle Time, Planning Time, Activity Time, Recall Time, Outdoor Time, Story Time, Lunch, Rest, Small Group Time, Quiet Activity Time, Circle Time, and Snack. I often see the children referring to the agenda between activities and hear them discussing what we will be doing next, throughout the day.

Taking Opportunities to Teach: During observations of their sprouting lima beans, my children were very interested in comparing the size of the roots. I showed them how we can use a ruler by putting its end at the beginning of the root and reading the number at the root's end. When they wanted to use rulers at the writing center the next day, I decided to make rulers the subject of a mini-lesson and introduced the tool. After the mini-lesson during small-group time, I gave them each a ruler and asked them to find out what they could do with it. They measured size and distance, did drawings, and read the numbers. They came back together and shared their discoveries, which I recorded. Some of the vocabulary they learned included *measure, distance, line, straight, ruler, number, inches,* and *long.*

Allowing for Possibilities: After carefully cutting out their handprint butterflies, several children discovered that they had created a cutout of a butterfly on their original paper. After finishing the designated activity, that of decorating the "positive space" butterflies, they glued the cutouts, or "negative space" butterflies, to another piece of paper and decorated those as well. I conferred with each of them about how they created the second butterfly, and they shared their creations with the other children.

Schedule: Since the schedule is posted at the children's eye level, I use it to help them move to the next activity. During a transition I ask them to read (find and point to) the activity that is ending and the activity that will be beginning. For the most part the schedule stays the same and is posted as: Breakfast, Circle Time, Planning Time, Activity, Recall Time, Outdoor Time, Story Time, Lunch, Rest, Small Group Time, Quiet Activity Time, Circle Time, and Snack. I often hear the children discussing what we will be doing next.

Word Box: We have a word box on one of the writing center shelves. Words that are part of our theme studies or words that the children often use are placed in the box. Usually I draw a picture to illustrate the word. In addition to using the words to create their drawings and stories, the children play together at reading the words.

Donna Yung-Chan, Kindergarten Teacher

classroom or center unless there is a consciousness about language use. Bloom proposes that the consciousness comes through frequent language-based interactions.

Agreeing that there is a need for consciousness about language use, Marie Clay (1991, p. 27) writes, "The teacher's task is to help children to make links between what they can already do with language and the new challenges of school." Here she is inclusive of children with a home language that is unlike the language of the school, as well as other differences. She shows how the expansion of talk by an adult—that is, an adult's repeating what a child has said, as a check on understanding—provides a model of language in word, structure, and meaning. She explains how language learning in this manner occurs and is practiced at the preschool level and continues at home after the child has gone to school. This language learning may or may not be in standard ("newscaster's") English. If it is not, the teacher must add standard English to the child's linguistic resources. The teacher first establishes communication and then helps children express their intentions so that they can eventually function and flourish in the school language. Clay cautions, however, that stimulating activities do not necessarily lead to language learning. We can evaluate activities by examining how much they provoke conversation with a mature speaker. In the case of English language learners, the "mature" speaker may be another child or children or peers to whom the child might apprentice himself or herself.

Recent research on young English language learners supports Clay's suggestion, revealing the importance of master conversationalists, whether adults and children. Fassler (1998), for example, studied a public school kindergarten classroom made up exclusively of children designated as ESL learners. In this room, the teacher, Mrs. Barker, not only provided consistent and continual modeling of English, she also allowed children to talk whenever possible, whether they were waiting in line for the bathroom or helping each other with an early literacy task. The children's languages represented nine different language groups, and so the children were often able to support each other's language growth in both the home language (in this classroom, most often a Chinese language or Russian) and English. Meyer, Klein, and Genishi (1994) report on a preschool classroom in which four children were Korean speakers. Progress in their second language, English, became evident only after the four had established communications and relationships among themselves, building on their shared linguistic and cultural knowledge.

With the increasing heterogeneity of the North American population, many children arrive in early childhood classrooms speaking different dialects of English or other languages, languages that may be as common as Spanish and as rare as Turkish (Genishi, Dyson, & Fassler, 1994). Many teachers must try to address the needs of one or two English language learners who do not have a conversational partner with whom to express intentions or ideas (Genishi, 1989). In these classrooms, teachers who speak only English are especially dependent on their abilities to observe nonverbal behaviors so that communication through language later becomes possible. We believe that Donna's teaching strategies would also be effective in these settings. Here, "translation" might take the form of exaggerated gestures and nonverbal messages, and teachers might occasionally invite additional adults or older students into the classroom to interact one on one with English learners.

Teachers increasingly confront the richness and complexity of working with linguistic and cultural differences (Ballenger, 1999; Dyson, 1993, 1997; Freeman & Freeman, 1999; Genesee, 1994). Across the small number of studies that describe what teachers like Mrs. Barker and Donna Yung-Chan do with their students, there are at least three striking commonalities. First, the teachers who observe their children making a transition from non-English speaker to beginning English speaker or from nonreader to reader show flexibility within a predictable daily schedule. They adapt the curriculum to allow for group preferences and for individual variation. They adjust to variation and do not require uniformity. Second, these teachers have high expectations. They expect every apprentice eventually to enter the community of speakers, listeners, readers, and writers—in short, to become master learners. Third, these teachers cherish communication and connection. They accept, even celebrate, everyone's need to be social, to have intentions and ideas and to communicate them freely and often to others.

Acknowledgment: We are grateful to the Spencer Foundation Practitioner Research program for the Communication and Mentoring Grant that made this study possible. The data and interpretations presented here are solely the responsibility of the authors.

Children's Books and Computer Software

Brown, M. W. (1947/1991). *Good night, moon.* New York: HarperCollins.

Dowell, P. (1991). *Zoo animals.* New York: Macmillan, Eye Openers/Aladdin Books.

Ling, M. (1992). *See how they grow: Butterfly.* New York: Dorling Kindersley.

Royston, A. (1992). *Sea animals.* New York: Macmillan, Eye Openers/Aladdin Books.

Weather Machine. (1994). *Sammy science house* (computer software). Redmond, WA: Edmark.

References

Ballenger, C. (1999). *Teaching other people's children.* New York: Teachers College Press.

Bloom, L. (1998). Language acquisition in its developmental context. In D. Kuhn & R. Siegler (Eds.), *Handbook of child psychology: Vol. 2. Cognition, perception, and language* (pp. 309–370). New York: Wiley.

Clark, E. V. (1973). What's in a word? On the child's acquisition of semantics in his first language. In T. E. Moore (Ed.), *Cognitive development and the acquisition of language.* New York: Academic Press.

Clay, M. M. (1991). *Becoming literate: The construction of inner control.* Portsmouth, NH: Heinemann.

Dyson, A. H. (1993). *Social worlds of children learning to write in an urban primary school.* New York: Teachers College Press.

Dyson, A. H. (with the San Francisco East Bay Teacher Study Group). (1997). *What difference does difference make? Teacher reflections on diversity, literacy, and the urban primary school.* Urbana, IL: National Council of Teachers of English.

Fassler, R. (1998). Room for talk: Peer support for getting into English in an ESL kindergarten. *Early Childhood Research Quarterly, 13,* 379–409.

Freeman, D., & Freeman, Y. S. (1999). The California Reading Initiative: A formula for failure for bilingual students? *Language Arts, 76,* Z41–Z48.

Genesee, F. (Ed.). (1994). *Educating second language children: The whole child, the whole curriculum, the whole community.* New York: Cambridge University Press.

Genishi, C. (1989). Observing the second language learner: An example of teacher's learning. *Language Arts, 66,* 509–515.

Genishi, C., Dyson, A. H., & Fassler, R. (1994). Language and diversity in early childhood: Whose voices are appropriate? In B. L. Mallory & R. S. New (Eds.), *Diversity and developmentally appropriate practices: Challenges in early childhood education* (pp. 250–268). New York: Teachers College Press.

Hohmann, M., Banet, B., & Weikart, D. (1979). *Young children in action.* Ypsilanti, MI: High/Scope Press.

Meyer, C., Klein, E., & Genishi, C. (1994). Peer relationships among four preschool second language learners in "small group time." *Early Childhood Research Quarterly, 9,* 61–85.

PART TWO

Instructional Strategies for Beginning Readers and Writers

Part Two deals with specific curricular issues related to beginning reading and writing. A substantial amount of classroom-based research in the past decade focused on determining the attributes of effective teachers and the teaching strategies that represent best practice. Building on a firm knowledge base accrued through earlier studies, this research has further advanced our understanding of what good teachers know and do to help children become successful learners. The chapters in Part Two represent the current knowledge base in relation to organizing and managing the classroom, working with struggling learners, promoting writing development, fostering decoding and comprehension skills, using children's literature, assessing students' progress, and making use of technology.

All learners, including adults, learn best when they are actively engaged in the process. With that in mind, we suggest that you continue to support your reading and thinking by keeping a response log in which you react to various ideas as they are presented. Remember to explore the entire range of your responses, including the ideas with which you agree or disagree or find confusing, perplexing, or surprising, as well as those that prompt you to react in other ways. Your response notes represent your personal interactions with the text and provide the basis for interactions with others.

If you are reading this book with a number of others, it may be possible to share your notes with a small group or a partner before sharing them with the entire group. As you read and respond, try to link the material presented in Part Two with the broader underlying foundations covered in Part One. For example, how does play or oral language development relate to organizing the classroom for literacy? What is the role of technology in literacy learning?

CHAPTER SEVEN

Organizing and Managing a Language Arts Block

Lesley Mandel Morrow

For Reflection and Action: Consider the instructional environment and allocation of time in a classroom of your choice. How does it compare with the ideas suggested here? Is the environment organized and managed in a way that is most conducive to learning? What changes would you make?

Lesley Morrow provides a wealth of concrete suggestions for organizing and managing the classroom environment for optimum literacy learning and teaching.

This chapter focuses on:

- Research findings about exemplary practices in the language arts
- Environmental factors in classrooms that enhance literacy instruction
  - Print that counts on classroom walls
  - Learning centers in content areas
  - The literacy center
- The outline of a well-organized and well-managed language arts block
- Descriptions of activities within the language arts block, including:
  - Morning meeting

- Organizing and managing center time
- Guided reading period
- Writing workshops

Investigations into exemplary practices in early literacy instruction attempt to capture as many dimensions as possible of expert performances to describe teaching excellence. In this type of research, investigators examine real-life situations in which many variables are successfully integrated. The results of the research on effective and exemplary teaching have many similarities. A list combining some findings about effective and exemplary teachers and their classroom practices includes the following characteristics (Morrow, Tracey, Woo, & Pressley, 1999; Pressley, Rankin, & Yokoi, 1996; Ruddell & Ruddell, 1995):

1. Varied teaching strategies are used to motivate literacy learning.
2. Teachers create excitement about what is being taught.
3. There are high expectations for student accomplishment.
4. Instruction is adjusted to meet the individual needs of students.
5. Guidance is provided through structured lessons for the acquisition of skills.
6. Extensive positive feedback is provided for students.
7. Children are treated with respect.
8. Opportunities are provided for children to practice the skills learned.
9. Classrooms are rich literacy environments with accessible materials.
10. Varied structures for instruction are utilized, including whole-group, small-group, and one-on-one settings with the teacher.
11. Opportunities exist for children to work independently of the teacher, either alone or in social cooperative groups.
12. Emphasis is placed on careful organization and management of strategies and structures for optimal literacy development to occur.

Of the items listed, the following are particularly relevant to this chapter:

- Classrooms are rich literacy environments with accessible materials.
- Varied teaching strategies are used to motivate.
- Varied structures for instruction are utilized, including whole-group, small-group, and one-on-one settings with the teacher.
- Emphasis is placed on careful organization and management of strategies and structures for optimal literacy development to occur.
- Children are treated with respect.
- Extensive positive feedback is provided for students.

The purpose of this chapter is to describe and demonstrate how the organization of the classroom environment and the management of the language arts block with varied structures for learning contribute to successful literacy instruction. These environmental and organizational factors are often overlooked, while strategies for instruction are emphasized. Without the support of the classroom's physical environment and the organization and management of instructional strategies, however, early literacy instruction is not likely to be effective or exemplary.

With this background, I will take you on a journey into an early childhood classroom. As you see the teacher in action, keep in mind that the story is based on a collective profile of six teachers identified as exemplary. I observed these teachers for a year as part of a study on exemplary literacy instruction in first grade. This investigation took place in five states where supervisors nominated exemplary teachers. These teachers were deemed experts based on supervisory observations, the achievement of their students, and their reputations with their colleagues, parents, and children. By synthesizing my findings on these expert teachers, I will present a composite sketch of exemplary classrooms that highlights (1) the classroom's physical environment and (2) the management of the language arts block, including the morning meeting, assignment of independent work in centers, and small-group instruction for meeting students' individual needs. I will describe characteristics in such classrooms and substantiate my descriptions by discussing research about classroom environments, classroom management, and the value of independent work and grouping to meet individual needs. Although the teacher portrayed is a composite of six teachers, for the purposes of this paper I shall call her Tracey Lyn Barclay.

The Physical Environment in Mrs. Barclay's Classroom

Tracey Lyn Barclay's room exemplifies her own philosophies regarding the physical design of a classroom. Tracey arranges her room so that it is "student-friendly." She stores materials so that they can be easily accessed, both visually and physically. Tracey finds that a rich supply of materials enables her to meet the different abilities and interests of her children. Her classroom, located in the basement of an old inner-city school, is by no means picturesque; however, it has adequate space for her 23 children and good lighting, and it is kept clean. The children's desks are arranged in groups of four to encourage social interaction. This arrangement also saves spaces for other materials. The room has provisions for whole-group instruction with students sitting at their desks or on a rug in the literacy center. The area for whole-group meetings has a chalkboard, a pocket chart, and an easel with an experience chart. Tracey has a rocking chair that she uses when teaching mini-lessons or reading stories to the children.

Tracey's morning meeting area includes functional print such as a calendar, a weather chart, a helper chart, and rules for the classroom. Signs communicate information, such as *Quiet, Please* and *Please Put Materials Away After Using Them.* A notice board is used to communicate with her children through writing. In addition, there is a word wall, and it is evident from the word wall that the class is reviewing long and short vowels. The featured words of the week—high-frequency words—are posted, and a bulletin board displays the thematic unit that is being studied, "People Around the World."

On one side of the room is a table where Tracey meets with small groups and individual children, based on need (see Figure 7.1). On this table Tracey has all the materials she uses for skill instruction. These include leveled books selected for the reading needs of children, a pocket chart, an experience chart, individual writing slates for work with word study and writing, and folders for students to assess their success and needs. On the windowsill are corrugated cardboard book bins, labeled with children's names, where they store individual work, such as their writing journals, books they are reading, homework assignments, and so on. These materials are packaged in Zip-Lock bags.

Learning Centers

To accommodate small-group, independent work, there are learning centers, each labeled according to content areas. Although there is a separate literacy center, all centers integrate literacy learning into content areas by featuring reading and writing activities. Tracey believes that literacy activities have more meaning when integrated into content areas. She uses themes for developing new vocabulary, new ideas, and purposes for reading and writing. Each of her centers has general materials that are typical of the content they represent, such as scissors, paste, crayons, and paper in the art center, but also special materials that are linked to the current thematic topic of study. For example, while the class is engaged in the unit entitled "People Around the World: Multicultural Education" the centers are equipped as follows:

- The *dramatic play center* is a Chinese restaurant with play money, a cash register, a menu, recipes, costumes, and checks. After a while this will be changed to an Italian restaurant, with a new and appropriate menu.
- The *music center* includes instruments from different countries, such as maracas from Mexico and a Caribbean steel drum. Tracey provides tapes and the sheet music for songs from the countries being discussed.
- The *art center* has blank flags for children to decorate to represent different countries, and there is a special paper and directions for folding Japanese origami figures.
- The *social studies center* features *National Geographic* magazines, maps of countries around the world, and foreign stamps.

Figure 7.1. The teacher meets with small groups for guided reading instruction.

- The *science center* offers cookbooks from other lands and the ingredients for making multicultural dishes.
- The *math center* has an abacus, foreign currency, and English and metric rulers.

Tracey has an organizational chart for center work. When she makes the assignment for center use, children know where to go by consulting the chart.

The Literacy Center: Tracey's literacy center (see Figure 7.2) includes space and materials for writing, reading, oral language, listening, comprehension, and word-analysis skill development. In this area she has her rocking chair and rug, since many of the activities in this center take place on the floor and it is where she holds group meetings, lessons, and story time. There are pillows and stuffed animals to add an element of softness.

Books are stored in open-faced shelving for displaying titles about themes being studied. These books are changed with the themes and to feature special selections. Tracey stores some books in baskets which she labels by genre, such as books about animals or seasons, poetry, biographies, and so on. To aid selection, other books are labeled with the letters A through E to represent the approximate difficulty of the book, so that children can read something easy for fun or difficult for a challenge.

In her classroom Tracey has five to eight book selections per child, or about 170 books. She has picture storybooks, poetry, informational books, magazines, biographies, cookbooks, joke books, novels, and fairy tales. She has acquired these books over the years by purchasing them at flea markets, through points gained from book club sales, through donations from parents, by using her allotted classroom budget, and by buying some herself. She rotates her books regularly to maintain children's interest in them, and children can check books out of the classroom to read at home. Literacy manipulatives such as puppets, taped stories with headsets, and felt

Figure 7.2. The literacy center.

boards with story characters are included in the literacy center materials to reach children through different modalities for learning. The literacy center includes foreign dictionaries and many books related to the multicultural theme, such as *Chinese Mother Goose Rhymes* (Wyndham, 1968).

There is a shelf of games that offer practice in word analysis. These materials—Bingo, Lotto, and Concentration, to name a few—teach the alphabet, long and short vowels, sound-symbol association of consonants, digraphs, and so on. For enhancing reading comprehension, Tracey creates activities that address strategies, such as mapping stories, retelling stories, creating Venn diagrams, story structure maps, sequencing story events, and predicting outcomes.

The Author's Spot: A portion of the literacy center called the author's spot is set aside and includes a table, chairs, and writing materials such as colored markers, crayons, pencils, paper, chalk, a chalkboard, and various types of paper. Index cards are used for recording words children request to read and write, called "Very Own Words"; the cards are stored in index boxes. Folders, one for each child, are used to collect writing samples. Tracey has two computers with excellent software for writing and reading activities.

In the author's spot, Tracey has materials for making books, including writing paper in many sizes, a stapler, construction paper, and a hole punch. Tracey prepares blank books keyed to themes, such as a booklet in the shape of a country studied. There is a place for children to display their written work, a mailbox, stationery, envelopes, and stamps for children to write to each other and to pen pals. Through the Internet, Tracey found a class in Mexico interested in corresponding with her class by e-mail.

Everything in this room has a function, a purpose, and a place to be stored. The teacher models new materials, their purposes, how they are used, and where they belong. Tracey starts the school year with a few items in the centers and adds to them slowly as the class studies different themes and skills.

The Research

Tracey's classroom organization and management practices echo findings from historical perspectives and research that deal with the manipulation of the environment and its effects on learning. The design of her classroom exhibits the characteristics described in research as beneficial for effective classroom instruction and management.

Historically, theorists and philosophers have emphasized the importance of the physical environment in early learning and literacy development. Pestalozzi (Rusk & Scotland, 1979) and Froebel (1974) described the preparation of manipulative materials that would foster literacy development in real-life environments. Montessori (1965) advocated a carefully prepared classroom environment to promote independent learning and recommended that each kind of material in the environment have a specific learning objective. She prepared her classroom with materials that were accessible for children.

Research has shown ways in which the physical design of the classroom affects the children's behavior (Loughlin & Martin, 1987; Morrow, 1990; Rivlin & Weinstein, 1984). Rooms partitioned into smaller spaces such as centers facilitate verbal interaction among peers and enhance cooperative and associative learning. When rooms are carefully designed for specific types of instruction, such as a table for meeting with a small group of children, productivity is increased and there is greater use of language than in rooms where no attention is given to setting (Moore, 1986).

Literacy-rich environments stimulate activities that enhance literacy skill development (Morrow, 1997a; Neuman & Roskos, 1992). Story props such as puppets or a felt board with story characters improve story production and comprehension, including recall of details and the ability to interpret text (Morrow, 1997b). Researchers have found that children like cozy corners with pillows and rugs to retreat to when things get hectic, and opportunities for privacy are important for children who are distractible and for those who have difficulty relating to peers (Weinstein & Mignano, 1996). Young children work best in rooms with variation; that is, they have warm and cool colors, some open areas and cozy spots, as well as hard and soft surfaces (Olds, 1987).

Organization and Management of the Language Arts Block

From the classrooms observed in the study dealing with exemplary practices in first-grade literacy instruction, I was able to outline a language arts block that was representative of all of the classrooms. The schedule is as follows:

8:30 to 9:00: Children enter school and engage in independent work until the day formally begins.

9:00 to 9:40: There is a whole-group morning meeting that includes opening exercises, a discussion of the calendar and weather, sharing time, morning messages with some word-analysis skill development, and storybook reading with some comprehension development. All of these activities are theme-related when possible.

9:40 to 9:50: The teacher describes independent and cooperative activities at centers and provides time for children to get organized to do this work productively. This is in preparation for the teacher to meet with individuals and small groups for direct instruction in reading and writing.

9:50 to 11:40: The teacher meets with the four or more groups of children she has organized based on similar needs for literacy instruction. Each group meets for about 20 minutes.

11:40: Writing workshop can occur during the language arts block. It can begin in the morning as part of the language arts block and continue after lunch. The entire workshop could also happen after lunch. Writing workshop includes a whole-group skill lesson, a writing assignment, and conferencing with peers and or the teacher for revising and editing.

According to research, effective classroom managers have clear rules, routines, and expectations for literacy goals. The rules are decided on by the children and their teacher, are consistent on a day-to-day basis, are taught in the first days of school and are reviewed often (Weinstein & Mignano, 1996). The teacher communicates the rules and expectations in a supportive manner, showing respect for students at all times.

We will now visit Tracey from the time her children enter the classroom in the morning and observe more closely the activities that occur in each of the segments of the morning devoted to language arts.

8:30 to 9:00: Beginning the School Day

When the children enter Tracey's room they engage in literacy activities immediately. All children locate their names and photographs on the attendance chart and turn their pictures face-up to indicate they are in school. Children who are buying lunch sign their names under their choices on the lunch chart. The children look for their names on a chart of daily jobs; Tracey changes the assignments frequently, which requires the students to read the chart when they enter the classroom. Those with jobs take care of their responsibilities. Kimberly and Dawn, for example, work on the calendar. Kim writes the date, and Dawn completes the days of the week. Jovanna and Tyrone complete the weather graph. Roseangela and Jordan are reporters and have to write about some daily news. Since the class is studying animals, Tracey borrowed a setting hen, which has laid several eggs. Charlene and Adalice have the job of reporting on what is happening with the hen.

Once these morning jobs are completed, children perform their daily tasks. One activity is to write an entry in their journals, which they do with a partner. Children discuss what they are writing about and offer each other input. When they finish, they read their pieces to each other and respond with comments. If there is still time before morning meeting, children can read independently or with a partner. At 8:55, Tracey rings a bell, indicating to the children that they have 5 minutes to finish what they are doing, clean up, and meet her on the rug for the morning meeting.

9:00 to 9:40: Morning Meeting

Tracey and the children gather for the morning meeting on the rug in the literacy center. This meeting is always a whole-group experience. Math and language concepts are woven throughout a discussion of the calendar and the weather. The children count how many days are left in the month and how many have passed. The daily reporters, who did their work when they got to school, read their news aloud. Others add to it.

Tracey shares her previously written morning message, which is related to the theme "Many Kinds of Animals." The message is about the class's upcoming visit to a zoo. Within this message, Tracey always misspells an occasional high-frequency word or leaves out some punctuation; the children need to be detectives and find the errors. She also tries to include new vocabulary or high-frequency words and some other word-analysis skill such as the *sh* digraph, or "chunk," as she calls it. Before asking the class to read the message, Tracey reminds them to look for new vocabulary, high-frequency words of the week, errors she may have made, and words containing the *sh* chunk. When children notice something, they come up and correct it or circle the word or digraph. Tracey takes the opportunity to ask children for other words they know that include the *sh* chunk, and they list those. She introduces a new digraph, *ch* (which she had purposefully used in the morning message), with a discussion about seeing chickens at the zoo.

After the morning message and mini-skill lesson, four children have the opportunity to share something brought from home related to the theme. These four children sit on a little bench set aside for them at the meeting area. The purpose of this activity is to promote language development and to encourage children to be responsible about bringing things to share. Finally, Tracey reads a theme-related story, using a Directed Listening and Thinking Activity format to teach a skill. Today she reinforces the concept that stories have a setting, theme, plot episodes, and a resolution. Children are to listen for all elements while the book is being read so that they can retell and then rewrite it during independent work. She reads an old favorite, *Ask Mr. Bear* (Flack, 1932), about a little boy who consults animals to find his mother a birthday gift. Tracey stops at appropriate places to ask children to predict what each animal might suggest as a gift for the boy's mother. At the end of the story she asks for volunteers to retell the story and to include the elements of story structure discussed earlier. She also asks the children to think about what they might give to their mothers for a birthday gift. She records their responses on an experience chart.

Tracey follows this routine of activities during morning meeting each day. The routine includes the discussion of the calendar, weather, and news. Then there is discussion of the morning message, with skills to reinforce and learn. The message relates to the theme being studied. Next, four children share something from home related to the theme. Tracey reads a theme-related book, emphasizes a literacy skill, and provides a mini-lesson for that skill. Children know what to expect and are comfortable with this portion of the day.

9:40 to 9:50: Independent Center Activities

Tracey now models independent activities for students to participate in alone or with a partner. Most activities are done at centers; some are done at desks. After modeling, she has an organizational chart with the activity options for children to select what they will do. Sometimes Tracey will assign jobs. The purpose of the independent work is to reinforce skills learned, help children work independently of the teacher (alone and in collaboration with one another), and engage the children in a productive manner so that the teacher can work with small groups of individuals to help with specific needs.

The activities that Tracey models are often skill- and theme-related. They are always in familiar places in her room, and they are familiar types of activities. At the beginning of the school year, Tracey spends time simply introducing children to the centers and the types of activities they include. She has her class practice working on the different activities. She helps the children so that eventually they will be able to work independently.

The children have some tasks they must do and others from which they may select. The tasks engage the children in reading and writing, which will help with skill development. The first four activities must be done by all students. Children can select to do activities 5 and 6 after they finish the required tasks. They do not have to do all of the optional activities, since there probably would not be time. These are the required activities on this morning:

1. *Partner reading.* Children pair off and read the same book together. They may also read separate books and then tell each other about the stories they read. Since they are studying animals, they are to select books from the open-faced bookshelves that include stories and expository texts about animals. Discussion about what is read is encouraged. Each child must fill out an index card with the name of the book read and one sentence about the story.
2. *The writing activity.* Children are to rewrite the story *Ask Mr. Bear* that Tracey during the morning meeting. In their rewritings, the children are to include the story elements discussed, such as setting, theme, plot episodes, and the resolution. They may consult copies of the book in the classroom if necessary. Each day there is a writing activity related to the story read earlier; however, the writing assignments vary.
3. *Working with words.* The children are to find words around the room that have the *sh* or *ch* digraph in them. They then classify these words by writing them on a sheet of paper

Figure 7.3. Children need to be accountable for completing independent work they do at centers.

under appropriate digraph headings. Children can look through books to find these digraphs as well.

4. *Listening center.* The children listen to taped stories about animals. For each story there is a sheet of paper with a question to answer about the story. Two titles on tape for this unit about animals are Kellogg's *Is Your Mama a Llama?* (1989) and Brown's *Arthur's Pet Business* (1990).

The optional activities take place in the art center and computer center:

5. *Art center.* Tracey has provided magazines with many photographs of animals; the children may create animal collages.
6. *Computer center.* Here the children may engage in a variety of math games and literacy activities.

Tracey has an organizational chart that she uses to assign children to centers. The rotations are coordinated with the reading groups that Tracey is meeting with for small-group instruction. If children finish a center activity before the group rotates, they can start one of the optional activities or go on to the next task, if there is space at the center. There is a basket for completed work, and every center requires some type of accountability: a sign-in sheet and a finished product to be handed in (see Figure 7.3).

Management of Centers: Tracey's center management is by no means the only course to follow. In fact, as many studies make clear, the organization of center time varies from one teacher to another. Some teachers assign children to groups and decide what activities they will participate in; others allow children to select the centers they will go to. In one classroom we observed, children can work at a center if there is a seat available for them. If there is no available seat, students can select another center or do a writing activity at their desks.

At the beginning of the school year, some teachers start center time in a structured fashion.

Check Activities to Do During Literacy Center Time

Name ______________________________ Date ______________

- ❑ 1. Read a book, magazine, or newspaper.
- ❑ 2. Read to a friend.
- ❑ 3. Listen to someone read to you.
- ❑ 4. Listen to a taped story and follow the words in the book.
- ❑ 5. Use the felt board with a storybook and felt characters.
- ❑ 6. Use the roll movie with its story book.
- ❑ 7. Write a story.
- ❑ 8. Draw a picture about a story you read.
- ❑ 9. Make a book for a story you wrote.
- ❑ 10. Make a felt story for a book you read or a story you wrote.
- ❑ 11. Write a puppet show and perform it for friends.
- ❑ 12. Make a tape for a story you read or a story you wrote.
- ❑ 13. Record activities completed in logs.
- ❑ 14. Check out books to take home and read.
- ❑ 15. Use activity cards with directions for activities you do.

Figure 7.4. Sample checklist of activities to do during a literacy center time.

They assign the groups and tasks. As children learn to function independently, they are given opportunities for decision making and select their tasks or groups to work with. Figure 7.4 shows a sample checklist of activities to do during a literacy center time.

The management of center time is crucial for its success. Students must know the choices before them, the activities in which to participate, the rules that guide participation concerning the selection of materials, and what is to happen in groups or when working alone. Children can help with the guidelines. For example, in Tracey's classroom the students generated the following rules for working independently:

1. Handle the materials carefully.
2. Speak in soft voices.
3. Put materials back in their place before taking a new one.
4. Record completed activities.

Rules formulated by Tracey's first graders about cooperating when working in groups include the following suggestions:

1. Decide whom you will work with or if you will work alone.
2. Make sure everyone in the group has a job.
3. Take turns talking.
4. Share materials.
5. Listen to your friends when they talk.

6. Say helpful things to your group members, such as

   "Can I help you?"
   "I like your work."
   "You did a good job."

7. Evaluate your work when it is done.

The opportunity to work independently of the teacher allows children to use judgment and to make decisions. It increases cooperation among children and enhances their independence, self-control, and socially responsible behavior (Solomon, Watson, Delucchi, Schaps, & Battistich, 1988).

Advantages of Cooperative Learning: Work during center time involves opportunities for interaction among students in collaborative settings. This brings children together so that they can teach and learn from each other through discussion and, often, debate. Social interaction and collaboration within small groups of children promotes achievement and productivity. According to researchers, cooperative learning succeeds because it allows children to explain material to each other, listen to each other's explanations, and arrive at a joint understanding of what has been shared. In cooperative settings students can accomplish together what they cannot do alone (Forman & Cazden, 1985).

In cooperative settings children form friendships and develop greater acceptance of differences. High and low achievers work together, as do children from varied racial and ethnic backgrounds. Children with special needs (physical disabilities, emotional handicaps, learning difficulties) and social isolates are more likely to be accepted in cooperative learning settings than in traditional classroom structures (Augustine, Gruber, & Hanson, 1989; Johnson & Johnson, 1987; Lew, Mesch, Johnson, & Johnson, 1986; Slavin, 1990).

From my observations in classrooms as well as the existing research, it appears that students benefit from the independent work they participate in during center time. The ability to self-direct, the time for practicing skills, and the opportunity to interact with peers should all bring positive outcomes.

9:50 to 11:40: Instruction Based on Need

According to Vygotsky, intellectual growth is fostered through collaboration with more capable peers and adults, who serve as coaches and tutors (Wertsch, 1985). Effective grouping occurs when groups are formed for a variety of reasons. One of them is for the purpose of direct instruction for students who need reinforcement of a particular skill currently being taught or studied during whole-group instruction. In addition, groups can be formed based on friendships, interests, and cooperative projects. Meeting with the whole class as well as in small groups is needed. Groups can have varied numbers of children based on the reason for the group.

Although there is controversy about grouping for ability, many have found that in the early grades, it is an effective means for building strategies and fluency (Routman, 1991).

We now visit Tracey's class again. Although grouping practices based on need and ability are controversial, Tracey believes it is the only way she can learn what individual children know and what they need to learn, and then design her instruction based on that information. The next section describes meetings with groups for direct instruction based on need.

After children begin their independent work and Tracey feels they are working well, she calls on her first group for reading instruction. During this time she must work without interruption. The strategy she uses to ensure that she is not bothered by children's questions is called "Ask Three, Then Me." Before she assembles her reading group, Tracey identifies students others can consult to answer questions or resolve problems. All children know that the rule means ask three students first if you need help; if they can't solve your problem, then ask the teacher.

The Shape of the Group Lesson: Tracey has organized the class into five groups of four to five children apiece who have similar reading needs, are capable of similar reading skills, and are reading at about the same level. Children frequently move from group to group based on Tracey's ongoing assessment of children's progress. She meets with each group four to five times a week for about 20 minutes. A typical lesson includes (1) reading something familiar for fluency and success, (2) working on a skill involving word analysis, (3) introducing a new book and the skills associated with it, whether it be for decoding or comprehension, (4) reading the new book with the support of the teacher and peers, (5) discussing the story after the reading, and (6) a writing activity. During these activities Tracey assesses the reading development of one or two children during each reading group session by making running records of their oral reading and recording errors and by listening to children's oral retellings of stories as a check of comprehension.

Tracey begins her small-group reading lesson with a familiar text that each child has in a plastic bag. She calls this "a book in a bag," and every day the children bring it to reading group. The book in the bag changes when the group is ready for a new one. This could be every few days, depending on the difficulty. Other materials in the bag could include skill-building and writing activities. Tracey uses a familiar text for fluency and to create a feeling of success. The children zip through the book and enjoy the ease with which they can read this old friend.

Next, Tracey engages the children in a minilesson, helping them with a skill she has found they need help with. She is interested in having the children use the text along with phonic clues to decode unknown words. She writes a sentence on a small white slate, leaving one word blank. She asks the children to predict what word might make sense in the blank. She then asks them to write the word onto their white boards. Tracey has prepared a practice sheet with three more sentences that are missing words but include the first letter of each of the missing words. She asks the children to work in pairs to figure out the missing words. They discuss how they are using the meaning of the sentence and the first letter of the word to figure it out.

At this time a new book is introduced that comes from a set of leveled books selected for the reading ability of the children with whom Tracey is working. She is able to find one that matches the animal theme they are studying. Tracey introduces some vocabulary words the children have not experienced before. The words are on 3 × 5-inch cards, and as the children recite the words, Tracey places the cards in a pocket chart. The children copy the words on their white slates. Tracey has sentence strips prepared that come from the text of the new book, with the new vocabulary words left out. She places the sentence strips in the pocket chart and the children fill in the blanks with the correct vocabulary word card.

For the first reading of the new book Tracey has the entire group chant the book along with her. After the first reading she invites the children to read the book independently all the way through. Because the children are beginning readers, they are to read aloud but in soft voices. Tracey pays close attention to one of the children beside her. This is her focus child of the day and the one for whom she annotates a running record, which is an assessment tool for determining the types of errors made when reading. Tomorrow when she meets with this group again, another child will sit by her side and be focused on for assessment purposes.

After this second reading, the children participate in a brief discussion about the story that includes answering questions relating to details in the text and questions that require them to connect the story to circumstances in their own lives.

As the lesson ends, Tracey writes a short note to all of the children's parents about the children's progress, what they were learning, what they needed help with, and what their homework is. Homework always requires the reading of the new book with a parent and their signatures. When the group finishes its work for the day, all members put their books in their plastic bags with their homework notes. They place their materials in their own boxes or book bins which sit on the windowsill for safe storage until it is time to go home (see Figure 7.5).

Tracey meets with another group with books selected for their reading instructional level and carries out an appropriate lesson for them. Tracey meets with her three other groups, and the morning ends at 11:45, when the children leave for lunch.

Figure 7.5. When guided reading is done, children place their work in their individual book bins.

Writing workshop can occur during the language arts block, if there is time, or after lunch. It begins with a whole-group lesson that includes a writing skill. The entire class is given the same writing assignment, and students meet with the teacher in one-on-one or small-group conferences to talk about their work. Children work in pairs to discuss and share their writing pieces. The conferences and pairs are different groupings of children from those in the reading groups or center groups.

The Pros and Cons of Grouping by Need: A survey of research on the possible benefits of ability-based grouping for reading instruction shows mixed results. There are achievement as well as self-esteem issues to consider. On the one hand, students who are consistently grouped together based on their low ability may come to view themselves as failures and subsequently live up to that image. On the other hand, if children are grouped and regrouped often, based on progress, shared interests, or other criteria, the stigma associated with grouping is less likely to occur. Students in groups based on need should be evaluated regularly and regrouped when change in student progress occurs (Anderson, Wilkinson, & Mason, 1991). Some group formations should be based on friendships and interests. These heterogeneous groups should exist along with the groups based on skill needs. With this type of organization and management of groups, students are likely to make their primary identification with the larger heterogeneous class rather than with any one group in which they work (Slavin, 1987). Small groups allow children to be more active and attentive learners, since they are able to interact more closely with their peers and focus their attention (Anderson et al., 1991).

Concluding Remarks About Organization and Management

As you can see from the profile presented, effective management begins with the physical design of the classrooms, which includes an environment rich with accessible materials. Early in the school year the children are introduced to the design of the classroom and how the different materials and areas are used.

From the first day of school, the teacher helps children become independent learners, so that they can think for themselves. Early in the school year, time is used to teach routines that include whole-class instruction, the use of learning centers, self-directed independent work, cooperative work, and behaviors in need-based groups. Children learn the protocols for sitting on the

AN IDEA FROM A TEACHER

Ideas for Accountability While Children Work Independently

While children are working independently at centers, it is important that the teacher be able to quickly check the status of the class to ensure that everyone is being productive. I have found two ideas that work extremely well for managing center time in my classroom.

First, I created an "In-and-Out" board for each center. I took two heavy pieces of construction paper ($11\frac{1}{2}$ by 17 inches) and, using a marker, divided it into an appropriate number of rows and columns based on the number of students in my class. (For example, I have 20 students, so I divided my board into two columns and ten rows.) In each box I write the student's name. Next to the board I have a basket of clothespins. As children complete work at each center, they put a clothespin next to their name.

My second strategy is an effective way to collect finished center work. Rather than have a single basket, or a basket at each center, I provide a cubby for each child to file his or her work in. An inexpensive way to do this is to buy cardboard shoe holders. One holder folds into nine cubbies. I label each cubby with a student's name. When it comes time to check the class's status, it is much easier to look at each individual student's cubby than to sort through piles of work for each center. I just check each cubby for the appropriate number of recording sheets.

Sarah Crane, First-Grade Teacher

rug during lessons and how to take turns. Rules are discussed and created by the class, so that children feel some responsibility to follow them. Children learn these rules and routines so that they can function much of the time without the teacher. Teachers are consistent in their routines and the enforcement of rules.

One of the more difficult times to manage during the school day is when children work in centers while teachers meet with small groups for direct instruction. Students need to master the system for using the centers, which the teacher simultaneously organizes for them. For instance, they need to know the number of children who can be at a center at one time and how many center activities need to be completed in a given day. Children have to account for work accomplished at centers as well. When the children become self-regulated learners, teachers can devote attention to working with small groups.

Teachers need to be aware of what is happening in their room all the time. They need to position themselves so they can see every child. Therefore, for small-group meetings the table is placed so that other children can be observed as they work.

In the classrooms I visited, the environment was designed to support the carefully planned activities that took place in whole-group, small-group, paired, and individual settings. The sequence of events was well thought out. For example, if children were sitting and listening during a whole-group activity, the next lesson would include some movement and small groupings. When interviewed, all of the teachers agreed that if children are actively involved in interesting experiences that are challenging but can bring success, they are likely to remain engaged in their work (Morrow, Strickland, & Woo, 1998).

The teachers observed always spoke to children in soft, pleasant voices. When a child was off task, the teachers used the same tone of voice that was used when giving positive feedback. The teachers had a large vocabulary filled with encouraging expressions, such as "You really do understand that, and I'll bet you can get it right if you try." If children were off task, teachers helped redirect their efforts. Teachers always respected their students, and the respect was reciprocated by the children. As one teacher said, "I treat the children as I would like to be treated. I never talk down to them. I address them in a manner that demonstrates respect since I think they appreciate this. In turn, I have found they treat me and each other similarly."

The teachers in the rooms we observed all created the routines, procedures, rules, and respectful atmosphere identified in the research on exemplary and effective teaching. These teachers had knowledge of literacy strategies and how to organize and manage instruction, thus providing for a productive instructional atmosphere for early literacy development.

References

Anderson, R. C., Wilkinson, I. A. G., & Mason, J. M. (1991). A microanalysis of the small-group, guided reading lessons: Effects of an emphasis on global story meaning. *Reading Research Quarterly, 26,* 417–439.

Augustine, D., Gruber, K., & Hanson, L. (1989). Cooperation works. *Educational Leadership, 46,* 4–7.

Brown, M. (1990). *Arthur's pet business.* New York: Little, Brown.

Flack, M. (1932). *Ask Mr. Bear.* New York: Macmillan.

Forman, E., & Cazden, C. (1985). Exploring Vygotskian perspectives in education: The cognitive value of peer interaction. In J. Wertsch (Ed.), *Culture, communication, and cognition: Vygotskian perspectives.* Cambridge: Cambridge University Press.

Froebel, F. (1974). *The education of man.* Clifton, NJ: August Kelly.

Johnson, D. W., & Johnson, R. T. (1987). *Learning together and alone* (2nd ed.). Englewood Cliffs, NJ: Prentice Hall.

Kellogg, S. (1989). *Is your mama a llama?* New York: Scholastic.

Lew, M., Mesch, D., Johnson, D. W., & Johnson, R. (1986). Positive interdependence, academic and collaborative skills group contingencies, and isolated students. *American Educational Research Journal, 23,* 476–88.

Loughlin, C. E., & Martin, M. D. (1987). *Supporting literacy: Developing effective learning environments.* New York: Teachers College Press.

Montessori, M. (1965). *Spontaneous activity in education.* New York: Schocken Books.

Moore, G. (1986). Effects of the spatial definition of behavior settings on children's behavior: A quasi-experimental field study. *Journal of Environmental Psychology, 6,* 205–231.

Morrow, L. M. (1990). Preparing the classroom environment to promote literacy during play. *Early Childhood Research Quarterly, 5,* 537–554.

Morrow, L. M. (1997a). *Literacy development in the early years: Helping children read and write* (3rd ed.). Boston: Allyn & Bacon.

Morrow, L. M. (1997b). *The literacy center: Contexts for reading and writing.* York, ME: Stenhouse.

Morrow, L. M., Strickland, D., & Woo, D. G. (1998). *Literacy instruction in half- and whole-day kindergarten: Research to practice.* Newark, DE: International Reading Association.

Morrow, L. M., Tracey, D., Woo, D., & Pressley, M. (1999). Characteristics of exemplary first grade instruction. *The Reading Teacher, 52,* 462–476.

Neuman, S., & Roskos, K. (1992). Literacy objects as cultural tools: Effects on children's literacy behaviors in play. *Reading Research Quarterly, 27,* 202–225.

Olds, A. R. (1987). Designing settings for infants and toddlers. In C. S. Weinstein & T. G. David (Eds.), *Spaces for children: The built environment and child development* (pp. 117–138). New York: Plenum Press.

Pressley, M., Rankin, J., & Yokoi, L. (1996). A survey of the instructional practices of outstanding primary-level literacy teachers. *Elementary School Journal, 96,* 363–384.

Rivlin, L., & Weinstein, C. S. (1984). Educational issues, school settings, and environmental psychology. *Journal of Environmental Psychology, 4,* 347–364.

Routman, R. (1991). *Invitations: Changing as teachers and learners K–12.* Portsmouth, NH: Heinemann.

Ruddell, R., & Ruddell, M. R. (1995). *Teaching children to read and write: Becoming an influential teacher.* Boston: Allyn & Bacon.

Rusk, R., & Scotland, J. (1979). *Doctrines of the great educators.* New York: St. Martin's Press.

Slavin, R. E. (1987). Ability grouping and student achievement in elementary schools: A best-evidence synthesis. *Review of Educational Research, 57,* 293–336.

Slavin, R. E. (1990). *Cooperative learning: Theory, research, and practice.* Englewood Cliffs, NJ: Prentice Hall.

Solomon, D., Watson, M. S., Delucchi, K. L., Schaps, E., & Battistich, V. (1988). Enhancing children's prosocial behavior in the classroom. *American Educational Research Journal, 25*(4), 527–554.

Weinstein, C. S. (1991). The classroom as a social context for learning. *Journal of Environmental Psychology, 2,* 23–25.

Weinstein, C. S., & Mignano, A. J., Jr. (1996). *Elementary classroom management.* New York: McGraw-Hill.

Wertsch, J. V. (1985). *Vygotsky and the societal formation of mind.* Cambridge: Harvard University Press.

Wyndham, R. (1968). *Chinese Mother Goose rhymes.* New York: Philomel Books.

CHAPTER EIGHT

Classroom Intervention Strategies: Supporting the Literacy Development of Young Learners at Risk

Dorothy S. Strickland

For Reflection and Action: Inquire about the special programs or classroom interventions offered to children experiencing difficulty in reading in a school with which you are familiar. Do special programs replace the regular classroom instruction? In the case of pullout programs, what kind of communication occurs about the interventions and the progress of children, and how often do these communications take place? What special attention is offered to struggling learners by the regular classroom teacher?

Dorothy Strickland makes use of what has been learned from successful special intervention programs for struggling learners to suggest strategies that might be applied in the regular classroom.

Addressing the needs of young learners at risk for failure is one of the most perplexing problems teachers face. Low achievers need extra time, materials with which they can feel successful, and strategies that work for them. Several factors have caused educators to turn to early intervention to help students who are experiencing difficulty learning to read and write.

The Case for Early Intervention

Research indicates that the cycle of failure often starts early in a child's school career. Stanovich (1986) argues, with good evidence, that children who encounter problems in the beginning stages of learning to read fall farther and farther behind their peers. Longitudinal studies (Juel, 1988) reveal that there is a nearly 90% chance that a child who is a poor reader at the end of grade 1 will remain a poor reader at the end of grade 4. As they move through the grades, poor readers are apt to experience continued failure and defeat, which may account for the tendency of low-achieving students to drop out of school.

Another compelling reason to promote early intervention is that supplementary remedial programs such as those funded by Title I and "replacement" programs that substitute for regular in-class instruction have had mixed results (Johnston, Allington, & Afflerbach, 1985). Some argue that such programs cause classroom teachers to rely too much on special help and neglect their responsibility toward less able students. Others suggest that where these programs exist, instruction within and outside the classroom are often at odds with one another. Supplemental programs appear to work best when there is a strong compatible instructional program in the regular classroom. Regardless of the supplemental help offered, however, more attention needs to be given to incorporating the best prevention and intervention procedures into regular classroom instructional practice (Allington & Walmsley, 1995).

Increased demands to make every child a reader by the end of the primary grades have also spurred early intervention efforts. National, state, and local school reform movements have raised expectations of what young learners should know and be able to do, and they specify the grade levels at which children should be able to reach these goals. Standards have been raised for all students regardless of who they are, where they live, their linguistic backgrounds, and whether or not they have a learning disability. The gradual trend away from long-term remedial programs at all levels and the growing emphasis on early intervention, prevention, and good "first teaching" have made the early grades a key focus of reform.

Those who have turned their attention to early intervention state that it is ultimately less costly than years of remediation, less costly than retention, and less costly to students' self-esteem (Barnett, 1998). Removing the onus on self-esteem may be the most compelling reason to institute early intervention: teachers in remedial programs often observe that students who feel they are failures frequently give up and stop trying to learn despite adequate instructional opportunities.

At this point, it seems fair to state that even though the press for early intervention is a worthy effort, later intervention remains a viable solution for some students who were not given adequate help during the early grades. Krashen and McQuillan (1998) argue that people can and do become good readers later, by reading a lot about whatever interests them. They suggest that the repeated act of reading itself makes them good readers. This is a good point. But poor readers are often caught in a catch-22: poor readers find reading difficult and unrewarding and so they avoid reading; reading is what makes good readers, but poor readers find reading difficult and unrewarding. Krashen and McQuillan caution that their arguments for late intervention are not arguments against early intervention but rather are offered to counteract the dogma of "once a poor reader, always a poor reader" (p. 409).

Numerous early intervention programs that target struggling readers and writers have been introduced successfully into school literacy programs (Pikulski, 1994). Analyses of these programs suggest some principles of instruction that may be helpful to struggling readers in the regular classroom. They also suggest ways in which external programs and regular classroom instruction might be made more compatible in order to support the struggling reader better. Regardless of the help children receive through special programs, ongoing attention to these learners in the regular classroom remains key to any attempt at early intervention.

This chapter addresses what teachers of young children should know about helping the struggling reader and writer within the regular classroom. The discussion includes

- What is known about the development of successful beginning readers and writers
- Factors that militate against success in learning to read and write
- What is known about successful intervention programs, and the application to teaching and learning in the regular classroom

Although this chapter places particular emphasis on children who are experiencing difficulty learning to read and write, the background information and specific strategies described are intended to improve the instructional program for *all* learners.

Successful Readers and Writers

For most children, learning to read and write follows a typical pattern and evolves in relatively predictable and satisfactory ways. Such children generally have average or above-average language skills and a fair amount of motivating and pleasurable early childhood experience with books and literacy. They are cared for by adults who involve them in purposeful literacy experiences during the early childhood years and provide them with opportunities to identify letters and environmental print, including their own names. Through rhyming, singing, and language play, these children are given opportunities to develop an awareness of the internal structure of spoken words. They also hear explanations about language from responsive adults who listen to them, talk with them, and help them develop an awareness of the contrasting nature of spoken and written language.

The schools these children attend offer experiences that help them understand and use reading to make meaning with print, give them frequent and intensive opportunities to read and write, and help them learn about the nature of our alphabetic writing system, the structure of spoken and written words, and the joys of literature. Although some of these children may have episodic difficulties with specific aspects of literacy learning, their overall progress is steady and sure. They build successfully on the informal experiences with literacy from their earliest years as they encounter the more formal and complex tasks involved in conventional reading and writing.

Young Learners at Risk for Failure

Just as we know a great deal about the characteristics of children who learn to read adequately through rather typical home and school experiences, so we also know a great deal about those for whom learning to read is a highly challenging and difficult task. This discussion identifies several factors that can place children at risk for failure in learning to read and write. They are not cited here to place blame on the child or the child's circumstances but to alert teachers to certain variables that may have an impact on the learning situation. Knowing learners as individuals who come to the classroom with well-defined influences on their lives is equally as important as (if not more important than) poring over the results of paper-and-pencil screening instruments designed to yield information about children's knowledge of letters, sounds, and words. It should be noted that some of the risk factors refer to the child's personal development and others refer to the group or situation in which the child's learning takes place. Learning to read and write may be extremely challenging and difficult for any of the following:

1. *Children with a history of preschool language impairment.* Although children vary widely in their early language development, there are indicators outside the normal range, such as severe delay in pronunciation accuracy and in the use of complex sentences, that signal language delay to parents, pediatricians, and caregivers (Scarborough, 1998). Language delay is often part of a broader condition such as general developmental disability, hearing impairment (Conrad, 1979), or a neurological condition. Reading problems are most likely to occur when the language impairment is severe, broad in scope, and persistent.

2. *Children with limited proficiency in English.* When a child's home language is other than English, the likelihood of reading difficulty is increased. This is particularly true if reading instruction in English begins before the child has acquired oral proficiency in English (August & Hakuta, 1997).

   Similarly, when a child's home language or dialect is other than standard English, the likelihood of reading difficulty is increased. As with second language learners, this difficulty is not a result of any inherent deficiency in the dialect or in the child. Rather, it arises from differences between the child's dialect and the dialect of instruction. Learning is impeded when these differences are not taken into consideration during instruction or when the child's language is viewed in a stereotypical way to make negative judgments about his or her learning capacity (Labov, 1995; Smitherman, 1977).
3. *Children whose parents had difficulty learning to read.* If a child is diagnosed with a reading disability, there is a higher than normal chance that other family members also had difficulties with reading (Gilger, Pennington, & DeFries, 1991; Volger, DeFries, & Decker, 1985).
4. *Children with attention deficit-hyperactivity disorder.* Long-term studies indicate that from the beginning of formal schooling, reading disability is relatively common in children with inattention problems (31% in first grade) and become even more frequent among these children as they mature (Shaywitz, Fletcher, & Shaywitz, 1995).
5. *Children who lack motivation to learn to read.* Children who have never experienced purposeful and pleasurable experiences with books and literacy are apt to be unenthusiastic about learning to read and write. Those who experience continued failure tend to avoid reading and thus deny themselves the most important means to improve their reading abilities (Snow, Barnes, Chandler, Goodman, & Hemphill, 1991).
6. *Children from poor neighborhoods.* Children who attend schools and live in communities where low socioeconomic status is widespread are more likely to be at risk for failure in reading. Families that lack sufficient resources to provide adequate housing, health care, and nutrition for their children are less likely to focus on their educational needs (Committee on the Prevention of Reading Difficulties in Young Children, 1998).
7. *Children who attend schools in which the classroom practices are deemed ineffective.* Classroom practices in ineffective schools (regardless of community socioeconomic status) are characterized by significantly lower rates of student time on task, less teacher presentation of new material, lower rates of teacher communication of high academic expectations, fewer instances of positive reinforcement, more classroom interruptions, more discipline problems, and classroom ambiance generally rated as less friendly (Teddlie, Kirby, & Stringfield, 1989).

Although classroom teachers need to be aware of the factors that often accompany low achievement in reading, none of these factors is an automatic barrier to the attainment of literacy. Nor do individual factors function alone as single causal determinants or predictors of an individual child's reading problems. For example, although low reading achievement is a widespread problem among Latino students, linguistic differences are not solely responsible for the high degree of risk faced by these children. Many children with limited English proficiency come from homes where the parents are poorly educated and the family income is low. Similarly, African-American students who speak a nonstandard dialect of English are apt to live in poor neighborhoods and to attend schools in which achievement is chronically low. In such cases, co-occurring group risk factors such as the socioeconomic circumstances of the child's family, the child's home literacy background, the neighborhood where the child lives, and the quality of the instruction in the school the child attends must be taken into account to fully comprehend the problem. A child from a low socioeconomic status background in a generally moderate- to upper-status school or community is at far less risk than that same child in a whole school or community of low-socioeconomic-status children

(Committee on the Prevention of Reading Difficulties in Young Children, 1998). Simply put, the factors listed here are those most often associated with reading difficulties and so must be considered when decisions regarding policy and practice are made for children who are experiencing difficulty with reading and writing.

Successful Intervention in the Regular Classroom

What can be done? Fortunately, the knowledge base for improving literacy has never been richer. Researchers and practitioners have filled the literature with an abundant research base as well as practical suggestions for educators, policy makers, and others as they consider how they might help *all* children meet today's higher literacy standards. Obviously, many children will need help from specialists beyond that of the regular classroom. Nevertheless, the instruction received in the regular classroom will remain at the center of the child's literacy program. Successful early intervention programs suggest some key areas requiring attention for students experiencing difficulty with reading (Pikulski, 1994):

- Time and timing
- School and classroom instructional organization and management
- Instructional experiences and materials
- The nature of the instruction
- Monitoring progress
- Home/school connections
- The professional development of teachers

Many of these factors are examined in depth in other chapters of this book. The purpose here is to present them as the basis for planning a unified program of early intervention within the regular program. Following is a more detailed description of these considerations with suggestions for addressing each within the regular classroom, regardless of the support programs available.

Time and Timing

Not only is the *timing* of intervention important (i.e., extra support should be timed during the early school years) for children who are experiencing difficulty, struggling learners also need more *time on task.* Pullout programs and other types of special intervention programs should be considered supplementary, not as replacements for the time spent in an instructional program that addresses individual students' needs within the regular classroom. Children who are given extra support outside the classroom often need continued support in the regular classroom even after they are released successfully from an external support program. Large blocks of uninterrupted time in which small-group, personalized instruction is offered should be regularly scheduled for learners who are experiencing difficulty. Fortunately, small-group instruction is beneficial for *all* learners, whether or not they need extra support.

School and Classroom Organization and Management

Issues related to classroom organization cannot be addressed apart from a consideration of the school's and the district's organizational structure. A district-wide and schoolwide infrastructure in which support services are identified and coordinated is needed to provide a supportive environment for what happens in the classroom. According to Crevola and Hill (1998), the experience of two prominent early intervention programs, described in *Success for All: A Summary of Research* (Slavin et al., 1996) and *Reading Recovery: A Guidebook for Teachers in Training* (Clay, 1993), indicates that ensuring that all students make satisfactory progress in early literacy is typically beyond the capacity of the individual classroom teacher working in isolation. As Creole and Hill put it, "Dramatic improvements are achievable within the context of a fully implemented, comprehensive program that involves both system- and school-wide commitment and coordination" (p. 133). Their Early Literacy Research Project (ELRP), currently in operation in Australia, makes use of some of the elements limned in *Success for All* and *Reading Recovery* to provide a comprehensive, schoolwide plan. Elements of the ELRP include a balanced classroom literacy program, in which children are involved in a variety of experiences with oral and written language; daily assessment, including running records; one-to-one tutoring using reading recovery–trained teachers; a special emphasis on preschool education; a home-school support program; ongoing professional development; additional assistance in the form of a schoolwide coordinator; and the fostering of high expectations for students, along with targeted goals for achievement.

In the United States, the focus of many federally funded educational programs has shifted from the program to the school to avoid compartmentalizing children's experiences as they approach literacy (Plunkett, 1998, p. 112). The importance of the classroom teacher working collaboratively with an entire instructional team is further defined by Plunkett:

> It is no longer acceptable for many at-risk children to be successful for only 10% to 20% of their time in school, during the "categorical" portion of the day. When 80% to 90% of the school time is not working for a large number of children, a change in the allocation and use of resources is very much in order. We must seek to generalize and export the practices and instructional strategies that are effective with the categorical programs and children across the entire school day in order to generalize the success of such children (p. 112).

One of the things that classroom teachers can do to provide an organizational structure that attends to the needs of struggling students throughout the day is to use flexible grouping for differentiated instruction. Flexible grouping addresses student variability by providing for varied grouping patterns, varied materials, and varied instructional tasks.

Small-group instruction is particularly crucial for the struggling reader, who often needs a second or third try at learning the reading strategies previously introduced to the entire class. Small similar-ability or similar-needs groups allow teachers to tailor instruction. They offer opportunities for guided practice under the watchful eye of the teacher, who uses these opportunities to monitor children's reading behaviors and adjust instruction accordingly. Moreover, when children work in small groups, the teacher is more likely to hold their attention. Children who are experiencing difficulty are likely to be the least attentive and focused. Flexible grouping also provides opportunities for children to work in pairs and in small groups with other children of different abilities and interests. Thus, the stigma long associated with long-term ability grouping is eliminated. Struggling learners also need opportunities for planned, indirect instruction. It is here that skills and strategies can be applied independently without benefit of constant teacher supervision. Independent activities yield the genuine products of learning.

Instructional Experiences and Materials

Struggling readers and writers need opportunities to work with a wide array of materials. Too often whole-group activities use materials well beyond their reading levels, and their independent work consists of a steady diet of worksheets and workbooks. Like all learners, these readers need materials that give them the confidence to take the necessary risks involved in gradually mastering harder and harder material. Guided reading instruction should make use of texts that are suited to students' ability levels and gradually increase in difficulty. Figure 8.1 lists the kinds of instructional experiences and materials that all children need opportunities to work with on a regular basis. These include reading aloud to students, shared reading, guided reading, and independent reading. The main strategies are further discussed below.

- *Reading aloud* by the teacher is an important component of the struggling reader's literacy program. Teachers should select stories, poems, and informational texts to read aloud that help expand and strengthen the background knowledge of their students. Many poor readers are unable to anticipate what a word might be simply because they lack background knowledge about the world and the familiarity with varied text structures that are required to make reasonable predictions.
- *Shared reading* and writing makes use of texts that an entire group of children can see and work with at once. This is extremely valuable for the child who is having trouble figuring

SELECTING AND USING MATERIALS FOR READING

Children experiencing difficulty need daily opportunities to read a variety of meaningful texts.

Reading Aloud

Teacher models reading process, students listen and respond.

MATERIALS: Storybooks, content materials, poetry, charts.
CHOICE: Usually teacher's choice.
GROUPING FORMAT: Usually whole group.
PURPOSES:

- To stretch students beyond their reading levels, particularly in content areas under study; expand vocabulary; develop concepts
- To expose students to varied forms of text (fiction, nonfiction, poetry)
- To enlist varied forms of response (discussion, writing, drama, art, movement, etc.)
- To study various genres, literary devices, writer's craft

Struggling readers benefit from listening, responding, and expanding their knowledge, vocabulary, and concepts.

Shared Reading

Teacher leads, students participate.

MATERIALS: Primarily enlarged texts visible to students; may include content materials, storybooks, charts, poems, songs.
CHOICE: Usually teacher's choice.
GROUPING FORMAT: Whole group or small group.
PURPOSES:

- To teach concepts about print and print conventions
- To teach comprehension and interpretation
- To analyze textual features: word study (e.g., phonics, word analogies, structural analysis)

Struggling readers benefit from highly visible demonstrations of the reading process. Concepts and conventions of print are made very accessible for them. Examination of textual features (letters, words, and parts of words) helps develop an understanding of the alphabetic principle and the nature of written language.

Word Study

Teacher leads, students participate.

At *prekindergarten level:* Largely oral activities fostering phonemic awareness.

At *kindergarten level and above:* phonics, structural analysis, and sight vocabulary.

MATERIALS: Core program, trade books, charts, environmental print.
CHOICE: Usually teacher's choice.
GROUPING FORMAT: Small or whole group.
PURPOSES:

- To provide systematic, focused instruction at the word level
- To provide additional support for students who need it

Struggling readers benefit from focused instruction and direct experiences applying the alphabetic code and sight vocabulary. The examination of textual features and linguistic patterns helps to support reading and spelling.

Guided Reading

Teacher monitors for application of strategies.

MATERIALS: Books or materials that modestly challenge the reader.
CHOICE: Usually teacher's choice.
GROUPING FORMAT: Small group.
PURPOSES:

- To practice application of specific strategies/skills in highly focused manner
- To provide opportunity for teacher-monitoring of application of skills and strategies
- To provide instruction as close as possible to students' instructional levels while gradually increasing the difficulty of the material

Struggling readers benefit when they read materials with which they can practice what they have learned.

Independent Reading

Teacher monitors for time on task.

MATERIALS: Books or materials with minimal challenge; varied types.
CHOICE: Usually student's choice; may be negotiated choice (teacher and student agree).
GROUPING FORMAT: Individual, pairs, small group (response circles).

Struggling readers develop fluency, automaticity, and confidence from frequent, intensive practice in reading familiar or new texts of minimal challenge.

Figure 8.1

out what reading is all about. During shared reading and writing, students observe and participate as the teacher demonstrates the use of reading and writing strategies such as using initial and final sounds, looking at word endings, breaking words into parts, and generally using various conventions of print to make meaning with text. All of this helps make the processes more transparent and accessible to the learner, a critical element for those children who need extraordinary assistance.

- *Word study* fosters recognition of the individual sounds of words and an understanding of the alphabetic principle and its application to reading and spelling. Activities involve phonemic awareness, phonics, structural analysis, and the development of sight vocabulary.
- *Guided reading* involves teachers' structuring a learning situation in which children work in small groups on material that is modestly challenging to them. Children's abilities to apply and practice the strategies they have learned are monitored by the teacher. Because the instructional material is tailored as closely as possible to learners' levels of achievement and needs, guided reading allows *all* children to apply their developing abilities to material they can handle.
- *Independent reading* is as important for low-achieving children as for any others. In fact, independent reading is what struggling readers most need to practice. Struggling readers and writers should be encouraged to select books that match their interests and reading abilities. Teachers can assist them in finding appropriate books by designating certain areas or baskets of books for their use and by giving them tips on how to select books on their own. Teachers should not feel reluctant to establish parameters for independent book selection. This is not a negative practice. Struggling readers may have difficulty selecting appropriate books on their own and may feel overwhelmed when there are too many books to choose from. Obviously, if a child wants to stretch a bit and read something that may be considered too difficult, he or she should be allowed to give it a try. Children will often stick with a difficult book if the content appeals to them.

Children should be allowed to reread familiar books. This helps build confidence and fluency, a skill that requires special attention for less capable readers. Opportunities for rereading may occur through choral reading, partner reading, reading selected parts aloud, and reading aloud at home.

Nature of the Instruction

All children need to be helped to become strategic readers who think with texts. This is no less true for the struggling child. Too often teachers treat these learners as if they were incapable of higher-level thinking. Skills should not be taught to them in a manner suggesting they can learn only by accumulating disparate pieces of information. Some instructional strategies that promote thinking with text for all students are (1) the use of multilevel activities that allow teachers to give the same task to the entire group, with the understanding that each child will respond to his or her best ability, (2) specific instruction in self-monitoring and self-assessment, (3) instruction that makes use of modeling and demonstrations, and (4) linking reading and writing instruction.

Documenting and Monitoring Learning

Keeping track of how well students are doing is at the heart of a successful program in which instruction is differentiated, and it is absolutely crucial if teachers are to identify and address the needs of children experiencing difficulty. Teachers who respect and respond to variability are constantly alert to individual needs, whether they indicate long-term additional support or short-term attention. But merely documenting progress is not enough. The instructional decisions that are based on that documentation are what really count. Increasingly, teachers are integrating a system of ongoing, informal classroom assessment into their instructional programs. They have discovered that this type of documentation reveals student needs more accurately

SAMPLE INDEPENDENT READING CONFERENCE RECORD FORM

Student's Name ______________________________ Grade 1

DATE	BOOK	COMMENTS
Feb. 3	*Freight Train* (Crews)	Rereading of big book, largely memorized. Knows some color words and the word *car* in isolation. Gaining confidence. Very proud of skills.
Feb. 10	*Fresh Fall Leaves* (Franco)	Likes this book, though some words are very hard. Will reread with a buddy
Feb. 17	*Wheels on the Bus*	Good for fluency, since student has sung this in kindergarten and grade 1. Matched and read individual words quite well, indicating he's really reading.

Figure 8.2

than norm-referenced standardized tests or even teacher-developed paper-and-pencil tests (Calfee & Hiebert, 1988).

Keeping district curriculum objectives in mind, teachers can engage students in literature-based activities and still chart progress on targeted strategies over time. Progress can be charted in several ways:

- as the progress of the individual learner in relation to him- or herself,
- as the progress of the individual relative to the group, and
- as the progress of the group as a whole.

All of these approaches offer insight into what skills need extra emphasis. Teachers must decide where that emphasis should be placed: at the whole-group level, at the level of small, needs-based groups, or at the level of individual conferences.

A variety of tools can be used to collect information about the progress of learners in the classroom. Establishing an assessment plan is important. Assessment may occur informally, through large-group and small-group observations and during one-on-one conferences. It may involve the systematic collection of information through the use of running records of students' oral reading, rubrics containing characteristics of acceptable student writing, and checklists of various performance indicators. Students should be encouraged to participate in the assessment process by commenting on their progress as they see it and by expressing opinions about where they think they need to make special efforts. The assessment methods should not be onerous or overly time-consuming. They should be integrated into the instructional program, be relatively easy to manage, and provide useful information. Assessment should be deliberate and systematic over time, not random or occasional. There should be some evidence that it is used to inform instruction. For example, observations during whole-group instruction may lead to short-term skills-based grouping for children experiencing similar difficulties. Learners should be evaluated in terms of their personal growth first, then compared with the group.

Figure 8.2 shows a useful form for tracking independent reading. Brief one-to-one conferences with children about their self-selected reading go a long way toward giving this kind of activity the stature it deserves as the most important practice for reading development (Anderson, Wilson, & Fielding, 1988). In the past, too often only those children who finished their work early had time for independent reading. Enlightened about its importance, today's teachers are more apt to make independent reading an integral part of their reading programs. As a part

FORM FOR BUDDY READING AT HOME

TO: AT-HOME READING BUDDY

FROM: ______________________________ (Teacher's name)

PLEASE READ THE ENCLOSED BOOK WITH YOUR READING BUDDY, DO AT LEAST ONE ACTIVITY, FILL OUT THE FORM, AND RETURN IT TOMORROW.

THANK YOU.

(Name of child) ______________________________

We read (Name of book) ______________________________ together.

We also (Briefly tell what else you did) ______________________________

____

____

Below are some suggested activities that can be done with any book:

Discuss the story.	Write a story like the one you read.
Read the story again with another reading buddy.	Make a puppet of one of the story characters.
Draw a picture to go with the book.	Act out parts of the story.
Tape record a second reading at home.	Write about your favorite part.

Signed by (Reading buddy) ______________________________ Date ______________

Figure 8.3

of their language arts standards, some school districts actually specify the number of books to be read each year. Teachers are also aware that independent reading is an effective way to adjust materials to students' reading levels and interests, an important goal for children experiencing difficulty.

Children can, of course, keep their own records of their personal reading. However, personalized conferences take no more than 5 minutes and allow the teacher to document and monitoring progress. A three-ring binder with pages for each child provides a quick and easy method for recording information. Pages should be arranged alphabetically by last name for easy reference. Brief conferences of no more than 5 minutes are scheduled for each child every week and should employ the following format: (1) a brief discussion of the book, (2) the student's reading aloud of selected parts, and (3) record keeping by the teacher. The independent reading conference, while not as specific or as detailed as running records (Clay, 1993) or miscue analysis (Goodman & Marek, 1996), is a quick way to gather information on a regular basis within the framework of flexible grouping.

Home-School Connection

A systematic program of home support, with a built-in monitoring system, should be in place. This program keeps parents and other caregivers informed of the school's expectations and their children's progress. Parents of students who are

AN IDEA FROM A TEACHER

Connecting to the Classroom Teacher

One of the biggest challenges I have is finding time to share with classroom teachers both the success stories and the concerns I have about students. This is important, since many students receive extra help from a variety of sources—Title I, in-school volunteer tutors, at-home tutors, and their classroom teacher. Although the variety of support seems on the surface helpful, a child's instruction can be fragmented if the help is not coordinated. For my part, I try to meet with teachers, if only briefly, as often as I can. This includes arranging once each marking period to suspend classes with students for one day and schedule meetings with teachers before, during, and after school—whenever they are available. I developed a simple system in which I provide a 5 × 8-inch card for each child and a package of permanent adhesive labels for myself. At the end of an instructional session I jot down a comment about at least one or two children. The cards facilitate discussion during the very brief periodic meetings I manage with teachers and as documentation for my records that goes well beyond what standardized tests and inventories reveal.

Gladys Napoli, Title I Teacher

experiencing difficulty are particularly concerned about their children's progress. They usually want to be involved and kept informed. Keeping them involved makes it less likely that they will be surprised about their children's progress. Home activities should emphasize independent reading and writing, should be easily monitored by parent and teacher, and should not be overly time-consuming. If the text is one that the child is to read aloud, it should be a familiar one that has been practiced at school and allows the child to "show off." Figure 8.3 is an example of a reading activity form that can be used over and over again with different books.

Professional Development

A program of ongoing professional development that stresses the responsibility of every staff member for struggling readers and writers can go a long way toward improving the instructional program for these students (Strickland, 1995, 1998). Areas of focus that need to be addressed include (1) how young children learn to read and write, and the implications for instruction, (2) instructional strategies that support what is known about how young children learn literacy, (3) merging instruction with assessment in beginning reading programs, and (4) evaluating the beginning reading program.

Early intervention is a concept whose time has come. Teachers of beginning reading will be involved in efforts to reform early education in ways that accelerate literacy learning for all children. Efforts to work with children experiencing difficulty will be initiated through special programs and in the regular classroom. It is important that these programs be coordinated so that the child experiences a unified approach to instruction. Recognizing the reality of learner variability and approaching it as a natural part of instruction rather than something to work around, correct, or complain about is important to the progress of every child. Providing quality, differentiated instruction and support so that all children have the opportunity to learn is the best way to express one's belief that all children can learn.

References

Allington, R. L., & Walmsley, S. A. (Eds.). (1995). *No quick fix.* New York: Teachers College Press.

Anderson, R., Wilson, P. T., & Fielding, L. (1988). Growth in reading and how children spend their time outside of school. *Reading Research Quarterly, 23,* 285–303.

August, D. A., & Hakuta, K. (Eds.). (1997). *Improving schooling for language-minority children: A research agenda.* Washington, DC: National Academy Press.

Barnett, W. S. (1998). Long-term effects on cognitive development and school success. In W. S. Barnett & S. S. Boocock (Eds.), *Early care and education for children in poverty* (pp. 11–44). Albany, NY: SUNY Press.

Calfee, R., & Hiebert, E. (1988). The teacher's role in using assessment to improve learning. In C. V. Bunderson (Ed.), *Assessment in the service of learning.* Princeton, NJ: Educational Testing Service.

Clay, M. (1993). *Reading recovery: A guidebook for teachers in training.* Auckland, New Zealand: Heinemann.

Committee on the Prevention of Reading Difficulties in Young Children. (1998). *Report.* Washington, DC: National Academy Press.

Conrad, R. (1979). *The deaf school child.* London: Harper & Row.

Crevola, C. A., & Hill, P. W. (1998). Evaluation of a whole-school approach to prevention and intervention in early literacy. *Journal of Education for Students Placed at Risk, 3,* 133–158.

Gilger, J. W., Pennington, B. F., & DeFries, J. C. (1991). Risk for reading disability as a function of family history in three family studies. *Reading and Writing: An Interdisciplinary Journal, 3,* 205–217.

Goodman, K., & Marek, A. (1996). *Retrospective miscue analysis.* Katonah, NY: Richard C. Owen.

Johnston, P. A., Allington, R. L., & Afflerbach, P. (1985). The congruence of classroom and remedial reading instruction. *Elementary School Journal, 85,* 465–478.

Juel, C. (1988, April). *Learning to read and write: A longitudinal study of fifty-four children from first through fourth grade.* Paper presented at the annual meeting of the American Educational Research Association, New Orleans, LA.

Krashen, S., & McQuillan, J. (1998). The case for late intervention: Once a good reader, always a good reader. In C. Weaver (Ed.), *Reconsidering a balanced approach to reading.* Urbana, IL: National Council of Teachers of English.

Labov, W. (1995). Can reading failure be reversed? A linguistic approach to the question. In V. L. Gadsden & D. A. Wagner (Eds.), *Literacy among African-American youth.* Cresskill, NJ: Hampton Press.

Pikulski, J. (1994). Preventing reading failure: A review of five effective programs. *Reading Teacher, 48,* 30–39.

Plunkett, V. R. (1998). A thoughtful look a resources and change through Title I schoolwide programs. *Journal of Education for Students Placed at Risk, 3,* 111–114.

Scarborough, H. H. (1998). Early identification of children at risk for reading disabilities: Phonological awareness and some other promising predictors. In K. Shapiro, P. J. Accardo, & A. J. Capute (Eds.), *Specific reading disability: A view of the spectrum* (pp. 77–121). Timonium, MD: York Press.

Shaywitz, B. A., Fletcher, J. M., & Shaywitz, S. E. (1995). Defining and classifying learning disabilities and attention-deficit/hyperactivity disorder. *Journal of Child Neurology, 10*(Suppl. 1), S50–S57.

Slavin, R. E., Madden, N. A., Dolan, L. J., Wasik, B. A., Ross, S. M., Smith, L., & Dianda, M. (1996). Success for all: A summary of research: *Journal of Education for Students Placed at Risk, 1,* 41–76.

Smitherman, G. (1977) *Talkin' and testifyin': The language of black America.* Boston: Houghton Mifflin.

Snow, C. E., Barnes, W. S., Chandler, J., Goodman, I. F., & Hemphill, L. (1991). *Unfulfilled expectations: Home and school influences on literacy.* Cambridge: Harvard University Press.

Stanovich, K. E. (1986). Matthew effects in reading: Some consequences of individual differences in the acquisition of literacy. *Reading Research Quarterly, 21,* 360–407.

Strickland, D. S. (1995). Pre-elementary programs: A model for professional development. In S. Wepner, J. Feeley, & D. Strickland (Eds.), *The administration and supervision of reading programs.* New York: Teachers College Press.

Strickland, D. S. (1998). Professional development models for program implementation. In P. D. Pearson (Ed.), *Final report, New York State Reading Symposium.* Albany, NY: State Education Department.

Teddlie, C., Kirby, P., & Stringfield, S. (1989). Effective vs. ineffective schools: Observable differences in the classroom. *American Journal of Education, 97,* 221–236.

Volger, G. P., DeFries, J. C., & Decker, S. N. (1985). Family history as an indicator of risk for reading disability. *Journal of Learning Disabilities, 18,* 419–421.

CHAPTER NINE

Teaching Young Children to Be Writers

Karen Bromley

Karen Bromley addresses what is known about young children's writing and offers strategies to develop and encourage it.

For Reflection and Action: Reflect on the dramatic changes in writing instruction in kindergarten and primary grade classrooms. What are the major developments? How is the new knowledge reflected in your classroom or in those you have observed?

Most kindergarten and first- and second-grade classrooms look very different today from the way they did a decade ago. One difference is the huge increase in the amount and kind of writing that occurs. Research on young children's language development and emergent literacy has changed teachers' understandings, philosophies, and literacy practices (Butler & Clay, 1982; Holdaway, 1979; Teale & Sulzby, 1989). Among the key ideas that have emerged from this research are the following:

- Children come to school knowing how to use language.
- Reading and writing develop together, not separately.
- Models, collaboration, and choices promote writing.
- The intentional teaching of writing develops young writers.

This chapter provides vignettes of several teachers who believe young children can be writers and who teach writing in different ways. The instructional strategies they use are fine examples of ways to promote writing development in young children.

Beth's First Grade: An Introduction

Beth Spiro teaches first grade in Benjamin Franklin Elementary School in Binghamton, New York. She considers many of her students to be at risk for failure because they have had few experiences with books and print. So, Beth builds her curriculum around writing. In September, students begin their careers as writers by scribbling, drawing, and experimenting with graphics. How does this activity relate to writing? Just as babbling precedes talk, scribbling and drawing pictures precede writing because they emerge before formal printed language develops. For most children, talk is also fundamental to writing. During "Share and Tell," young children delight in telling each other about their first writing attempts.

When children begin formal writing, their oral language is the basis for much of what they write. They quickly realize that speech can become print and that what they say can be written down. Later, as writing proficiency develops, the vocabulary and language patterns used in writing often become more sophisticated than the spoken language.

Years of teaching have shown Beth that for students to become literate, they need *engagement* with language through *immersion* in texts of all kinds and *demonstrations* of how texts are constructed and used (Cambourne, 1988). As a result, she fills her classroom with all kinds of print and media that she and her students use, including books, magazines, newspapers, pamphlets, the Internet, stories, letters, lists, art, poetry, directions, and recipes. Beth models reading and writing. She has high expectations of her students and communicates a "can-do" attitude to them about their abilities.

Beth also believes that collaboration among students and with colleagues enriches and strengthens teaching and learning. She knows the power of social interactions for learning and that students need to have real purposes and audiences for their work. She knows how important it is for students to receive appropriate and positive feedback and to feel comfortable enough to make mistakes as they try new strategies and ideas. For these reasons, Beth and her students create many collaborative books as a class. How does she manage this with first graders, many of whom are struggling with literacy? First, she promotes collaborative literacy learning, with lots of shared reading and intentional demonstrations and modeling of the writing process with her students. Beth encourages students to collaborate as they read and write by reminding them that everyone in the class is a literacy teacher.

Shared Reading

Shared reading stimulates language and concept development in young learners and builds their familiarity with and understanding of printed texts (Fountas & Pinnell, 1996; Holdaway, 1979). Shared reading is a social activity in which children engage together in reading and listening to meaningful, predictable stories. It is an enjoyable activity through which children acquire reading-like behaviors as the teacher models the reading process, pointing to words as they are read aloud. Young students learn the concepts of print (e.g., letter, word, sentence, paragraph, punctuation marks). They learn book concepts (e.g., title, author, illustrator, left-to-right progression, story grammar). When students are familiar with the text they can fill in words or phrases the teacher leaves out, predict what might happen next, or read along with classmates.

Typically, shared reading is done with a "big book," an enlarged version of a children's book, that sits on an easel or chalkboard ledge and is big enough for the entire class to see as they read together. The predictable books listed in Figure 9.1 are characterized by simple language, rhyme, repetition, and a close relationship between text and illustrations, and many have a cumulative pattern or easily distinguished sequence of events.

A SELECTED LIST OF PREDICTABLE STORIES

Carlstrom, N. (1986). *Jesse Bear, what will you wear?* New York: Macmillan.

Carle, E. (1981). *The very hungry caterpillar.* New York: Putnam.

Carle, E. (1993). *Today is Monday.* New York: Philomel.

DeRegniers, B. (1995). *What can you do with a shoe?* New York: HarperCollins.

Hawkins, C., & Hawkins, J. (1987). *I know an old lady who swallowed a fly.* New York: Putnam.

Hurd, T. (1984). *Mama don't allow.* New York: Harper.

London, J. (1997). *I see the moon and the moon sees me.* New York: Viking.

Martin, B. (1970). *Brown bear, brown bear, what do you see?* New York: Holt.

Neitzel, S. (1995). *The bag I'm taking to Grandma's house.* New York: Greenwillow.

Shaw, N. (1992). *Sheep eat out.* New York: Houghton Mifflin.

Weeks, S. (1994). *Crocodile smile.* New York: HarperCollins.

Figure 9.1

Big books are best used in a relaxed, cooperative, read-aloud environment in which children can make mistakes without fear of negative consequences (Morrow, 1997). Shared reading helps most readers, but it particularly helps emergent readers, struggling readers, and those learning English as a second language because they learn *how* to read in an environment in which they can take risks to successfully figure out what print says.

Many companies publish big books, and several basal reader series include them with their materials for early readers. In addition, teachers enlarge poems, songs, riddles, jingles, jump-rope rhymes, and language experience stories to add to their collections of classroom reading materials (Slaughter, 1993). As well as published big books, Beth also uses books created by previous students for shared reading. Often the children's friends or older siblings are the authors, and this delights them.

Interactive and Collaborative Writing

How does shared reading relate to writing? Much as steel beams support an office building, so does reading support writing. Written texts demonstrate standard form and spelling for young writers (Bean & Bouffler, 1997). Beth knows that as her students read, they learn the structure of stories and the form of written language.

Beth guides her students in various forms of interactive writing (Fountas & Pinnell, 1996). They create large-print lists, charts, letters, poems, recipes, stories, and retold group experiences together. Each piece of writing is read together many times. Through these experiences, Beth models speech-to-print correspondence, left-to-right directionality, the concept of word, word analysis, sound-to-print matching, letter formations, spelling patterns, capitalization, punctuation, and self-correcting.

Beth uses all kinds of children's literature throughout the year, but in September she and her students read alphabet books and counting books, which become the stimulus for interactive writing and collaboration. Before expecting her students to draw and write, Beth models by drawing a picture and creating letters and words for a page in an alphabet or counting book. Class books have titles like *Our Book of Mm* (*Bb, Rr, Pp, . . .*) and *Our Book of Five-5* (*Six-6, Seven-7, . . .*).

To create an alphabet book, each child takes a piece of paper, chooses a letter, and draws objects of his or her choice—such as monkey, mailbox, mitten—that begin with the same letter. Beth moves among the five large tables in her classroom where children sit in groups, and she prints each child's word on a label so the child can copy it onto his or her own page. As children become more capable, they write their own words.

In many classrooms, teachers set up writing centers equipped with crayons, regular pencils, colored pencils, felt-tipped markers, correction tape and fluid, erasers, stapler, scissors, hole punches, metal rings, and all kinds and colors of paper (e.g., plain white and colored, lined and unlined, colored construction, tagboard for book covers) where children can write. When the writing center is close to the classroom library, children have books nearby to read and use as models. Beth encourages her ESL students and struggling first language users to work in pairs in her writing center to support each other.

One special kind of book often found in writing centers, the shape book, inspires young children to write. Beth makes blank books in shapes keyed to the season or a special occasion and keeps her writing center stocked with them. In the fall she makes stapled books with plain white paper pages and orange construction paper covers in pumpkin shapes. She makes apple-shaped books with red covers, valentine books with pink covers, dinosaur books with green covers, and so on.

These shape books work well for pattern poetry (see Figure 9.2). After the class chooses a topic—say, pumpkins—the students examine several pumpkins, cut one open, taste cooked pumpkin, and read about the life cycle of a pumpkin. Then Beth helps her children come up with a list of words to describe pumpkins. Next she models how to write a poem in a pumpkin shape, for example, five lines of one, two, three, three, and one word per line:

Authors
Good, creative.
Think, plan, write.
Revise pumpkin poems.
Excellent!

Beth teaches her students to write this kind of poetry as a way to build vocabulary, increase spelling awareness, and develop early counting skills. For many children she focuses on punctuation and capital letters later, since choosing and copying words is challenging enough for some.

Beth laminates each child's poem after the child has made corrections and read it to her and the class. Then she punches holes in each poem and inserts rings to hold the book together. She leaves these books in the writing center. Her children enjoy reading them, and they become some of the most popular books in the classroom.

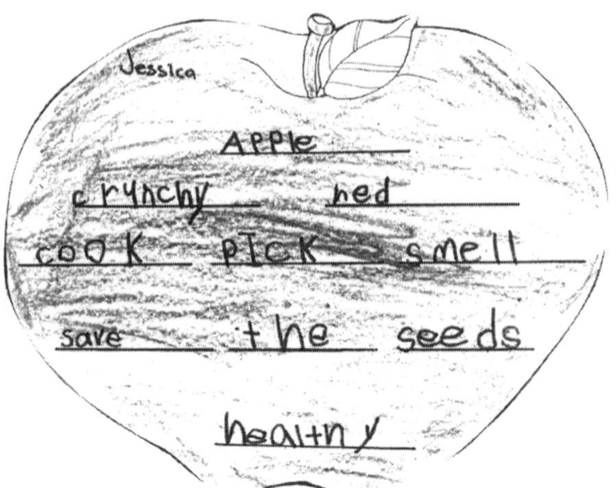

Figure 9.2. A shape book.

Modeling Mechanics

There are plenty of opportunities in a school day to engage children in writing and to model standard form for them. Beth and her children create a large-print "morning message" each day when she transcribes their discussion of the coming day's activities onto chart paper. As she does this, Beth demonstrates how oral language can be written down. When children read and reread the message together, they begin to match spoken language with print. Beth uses this opportunity to reinforce children's notions of lowercase and capital letters, words, paragraphs and punctuation marks. She teaches them the importance of a "finger space" between words and focuses their attention on neatness. As well as learning to sound out and spell words, children learn left-to-right print progression and voice inflections signaled by punctuation.

Before children write, many teachers focus children's attention on a particular skill and teach brief lessons. For example, Beth noticed an overgeneralization and use of the period in Stevie's work ("Leaves. Fall. In. October."). So, before making an *October* book, Beth taught a lesson on how periods function. She read several sentences with and without periods from a big book the class had recently finished.

Beth noted later that Stevie used periods more appropriately when she wrote, "I can ride a

Figure 9.3. Beth's students draw and write about what they know.

horse." (see Figure 9.3), "I love my family.", and "I can write. My mommy tought me." Beth's children often select book topics like these: "I Can . . . ," "I Love . . . ," "I Eat . . . , "Thanksgiving Is . . . ," and "Being a Good Friend Means. . . ." For these books, children use 8 × 11-inch paper with several lines along the 11-inch side and the rest of the page blank for a picture. Children make the cover from tagboard or a file folder and use a three-hole punch and metal fasteners to make the book. In some classrooms, teachers cut up brown paper bags to make pages for large class books.

To avoid anxiety over mistakes and holes in paper when children erase unwanted pencil marks, Beth provides fine felt-tipped markers to write with because she feels they are easier to control than pencils and they don't need sharpening, as pencils do when children apply too much pressure and the lead breaks. Plus, her children love writing with them. Beth also provides white correction tape, which she calls "boo-boo" tape. Stevie used correction tape to change her "*kan*" to "*can*" and to omit an inappropriate period after "*tought.*" The freedom to use this tape or white correction fluid may help focus the novice writer's attention on the conventions of written language and encourage the use of standard English so that writing becomes more legible.

Beth models how to fix mistakes. She might say, "Oh, look what I did! Oh, well, I'll just change it a little bit to make it right." Or "I'll use tape to fix that." Before long she finds her students pick up on this and say things to each other like "Just put a line through it and fix it" or "Make it into a worm that's coming out of your apple." Beth encourages her students to use standard spelling, especially when others will read their work. Her opinion makes good sense. She says, "For too long we've been too lax with mechanics, and I think children learn to repeat their mistakes. Why not help them get it right the first time so they can practice it correctly?"

Songs as Writing Models

Songs are particularly effective for shared reading that leads to writing because children are naturally drawn to music. Once students have learned to sing the song, matching the words to the printed lyrics seems to come easily. One of the song picture books Beth uses is *This Is the Way We Eat Our Lunch* (see Figure 9.4 for a listing of song picture books).

First Beth reads the song, then she teaches the children how to sing it. Next, she writes the lyrics on chart paper and points to the words as the children sing the song. When they can match print to the sung lyrics, Beth leads the children to experiment with their own lyrics. She writes each child's words at the bottom of unlined art paper, and then the children draw pictures to illustrate their pages. Beth encourages students to focus on school behavior, and the completed book becomes a record of their activities and routines. For example, the children illustrate "This is the way we

- come to school
- make our books
- look at words
- read a book
- sit in a circle
- eat our snack
- eat our lunch
- do our work
- throw the koosh ball
- cut and paste
- tell the date
- graph the weather
- write the numbers
- stretch up high
- raise our hands
- pick up stuff

in Mrs. Spiro's class!"

A SELECTED LIST OF SONG PICTURE BOOKS

Aliki. (1968). *Hush little baby.* Englewood Cliffs, NJ: Prentice Hall.

Allender, D. (1987). *Shake my sillies out.* New York: Crown.

Baer, E. (1995). *This is the way we eat our lunch: A book about children around the world.* New York: Scholastic.

Berry, H. (1994). *Old Macdonald had a farm.* New York: Morrow.

Hague, M. (1992). *Twinkle, twinkle little star.* New York: Morrow.

Krauss, L. (1993). *The first song ever sung.* New York: Lothrop Lee.

Slavin, B., & Tucker, K. (1992). *The cat came back.* New York: Albert Whitman.

Trapani, I. (1993). *The itsy bitsy spider.* New York: Whispering Coyote.

Weiss, N. (1987). *If you're happy and you know it.* New York: Greenwillow.

Weiss, N., & Thiele, B. (1994). *What a wonderful world.* New York: Atheneum.

Figure 9.4

Children who are not yet familiar with the computer keyboard can use a word processor to write these lyrics and other stories on the computer. For the story in Figure 9.5, the class read Arnold Lobel's *Frog and Toad Together* and wrote about their favorite parts. Beth encourages children to illustrate their work, and Courtney drew four separate pictures of frog looking for spring "just around the corner." Beth puts everyone's finished work into a stapled book with a cover. These books are popular reading for her class all year long.

The Writing Process

Teachers of young children recognize the power of an experience, a concrete object, a discussion, a picture, or a drawing as a lead-in to writing. What happens during the prewriting or planning stage of writing can be important in determining what and how a child writes. Webs and other graphic organizers also help children plan their writing. Because organizers hold key ideas and vocabulary, they scaffold children's interactive and independent writing (Bromley, Irwin-DeVitis, & Modlo, 1995). They can be a way to link visual and verbal language as the teacher writes down key words from a class discussion or a child writes key words to show what he or she is thinking.

Many children rely on the stimulation of a prewriting event or activity to carry them through the writing of a piece. For example, to prepare for writing a story about his father, 7-year-old Ian created a web. Ian's notes show his use of invented spelling and remind him to include "hokiey" (hockey), among things his father likes, "dert" (dirt), among things he doesn't like, and "berd" (beard) among other words to describe what his father looks like.

For beginning or struggling writers, connector words written on the spokes of a web often help a child see how he or she can form complete sentences from the key words on a web. For example, with the addition of "says" on each of the spokes of Ian's web, he can create several sentences and write a story called "Things Dad Says." But Ian may well not need this prescribed way of creating a story. With guidance from his

Figure 9.5. Courtney's story drafted on the computer and illustrated.

teacher about how to introduce the story in a first sentence, Ian may see that he can develop this three-part story about his father.

Many first-grade teachers post the steps in the writing process—PLAN, WRITE, REVISE, and PUBLISH—on classroom wall charts and refer to these often as they teach. Jan, a first-grade teacher, adds CONFERENCE, and manages her writing workshop with the help of color: PLAN and WRITE are in green, CONFERENCE is in yellow, and REVISE and PUBLISH are in red (Bromley, 1998). When they begin writing independently, she gives each child a set of 6-inch laminated colored construction paper circles and a writing folder to hold their work. At the end of the writing time, each child clips a circle on the outside of the folder to show what he or she will be doing the next day—green for planning or writing, yellow when ready for a conference with Jan, and red for revising and editing or ready to share. In this way Jan can see at a glance where everyone is in the writing process and who is ready for a conference. Jan has a worktable at the back of her room where she holds conferences with individuals and small groups.

Collaboration with Second Grade

Beth and her students collaborate with Kaye Debnar's second graders down the hall because, Beth says, "Our kids learn so much from it and we complement each other beautifully. I have lots of ideas, and Kaye makes me see an idea through to completion. She gives me the support I need since when I work alone, I always wonder if what I'm doing is most effective." Kaye chooses collaboration with Beth because "it gives me a chance to talk about the hows and whys of my teaching with another professional. And we end up doing exciting projects I might not ordinarily do on my own. It's good for the kids, too, because they learn from each other and they learn to care about each other. I see collaboration as a way to really move kids along in their literacy."

To extend the literacy of both groups of students, Beth and Kaye pair children, a first grader with a second grader, and schedule times when the two classes can socialize and get to know one another. The classes meet together regularly for short sessions so buddies can share their work with each other, read books together, and eat snacks together. Buddies could also occasionally sit together at lunch and play games with each other at recess to cement friendships.

One successful collaborative project entailed creating an original three little pigs story. Beth and Kaye chose four different versions of the traditional story, and each teacher read two versions to the buddies and helped them compare and contrast the stories using data charts. On another day, the children created their own version of the story as the teachers transcribed. It was revised with the children's suggestions, and students typed the final version in a font large enough to be used for a big book. Beth cut up the words from each sentence and put the cut-up sentences into individual envelopes. Then each buddy pair took words from an envelope and arranged them to make a sentence. This required children to read and manipulate words, talk together, and produce a meaningful sentence that they practiced reading. Then everyone decided on the proper order for all the sentences and pasted these sentences onto 12 × 18-inch paper, leaving space for their illustrations (see Figure 9.6). Beth laminated the pages and punched holes for metal rings to create *"The Three Little Pigs & the Big Bad Wolf,"* Written by Grade 1 & 2 Buddies.

Beth and Kaye realize the importance of a real audience for written work, and they make time for children to read their writing to each other. They both see remarkable improvement in children's attention to content and meaning as well as to mechanics such as spelling, punctuation, and neatness when children know who will read their work. One end-of-year project that Beth's children find particularly satisfying is sharing a book called *We Are Proud*. Each child contributes a page like Melissa's (see Figure 9.7), which shows her progress. At the beginning of the year, Melissa could not read her own name.

Well, he huffed, and he puffed,

and he huffed, and he puffed, and

huffed, and he puffed,

but he could not blow the house

in! John and Bryan

Figure 9.6. John and Bryan manipulated 25 words to make this sentence.

Beth and Kaye report that collaboration for the purpose of reading and writing benefits their first and second graders, who eagerly work together and support each other's literacy growth. Collaboration provides rich opportunities for listening, speaking, reading and writing abilities to develop in an enjoyable setting. Both teachers see children's confidence and ability to work independently grow.

Writing Across the Curriculum

There are many ways to develop and nurture the learning of young children through writing in math, science, and social studies. Some examples from classrooms where children are writing in a variety of ways across the curriculum follow.

- In science, as part of Randy's kindergarten nutrition unit, children write a letter to the school's cafeteria staff. In the letter the children connect what they are learning about the four food groups with some of their favorite lunches. They also suggest ways the staff can include healthy snacks in their not-so-favorite lunches.
- Jennifer's kindergartners create a large-print, four-column, KWHL chart on a bulletin board to begin a study of the rain forest in science. They fill the *K* column with what they know and form questions about what they want to know, which Jennifer writes in the *W* column. Then they fill the *H* column with how they will find the answers. As the unit progresses, they fill the *L* column with what they have learned.
- In math, children in Lisa's and Mary Jo's first-grade classrooms interview each other about such things as birthdays, favorite colors, and number of siblings. Then the classes create bar graphs and pictograms to show what they have learned about each other, and they write about what the graphs mean. Together, the classes compare their data to see how they are similar and different.
- In Katy's library-media center, pairs of first and second graders use a CD-ROM encyclopedia and nonfiction books to find information about specific animal behaviors, habitat, food, predators, and so forth to include in the fictional stories they are writing in science. Each story is word processed on the computer and revised after peer evaluation and teacher

Figure 9.7. Melissa is a fluent writer with beginning knowledge of capitals and periods.

AN IDEA FROM A TEACHER

Language Charts in Kindergarten

I first read about language charts in a chapter of a book entitled *Booktalk and Beyond* (Roser, Hoffman, Labbo, & Farest, 1995). I was especially interested in the idea of transcribing my kindergarten children's talk about stories they read, since some of them seemed ready to draw and write. The language chart, among other things, is a way to "display the oral to written language connection," and I believe this is critical to beginning writers. I wanted a way to value my children's drawings, encourage their writing, and make discussions more concrete. Since I taught both morning and afternoon classes, I wanted each group to be aware of what the other was learning. So I decided to adapt the idea to fit my needs.

First, my morning and afternoon classes chose three versions of "The Three Little Pigs" they wanted to read, out of five that I introduced. Then we created a huge chart on butcher paper that I divided into four horizontal and four vertical sections. I divided each section on the chart with a diagonal line, so that the morning class could use the top portion and the afternoon class the bottom portion. Each portion was large enough for me to transcribe a sentence, with room left for children's drawings. I posted the chart on a bulletin board and explained the title of each section—"Title/Author," "Problem," "Ending," and "Vote"—to my children. Over the next few days I read each story several times and invited children's oral responses. I transcribed their ideas for the "problem" and "ending" of each story, and volunteers added drawings. When both classes had heard the three books and the appropriate information was charted, they reviewed their work and what they enjoyed about each story. I had my children vote for the story they liked best by writing their name in the appropriate section on the chart.

The language chart achieved my objectives and was an effective way to engage children in shared writing. It also helped develop their sense of story and of the similarities and differences between like stories.

***Renee Hare,** Kindergarten Teacher*

conference before becoming part of a class book for the school library.

- In Carol's multi-age (6 to 8 years) classroom, children read an Iroquois Indian creation story as part of a social studies unit. A small group retold the story, drawing pictures on the computer using *Kid Pix,* a software program, and then wrote text to accompany the pictures. Using their recorded text and the pictures, they created a movie retelling of the creation story.
- In a social studies unit with the title "Changes All Around Us," Rebeccca's second-grade class in North Carolina and Natalie's class in New York communicate on-line as electronic "key pals." They use e-mail to ask and answer questions and compare themselves, their families, schools, and communities.
- To develop math concepts, Venita's second graders write daily in journals, where they also make diagrams and drawings. Venita's purpose is to encourage children to explain

their thinking and the processes they use to solve problems. She writes comments in the journals and children often share entries in pairs or volunteers read entries to the class.

Conclusion

There are many ways to encourage young children to write, and several things to keep in mind as you nudge young writers toward becoming fluent and proficient language users. Like Beth and Kaye, many teachers are teaching young children in ways that link reading and writing by modeling and demonstrating literacy. These teachers provide direct instruction in the form of standard written language. They provide opportunities for children to interact and collaborate as writers. They incorporate writing into science, social studies, and math. They give children a range of experiences writing in a variety of forms. Above all, they believe young children can be writers, and they make time for writing in their classrooms every day.

References

Bean, W., & Bouffler, C. (1997). *Read, write, spell.* York, ME: Stenhouse.

Bromley, K. (1998). *Language arts: Exploring connections.* Boston: Allyn & Bacon.

Bromley, K., Irwin-DeVitis, L., & Modlo, M. (1995). *Graphic organizers: Visual strategies for active learning.* New York: Scholastic.

Butler, D., & Clay, M. (1982). *Reading begins at home.* Exeter, NH: Heinemann.

Cambourne, B. (1988). *The whole story: Natural learning and the acquisition of literacy in the classroom.* Auckland, New Zealand: Scholastic.

Fountas, I., & Pinnell, G. S. (1996). *Guided Reading.* Portsmouth, NH: Heinemann.

Holdaway, D. (1979). *The foundations of literacy.* Sydney, Australia: Ashton Scholastic.

Kid Pix. (1998). San Rafael, CA: Broderbund Software.

Lobel, A. (1972). *Frog and toad together.* New York: Harper & Row.

Morrow, L. M. (1997). *Literacy development in the early years: Helping children read and write* (3rd ed.). Englewood Cliffs, NJ: Prentice Hall.

Roser, N. L., Hoffman, J. V., Labbo, L. D., & Farest, C. (1995). Language charts: A record of storytime talk. In N. L. Roser & M. G. Martinez (Eds.), *Booktalk and beyond: Children and teachers respond to literature* (pp. 80–89). Newark, DE: International Reading Association.

Slaughter, J. P. (1993). *Beyond storybooks: Young children and the shared book experience.* Newark, DE: International Reading Association.

Teale, W. H., & Sulzby, E. (1989). Emergent literacy: New perspectives. In D. S. Strickland & L. M. Morrow (Eds.), *Emerging literacy: Young children learn to read and write* (pp. 1–15). Newark, DE: International Reading Association.

CHAPTER TEN

Phonics Instruction

Margaret Moustafa

For Reflection and Action: Discuss tensions in the field that you know about or have heard about concerning the teaching of beginning reading, particularly tensions related to phonemic awareness and phonics. Using this book and other resources, describe some strategies that might be effective in achieving a balanced approach.

Margaret Moustafa discusses the roles of phonemic awareness and phonics in children's literacy development, and some of the controversy and confusion surrounding these topics.

We have a long tradition of teaching children letter-sound correspondences and then giving them passages to read that use those letter-sound correspondences. This practice dates back to the first century A.D., when a Roman educator, Quintilian, used tablets with letters on them to teach children to read (N. B. Smith, 1965).

Some of the earliest concerns with traditional phonics instruction came from the empirical discovery that in English, the usual phonics generalizations are generally unreliable. For example, the popular "silent e" rule, which says that a vowel followed by an *e* is long and the *e* is silent, works in only 63% of the words in which the vowel plus *e* combination appears (Bailey, 1967; Burmeister, 1968; Clymer, 1963; Emans, 1967).

The discovery that phonic generalizations were unreliable was soon followed by the discovery that there are over 211 letter-phoneme correspondences that apply to at least five of the one- and two-syllable words within the comprehension vocabularies of children ages 6 to 9 years (Berdiansky, Cronnell, & Koehler, 1969; Venezky, 1967). To illustrate the complexity of English letter-sound correspondences, in my dialect, in the last sentence, when the letter *o* does not come right before a *w* or *r* or another *o* (as in *ow, or,* or *oo*) and is not between *ti* and *n* (as in *tion*), it is pronounced one way in *discovery, of,* and *one,* another way in *phonic, followed,* and *comprehension,* another way in *over, phoneme,* and *vocabularies* (which is the same as the *ow* in *followed*), and still another way in *two* and *to* (which is the same as the *oo* in *soon*). The letters *or* are pronounced one way in *correspondences* and another way in *word.* The /w/ sound is written in *word* but not in *one.*

Today we know that reading programs that emphasize meaning are more effective than traditional parts-to-whole phonics instruction (Anderson, Wilkinson, & Mason, 1991; Cantrell, 1999; Elly, 1991; Mullis, Campbell, & Farstrup, 1993, p. 30; Reutzel & Cooter, 1990; Ribowsky, 1986; Richek & McTague, 1988; Sacks & Mergendoller, 1997). We also know that children taught phonics in context are almost twice as successful in sounding out unfamiliar words as children taught traditional phonics (Freepon, 1991).

In the following pages we will review research underlying contemporary phonics instruction and observe several teachers as they implement different aspects of it. We will toggle back and forth between research and instruction, looking at research, then looking at instruction consistent with the research, as follows:

- Children's early reading
- Teaching a whole text
- Children's phonological and cognitive processes
- Teaching letter-sound correspondences within the text

Children's Early Reading

The first print words children learn to read, such as their names or the word *stop* on a stop sign, they learn to recognize holistically, not letter by letter (Ehri, 1994; K. Goodman & Goodman, 1979; Gough & Hillinger, 1980; Perfetti, 1985; F. Smith, 1988). Early readers read better in context than outside of context (e.g., K. S. Goodman, 1965; Nicholson, 1991; Nicholson, Lillas, & Rzoska, 1988; Stanovich, 1991, 1994) and comprehend print written with familiar language better than print written with unfamiliar language (e.g., Kucer, 1985; Rhodes, 1979; Ruddell, 1965; Tatham, 1970). Let's look in on Mrs. Jones, a kindergarten teacher, and see how she builds on these competencies of children.

Teaching the Whole Text

It's the third week of kindergarten. Mrs. Jones is creating a context within which she will teach the children letter-sound correspondences. She is in an instructional circle with her emergent readers. The children each have a copy of the words to the song "If You're Happy and You Know It." Mrs. Jones is asking the children their favorite words in the song and writing each word they choose on a specially prepared piece of card stock (see Figure 10.1). As she writes each word, she holds it up for the children to see and says, "This word is _____. Can you put your finger under this word in our song?" The children point to the words on their papers.

A child who is new to the class says his favorite word is "clap your hands." Smiling, Mrs. Jones responds "Yes, that's three words." She turns to the copy of the song on the chart rack beside her and points to each word as she reads "clap . . . your . . . hands." "Which word do you like best, *clap* or *your* or *hands?*" The child chooses *clap,* and Mrs. Jones writes *clap* on a piece of card stock. She asks the children to find *clap* on their papers.

Shared Reading

In a series of lessons, Mrs. Jones has brought the children to the point where they are able to locate

PREPARING WORD CARDS FOR PHONICS INSTRUCTION

1. Divide standard-size photocopy paper into equal parts. (The number of parts depends on the size you will want the word cards to be.) Copy a picture that represents the text to be taught and tape identical copies on the left-hand side of each section of the paper.
2. Photocopy onto paper or card stock.
3. Cut the photocopies into equal parts so that there is one picture on each part.
4. Save the photocopy master for future use.

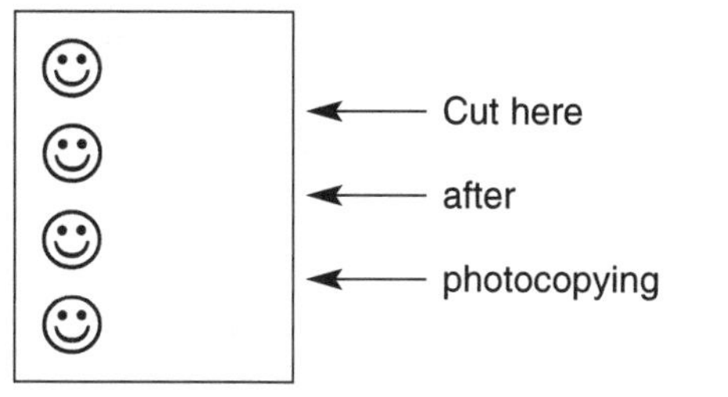

Figure 10.1

words in a text. She carefully selected the text she would use for teaching the children to read by making sure that the language of the text was the type of language children use and are familiar with. The first day of school she sang "If You're Happy and You Know It" to and with the children, clapping her hands as she sang "clap your hands" and stamping her feet as she sang "stamp your feet."

After the class had sung the song daily for several days, Mrs. Jones began to teach the children to read the words in the song. She copied the words onto chart paper, which she placed in the chart rack. Then she taught the children to read the words of the song by shared reading, a technique pioneered by Don Holdaway (1979) and used with great success by others (Eldredge, Reutzel, & Hollingsworth, 1996; Fayden, 1997; Heald-Taylor, 1987; Slaughter, 1983; Trachtenburg & Ferruggia, 1989). In shared reading, also known as the shared book experience, the teacher points to the words in full view of the children as she or he reads *to* and *with* the children. Mrs. Jones read the words to the song *to* and *with* the children twice the first day, twice the next day, and so on, for several days. Then she used a *cloze procedure* to ascertain whether the children had memorized the language of the text: she began reading a sentence while pointing to the text, but let the children complete the sentence as she continued pointing to the text.

Partner Reading

Once the children had memorized the language of the text, Mrs. Jones taught them to partner read, or to sit side by side taking turns reading and listening to each other. First she asked for two volunteers in her class to demonstrate for the other children. She had the volunteers sit side by side holding a copy of the words of the song and asked the volunteers, "Who will be the first reader and who will be the first listener?" Once the children decided, she said to the first listener, "When Maria is reading, if she comes to a word she doesn't know, will you give her time to think?" (The child nodded.) "Thank you. Then, if she wants help, she can ask you." Maria read the text. Elijah listened attentively. Mrs. Jones said to the class, "Didn't Maria do a good job of reading? Didn't Elijah do a good job of listening?" and led the group in applauding the two children. Mrs. Jones continued the demonstration: "Now, Elijah, it's your turn to be the reader, and Maria, it's your turn to be the listener." Elijah read to Maria. Mrs. Jones again led the group in applauding the children.

Now the children were ready to begin partner reading. Mrs. Jones asked them to line up with partners. During the first week of school she had assessed the reading proficiency of each child. She knew everyone in this group was an emergent reader. She also knows that learning to read is a social process. Therefore, she had the children choose their partners from among the children in the group. As the children lined up, two by two, Mrs. Jones handed each pair of students a copy of the words to the song and the children went to their seats or spots on the carpet to read to each other.

Once the children had settled down with reading partners, Mrs. Jones passed among the children listening to them read and coaching those who were sitting face to face to sit side by side so that all the children would be looking at the text right side up.

One-to-One Matching

The following day Mrs. Jones assessed each child's ability to match spoken words to printed words. She gathered the children around the chart rack, did another shared reading, and again passed out copies for the children to read to their partners. This time, as the children were reading, Mrs. Jones passed among the children and assessed the children. Choosing words past the first two-syllable word in the text, she asked each child to put a finger under such-and-such a word. She knew that those who perceived each cluster of letters as a syllable would not be able to track words past the first two-syllable word. She took notes on which children were able to track print words and which were not yet able to. She found that many of her students did not have one-to-one matching.

The following day, working with the whole group, Mrs. Jones began teaching one-to-one matching. She began with a "word hunt." She gathered the children around the chart rack, did another shared reading with the children, and then asked the children, "Who can find the word *clap* in our song?" Several children raised their hands. Mrs. Jones invited one child to come up and point to the word, guiding her to stand by the side of the chart rack so that all the children could see. When the child pointed to the word *clap*, Mrs. Jones said, "That's right! Can you tell the boys and girls how you found it?" The child explained. If she had not been able to explain, Mrs. Jones would have said, "I bet I know how you found it. I bet you started here at the beginning and said . . ."—pointing to the words as she read—" 'If you're happy and you know it, clap—' Oh, here it is! Here's *clap*." This technique guides the children to use their knowledge of language to find a print word in text. Mrs. Jones then asked the children to find several other words in the text, coaching them as needed.

Every day over the next week Mrs. Jones promoted one-to-one matching through this activity and others. She invited the children to take turns being teacher and pointing to the words on the card stock in view of the other children; she passed out copies of the words to the song and asked the children to put their fingers under a particular word in the text; and she had the children cut one of the sentences of the song into its constituent words, scramble the words, and reassemble them in the correct order. Through feedback in each of these activities the children learned to match spoken words to printed words. Each lesson on one-to-one matching was preceded by shared reading and followed by partner reading. Now when Mrs. Jones holds up the children's favorite words on the card stock, the children can match the words to the text in front of them.

Mrs. Jones has been laying the foundation for contemporary phonics instruction. Through shared reading she has demonstrated the reading process to the children. Through partner reading the children have engaged in reading and are coming to see themselves as readers. Now that the children have the concept of what a printed word is and can locate words in familiar text, Mrs. Jones can begin to teach letter-sound correspondences to foster eventual independent reading.

Children's Phonological and Cognitive Processes

Phonemes, Onsets, and Rimes

Traditionally we have taught children learning to read letter-phoneme correspondences: for example, the letter *l* says /l/ (Balmuth, 1982; N. B. Smith, 1965; Venezky, 1967). *Phonemes* are the smallest unit of speech that, if changed, change the meaning of a word. The word *smiles* consists of five phonemes: /s/, /m/, /i/, /l/, and /z/.

There is a body of research which concludes that children's knowledge of letter-phoneme correspondences is the best predictor of children's early reading proficiency (see Adams, 1990, for a review of this research). Adams and others have interpreted this finding to mean that children need to know letter-phoneme correspondences to become independent readers. However, in statistics the word *predicts* means that two phenomena are highly correlated. It does not mean one phenomenon causes the other.

Children who have not yet learned to read have difficulty consciously analyzing spoken words into their constituent phonemes (Bruce, 1964; Ehri & Wilce, 1980; Liberman, Shankweiler, Fischer, & Carter, 1974; Mann, 1986; Rosner, 1974; Treiman, 1983, 1985, 1986; Treiman & Baron, 1981; Tunmer & Nesdale, 1985). That is, they have difficulty analyzing the spoken word *smiles* into /s/, /m/, /i/, /l/, and /z/.

Some researchers (e.g., Foorman, Francis, Fletcher, Schatschneider, & Mehta, 1998; Lyon, 1997; Stanovich, 1986) propose to address this problem by establishing phonemic awareness training as part of the curriculum—teaching children who do not yet read to consciously analyze spoken words into their individual phonemes. However, if phonemic awareness is a consequence rather than a cause of becoming literate, as a growing body of noncorrelational research suggests (Bryant, 1993, p. 93; Goswami, 1986, 1988; Moustafa, 1995, 1997; Scholes, 1998; Treiman, 1983, 1985, 1986), then this is a cart-before-the horse approach. Bus and van IJzendoorn (1999) found that phonemic awareness in kindergarten accounts for 0.6% of the total variance in reading achievement in the later primary grades. Troia (1999) reviewed 39 studies of phonemic awareness training and found no evidence to support its use in classroom instruction. Krashen (1999a, 1999b) conducted similar reviews and had similar findings. As Taylor (1998, p. 23) has said, "phonemic awareness research is based on the false assumption that children's early cognitive functions work from abstract exercises to meaningful activity" rather than vice versa, as in other learning.

Fortunately, children who have not yet learned to read can and do analyze spoken words into other, larger units of speech. In English, spoken syllables can be analyzed into phonemes *or* into *onsets* and *rimes* (MacKay, 1972). Onsets are any consonants before a vowel in a syllable; rimes are the vowel and any consonants after it in a syllable. Onsets and rimes may have one, two, or three phonemes. The spoken word *smiles* consists of a two-phoneme onset, /sm/, and a three-phoneme rime, /ilz/. Linguists consider onsets and rimes the "psychological units" of spoken English.

In poetics, when words begin with the same onsets (e.g., *phone* and *fix*) it is called alliteration. When words have the same rime in the last syllable (e.g., *rendezvous* and *Kalamazoo*) they are said to rhyme.

Reading teachers have traditionally called letters that represent onsets with more than one phoneme (e.g., *sm-*) consonant clusters or consonant blends. They have called letters that represent rimes with more than one phoneme (e.g., *-ile)* phonograms or word families.

English-speaking children who have not yet learned to read can and do analyze spoken English into onsets and rimes (Calfee, 1977; Goswami & Bryant, 1990). That is, they can analyze *smiles* into its component onset, /sm/, and rime, /ilz/, without being taught to do so.

Treiman (1983) has suggested that developmentally, children first learn to divide syllables into onsets and rimes and only later learn to subdivide them into phonemes. English-speaking children learning how to read make letter-onset and letter-rime correspondences better than letter-phoneme correspondences (Goswami, 1986, 1988; Goswami & Mead, 1992; Moustafa, 1995, 1997; Wylie & Durrell, 1970).

In Spanish, syllables do not divide into onsets and rimes. The psychological units of spoken Spanish words are syllables. Traditionally, instruction in Spanish letter-sound correspondences has been syllabic: teachers teaching Spanish-speaking children to read in Spanish teach sets of syllables that vary by one vowel, such as *sa, se, si, so, su,* and/or teach children to break print words into syllables–for example, *casa* = *ca* + *sa*—and to recombine the syllables to make new words (e.g., *ca* + *ma* = *cama; sa* + *po* = *sapo*) (Moustafa & Maldonado-Colon, 1999). Hence, while Mrs. Jones teaches her English-speaking students English letter-onset, letter-rime, and letter-syllable correspondences, Mr. Jimenez next door, who teaches Spanish-speaking students to read in Spanish, teaches Spanish letter-syllable correspondences.

Analogy

Children who have begun to read make analogies between familiar and unfamiliar printed words to pronounce unfamiliar printed words (Goswami, 1986, 1988; Goswami & Bryant, 1990; Goswami & Mead, 1992; Moustafa, 1995, 1997). That is, by learning to recognize the print words *small* and *smile,* children figure out that *sm-* is pronounced /sm/. They then use their knowledge that *sm-* is pronounced /sm/ to pronounce *sm-* in other words they encounter with *sm-*. Similarly, by learning to recognize the print words *part* and *cart,* children figure out that *-art* is pronounced /art/. They then use that knowledge to pronounce *-art* in other words they encounter with *-art*. Once they know how to pronounce *sm-* and *-art,* they can independently pronounce *smart*. By teaching children a part of each word in whole words they have learned to recognize, where the parts represent familiar units of sound, teachers facilitate children's future ability to make analogies between familiar and unfamiliar printed words to pronounce unfamiliar printed words.

Teaching Letter-Sound Correspondences

The First Story

School is over for the day. Mrs. Jones plans the letter-sound correspondences she will teach the children the next day. Taking the words the children have chosen as their favorite words, she lightly underlines a letter or string of letters representing an onset, a rime, or a syllable in each word (see Figure 10.2).

Mrs. Jones lightly underlines the *h* in *happy* and *hands,* the *f* in *feet* and *face,* the *y* in *you, your,* and *you're,* and the *ow* in *know* and *show*. The words *if, it,* and *and* are all one-rime words, so she underlines all the letters in each of these words. Choosing a letter or letter string in each word the children have chosen from the song, she underlines the *w* in *will,* the *s* in *surely,* the *cl* in *clap,* and the *st* in *stamp*. She does not plan to teach every part in each word. Her objectives are to help children understand the alphabetic principle—that letters represent sounds within words—in the context of printed words they have learned to recognize, and to help them see the parts in the whole so that they can eventually make analogies between familiar and unfamiliar printed words to pronounce unfamiliar printed words.

Mrs. Jones does not attempt to be sure that the children have chosen every word in the song. She knows that whatever letter-sound correspondences she would have taught in the words the children didn't choose will come up again in other texts. She tapes the words in random order to an area on the wall she has covered with vinyl. She places the transparent tape horizontally at the top of the pieces of card stock rather than vertically, to facilitate the later regrouping of the words.

The next day Mrs. Jones gathers her students around the area where she has taped their favorite words and passes out copies of the words to the song. She points to the word *happy* on the wall, saying, "Can you put your finger under this word in our song?" "What is it?" "Yes, that's right. It's *happy,* and"—highlighting the letter *h,* which she has underlined—"this letter is *h*. It says /h/. Can you say /h/?" Mrs. Jones continues with other words.

After Mrs. Jones has highlighted and talked about the sound represented by a letter or letter string in each word, she leads the children in grouping words by like letters highlighted. She begins by modeling the process. She points to the words *happy* and *hands* and says, "Oh, look! These words have a yellow square around the same letters. I'm going to put them together." (She moves them to a clear place on the vinyl, placing one word under the other. The tape easily detaches and re-adheres to the vinyl.) "Who can find some other patterns?" She chooses a child from among the volunteers. The child groups the words *face* and *feet* together. Mrs. Jones says, "That's right! *Face* and *feet* both have a yellow square around the *f*. *f* says /f/." Another child groups *you, your* and *you're*. Still another child groups *know* and *show*. As the children group these words, Mrs. Jones talks about the sounds the highlighted letters represent in the context of these words. Finally, there are four

HIGHLIGHTING, GROUPING, AND RE-HIGHLIGHTING LETTERS IN FAVORITE WORDS

1. Highlight letters representing onsets, rimes, syllables, words in compound words, or root words.

Correct examples:

Onsets:	boat	lamb	smile	
Rimes:	smile	boat	lamb	is
Syllables:	unlock	lovely	jumping	
Words in compound words:	skateboard	baseball		
Root words:	breakfast	television		

Incorrect examples (letters representing units of sound smaller than onsets or rimes):

smile smile boat lamb is

2. Group words that have identical letters highlighted.

Correct examples:

ate cat
late what

Incorrect examples:

late (The sounds match
freight but the letters don't.)

late (Only the first letters match.
fall All the letters should match.)

3. After grouping words that have identical letters highlighted, check for multiple pronunciations of the highlighted letters in each group. When identical letters have different pronunciations (e.g., the *-at* in *cat* and *what*), use one color for each pronunciation (e.g., color the *-at* in *cat* and *bat* one color and the *-at* in *what* another color).

Correct examples:

cat breaks show sun show you
bat steak know some shirt yellow
what streak now sure happy
cow eensy
weensy

Figure 10.2

words that do not group with the other words: *will, surely, clap,* and *stamp.* Pointing to these words, Mrs. Jones says, "These words don't make a pattern, but they will as we learn more and more words."

Mrs. Jones shows the children how to put the words on the word wall. Before the school year began Mrs. Jones created a phonics word wall by securing two vinyl shower curtain liners to the wall and placing the letters of the alphabet across the shower curtain liners. Since the beginning of the year she has sung the ABC song with the children while pointing to the letters as she sings. Now she will help the children use the wall to create their own phonics generalities. Pointing to the *h* in *happy* and the *h* in *hands,* Mrs. Jones says, "Look, the letter in the yellow square in these words is *h.* I'm going to put these words under the *h* on our word wall." She continues with the words *know* and *show,* saying, "The letters in the yellow square in these words are *ow.* I'm going to put them under the *o* on our word wall." The children take turns putting the other words on the phonics word wall (see Figure 10.3).

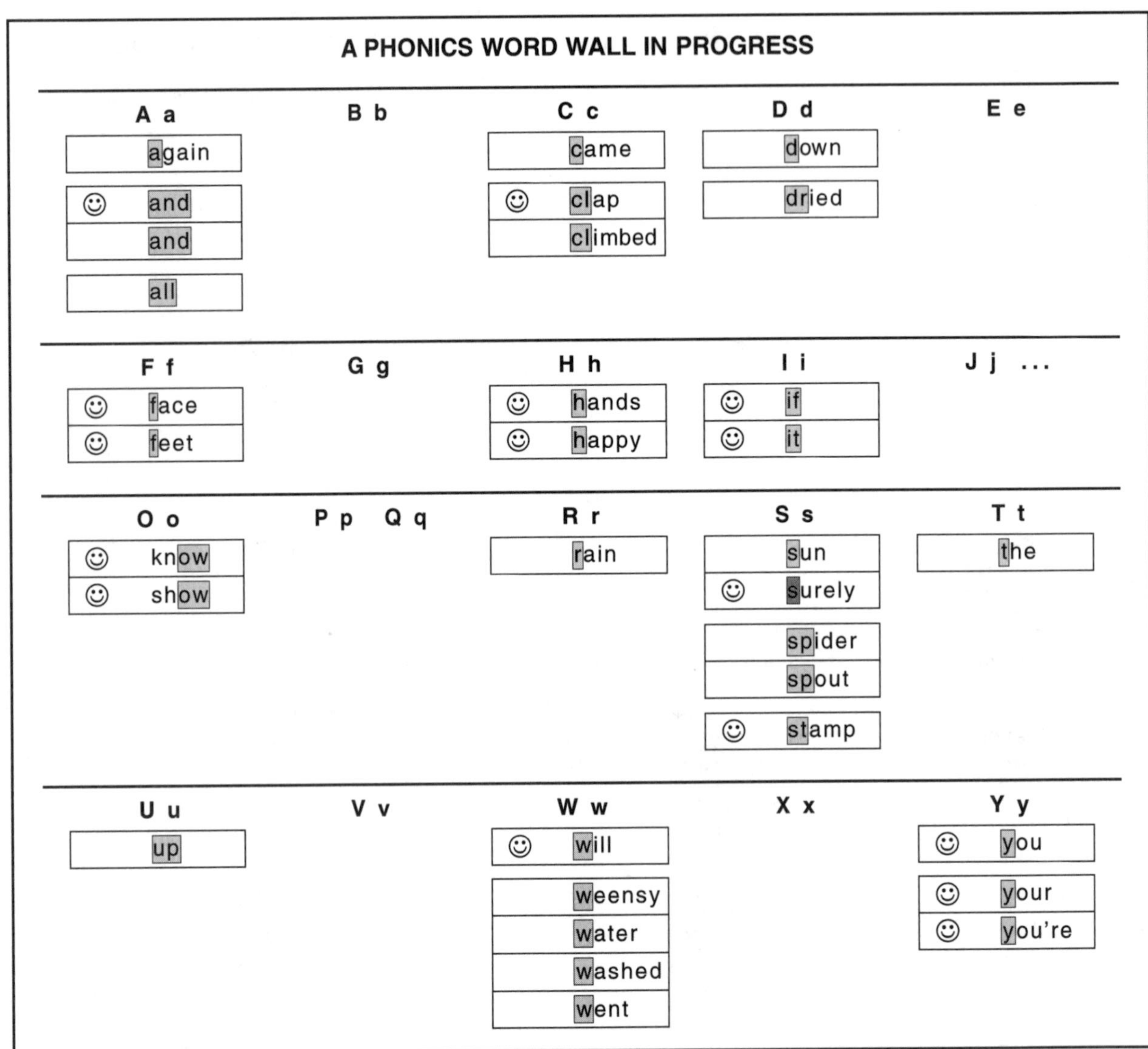

Figure 10.3

Subsequent Stories

The next day Mrs. Jones begins a shared reading with *The Eensy Weensy Spider.* She has been singing the song while doing the hand motions with the children since the second week of school. Now she repeats the pattern of daily shared reading and partner reading until the students can read it independently with one-to-one matching. Then she asks the children their favorite words in the story. This time Mrs. Jones writes the children's favorite words on pieces of card stock that have a picture of a spider on the left-hand side. A child chooses the word *and.* Although the children chose this word in the previous text, she writes it again on a card stock with a picture of a spider.

After school Mrs. Jones lightly underlines the *w* in *weensy, water, washed,* and *went.* She underlines the *d* in *down,* the *c* in *came,* the *r* in *rain,* the *s* in *sun,* and the *a* in *again.* She underlines all of the letters in the one-rime words *up, and,* and *all.*

AN IDEA FROM A TEACHER

Spelling by Analogy

I teach children to spell by analogy. We use words they know how to spell to spell words they don't yet know how to spell. During writing aloud (Dorn, French, & Jones, 1998) I divide a chart tablet into two sections, one for the message and one for practice. As I compose the message, I use the practice section to demonstrate spelling by analogy. For example, if I want to write **sock**, I might say, "Let's see, **sock** sounds like **rock**. So I can use **rock** to spell **sock**." I write **rock** in the practice section, circle **-ock**, and say, "I can use the **-o-c-k** in **rock** to write **dock**." I then write **dock**, first on the practice page beneath **rock** and then in the message section. During interactive writing, one child comes to the front of the instructional group, and composes a message on a chart tablet while the other children write the same message on their wipe-off board. Again, I divide the chart tablets into a practice section and a message section. When the children want to write a word they don't know how to spell, I guide them to make analogies using words they already know how to spell. For example, if a child wants to write **pot**, I say, " If you know how to spell **got** you can spell **pot**." I then guide them to write **got** and then **pot** on the practice section, and then to write **pot** in the message section, as I do in the writing aloud lesson.

During daily journal writing I have the children use one page of their journal for practice and the opposite page for their message. Then, as they are writing their individual messages, I guide them to use the practice page to work out spellings of unknown words using analogous words they already know how to spell. Eventually they are able to make analogies in their minds without the practice pages.

Rosalie Franzese, Second-Grade Teacher

She underlines the *sp* in *spider* and *spout*, the *cl* in *climbed*, the *dr* in *dried*, and the *th* in *the*. Even though she has underlined the *ow* in *know* and *show* in the previous text, she does not underline the *ow* in *down* because it represents only part of the rime in *down*. Mrs. Jones tapes the words in random order on the area on the wall covered with vinyl.

The next day Mrs. Jones gathers her students around the area where she has taped their favorite words from *The Eensy Weensy Spider*. She passes out copies of the song. She points to the word *water*, saying, "Can you put your finger under this word in the story?" "What is it?" "Yes, that's right. It's *water* and"—highlighting the letter *w*—"this letter is *w*. It says /w/. Can you say /w/?" Mrs. Jones continues with other words.

Then Mrs. Jones has the children group the words by identical letters highlighted on the phonics word wall along with the words from *If You're Happy and You Know It*. The logo on the left-hand side of each piece of card stock will help the children remember which text each word came from.

As the children put the word *and* from *The Eensy Weensy Spider* on the phonics word wall, they see the word *and* from *If You're Happy and You Know It*. Mrs. Jones and the children talk about the word being the same in both songs.

Teaching Multiple Ways of Pronouncing the Same Letter or Groups of Letters: After the children finish putting all the words on the word wall, Mrs. Jones points out the multiple pronunciations of the letter *s* within the context of the words the children are learning to recognize. "Look, boys and girls. The *s* in *surely* says /sh/. The *s* in *sun* says /s/. Let's color the two *s*'s differently. What color would you like to color the *s* in *surely*?" As words that begin with the letter *s* come up within the context of the children's reading in future texts, Mrs. Jones will lead the children in deciding whether the *s* represents /s/ or /sh/, coloring *s*'s that are pronounced /s/ one color and *s*'s that are pronounced /sh/ another color. She will do the same for other letters and letter strings with multiple pronunciations, such as the *ow* in *show* and *know* versus the *ow* in *cow* and *now,* or the *eak* in *steak* versus the *eak* in *beak.* In this way the children learn about the multiple pronunciations of letters and letter strings within the context of their own literacy experiences. This makes the learning meaningful and avoids the problem of unreliability of traditional phonics generalizations with which we began the chapter.

Next Mrs. Jones begins a shared reading with *Bears in the Night* (Berenstain & Berenstain, 1971). She has already used this book as a read-aloud with the class, and the children have acted out the story (going around a "lake" made of blue butcher paper, and so on) as she read it. She places a big book version of the story on an easel. She repeats the pattern of daily shared reading until the children have memorized the story. Once the children have memorized the story, she has them do partner reading. The routine of shared reading followed by partner reading is repeated over several days until the children can read the story independently. Then Mrs. Jones asks the children their favorite words in the story. This time she writes the children's favorite words on pieces of card that which have a picture of a bear from the story on the left-hand side. The children choose, among other words, the words *wall* and *window.*

After school Mrs. Jones again plans which letter-sound correspondences she will teach the children. Among other things, she underlines the *w* in *wall* and *window.* Then, making connections across texts, Mrs. Jones writes the words again. This time she underlines the *all* in *wall* and the *ow* in *window* so the children will be able to group *wall* with *all* and group *window* with *know* and *show* from their first text.

Teaching Letters That Represent Ideas Rather Than Sounds: Mrs. Jones decides to take advantage of the fact that regular noun plurals have come up within the context of the children's learning. She writes *hands* on a piece of card stock with a smiley face on it and *bears* and *rocks* on pieces of card stock with a picture of a bear on them and underlines the *s* in each of these words. Although the *s* in these words represents only part of the rime, she knows that singular and plural forms of regular nouns are meaningful units of speech to the children. She is still working with units of language the children understand.

Again Mrs. Jones highlights the letters in front of the children and has them group the words by identical letters highlighted. This time as she is highlighting she shows the children the difference between *hand* and *hands, bear* and *bears,* and *rock* and *rocks.* Although the *s* in *hands* and *bears* is pronounced differently than the *s* in *rocks,* Mrs. Jones doesn't talk about the difference in sound but only says that the *s* means there are two or three or more. Again the children group the words on the phonics word wall. Mrs. Jones creates a special place beside the phonics word wall for *hands, bears,* and *rocks.* Later in the year she will use the same place for grouping regular past tense verbs, such as *jumped* and *played*, and compound words, such as *baseball*.

Clearing Space on the Phonics Word Wall: The phonics word wall is getting crowded. There are seven words on the wall where the *w* is highlighted. To make room, Mrs. Jones explains to the children, "We need more room on the wall for our words. I'm going to put all these words that begin with *w* except one in the literacy center. Which word would you like me to keep on the wall?" The children choose a word, and Mrs.

Jones puts the others on a ring and places them in the children's literacy center.

Mrs. Jones continues the cycle of read-aloud, shared reading, partner reading, and whole-to-parts phonics instruction with more and more texts throughout the year. As more and more words the children have chosen go up on the phonics word wall, the children take ownership of the wall. They also use the words on the wall for reference for conventional spelling in their writing.

Addressing Children's Varying Proficiencies: Miss Jamal, who teaches first grade across the hall, also assessed her students' reading proficiency at the beginning of the year. Some of her students are emergent readers and others are early readers. She uses shared reading with her emergent readers and guided reading with her early readers. Therefore, she needs two phonics word walls, one for words from the texts the emergent readers are reading and one for the words from the texts the early readers are reading. To save space, Mrs. Jamal has lined two presentation boards with shower curtain liners. She uses one for one group and the other for the other group. She and the children stand each board on the floor or a table when they are using it and move it out of the way when they are not using it. In a variation of Mrs. Jones's teaching strategy, when Miss Jamal asks her children their favorite words, she provides the children with specially prepared pieces of paper similar to her specially prepared pieces of card stock (as in Figure 10.1) and has the children write the words on their papers as she writes them on the card stock.

Finally, Mrs. Jung, who teaches second grade down the hall, has early readers and independent readers. She has a phonics word wall for her early readers but not for her independent readers. After two years of read-alouds, shared reading, guided reading, self-selected reading, home reading, reading-writing connections, and contemporary phonics instruction, these children have outgrown the need for phonics instruction, and Mrs. Jung wisely spends instructional time addressing other educational needs.

References

Adams, M. (1990). *Beginning to read: Thinking and learning about print.* Cambridge, MA: MIT Press.

Anderson, R. C., Wilkinson, A. G., & Mason, J. M. (1991). A microanalysis of the small-group guided reading lesson: Effects of an emphasis on global story meaning. *Reading Research Quarterly, 26,* 417–441.

Baily, M. H. (1967). The utility of phonic generalizations in grades one through six. *The Reading Teacher, 20,* 413–418.

Balmuth, M. (1982). *The roots of phonics.* New York: Teachers College Press.

Berdiansky, B., Cronnell, B., & Koehler, J. (1969). *Spelling-sound relations and primary form-class descriptions for speech comprehension vocabularies of 6–9 year olds* (Technical Report No. 15). Los Alamitos, CA: Southwest Regional Laboratory for Educational Research and Development.

Berenstain, S., & Berenstain, J. (1971). *Bears in the night.* New York: Random House.

Bruce, D. J. (1964). The analysis of word sounds. *British Journal of Educational Psychology, 34,* 158–170.

Bryant, P. (1993). Phonological aspects of learning to read. In R. Beard (Ed.), *Teaching literacy, balancing perspectives* (pp. 83–94). London: Hodder & Stoughton.

Burmeister, L. E. (1968). Usefulness of phonic generalizations. *The Reading Teacher, 21,* 349–356.

Bus, A. C., & van IJzendoorn, M. H. (1999). Phonological awareness and early reading: A meta-analysis of experimental training studies. *Journal of Educational Psychology, 91*(3), 403–414.

Calfee, R. (1977). Assessment of individual reading skills: Basic research and practical applications. In A. S. Reber & D. L. Scarborough (Eds.), *Toward a psychology of reading* (pp. 289–323). New York: Erlbaum.

Cantrell, S. C. (1999). Effective teaching and literacy learning: A look inside primary classrooms. *The Reading Teacher, 52*(4), 370–378.

Clymer, T. (1963). The utility of phonic generalizations in the primary grades. *The Reading Teacher, 16,* 252–258.

Dorn, I. J, French, C., Jones, T. (1998) *Apprenticeship in literacy: Transitions across reading and writing.* York, ME: Stenhouse.

Ehri, L. C. (1994). Development of the ability to read words: Update. In R. Ruddell, M. Ruddell, & H. Singer (Eds.), *Theoretical models and processes of reading* (pp. 323–359). Newark, DE: International Reading Association.

Ehri, L. C., & Wilce, L. S. (1980). The influence of orthography on readers' conceptualization of the phonemic structure of words. *Applied Psycholinguistics, 1,* 371–385.

Eldredge, J. L., Reutzel, D. R., & Hollingsworth, P. M. (1996). Comparing the effectiveness of two oral reading practices: Round-robin reading and the shared book experience. *Journal of Literacy Research, 28*(2), 201–225.

Elly, W. (1991). Acquiring literacy in a second language: The effect of book-based programs. *Language Learning, 41*(3), 375–411.

Emans, R. (1967). The usefulness of phonic generalizations above the primary grades. *The Reading Teacher, 20,* 419–425.

Fayden, T. (1997). What is the effect of shared reading on rural Native American and Hispanic kindergarten children? *Reading Improvement, 34,* 22–30.

Foorman, B. R., Francis, D. J., Fletcher, J. M., Schatschneider, C. S., & Mehta, P. (1998). The role of instruction in learning to read: Preventing reading failure in at-risk children. *Journal of Educational Psychology, 90*(1), 37–55.

Freepon, P. (1991). Children's concepts of the nature and purpose of reading in different instructional settings. *Journal of Reading Behavior, 23*(2), 139–163.

Goodman, K., & Goodman, Y. (1979). Learning to read is natural. In L. B. Resnick & P. A. Weaver (Eds.), *Theory and practice of early reading* (Vol. 1, pp. 137–154). Hillsdale, NJ: Erlbaum.

Goodman, K. S. (1965). A linguistic study of cues and miscues in reading. *Elementary English, 42,* 639–643.

Goswami, U. (1986). Children's use of analogy in learning to read: A developmental study. *Journal of Experimental Child Psychology, 42,* 73–83.

Goswami, U. (1988). Orthographic analogies and reading development. *The Quarterly Journal of Experimental Psychology, 40A,* 239–268.

Goswami, U., & Bryant, P. (1990). *Phonological skills and learning to read.* Hillsdale, NJ: Erlbaum.

Goswami, U., & Mead, F. (1992). Onset and rime awareness and analogies in reading. *Reading Research Quarterly, 17,* 150–162.

Gough, P. B., & Hillinger, M. L. (1980). Learning to read: An unnatural act. *Bulletin of the Orton Society, 30,* 180–196.

Heald-Taylor, G. (1987). How to use predictable books for K–2 language arts instruction. *The Reading Teacher, 40,* 656–661.

Holdaway, D. (1979). *The foundations of literacy.* Portsmouth, NH: Heinemann.

Krashen, S. (1999a). Effects of phonemic awareness training on delayed tests of reading. *Perceptual and Motor Skills, 89,* 79–82.

Karshen, S. (1999b). Training in phonemic awareness: Greater on test of phonemic awareness. *Perceptual and Motor Skills, 89,* 412–416.

Kucer, S. B. (1985). Predictability and readability: The same rose with different name? In Douglass M. (Ed.), *Claremont Reading Conference forty-ninth yearbook.* Claremont, CA: Claremont Graduate School.

Liberman, I., Shankweiler, D., Fischer, F. W., & Carter, B. (1974). Explicit syllable and phoneme segmentation in the young child. *Journal of Experimental Child Psychology, 18,* 201–212.

Lyon, R. (1997, July 10). Statement of G. Reid Lyon before the Committee on Education and the Workforce, U.S. House of Representatives, Washington, D.C.

Mann, V. A. (1986). Phonological awareness: The role of reading experience. *Cognition, 24,* 65–92.

MacKay, D. G. (1972). The structure of words and syllables: Evidence from errors in speech. *Cognitive Psychology, 3,* 210–227.

Moustafa, M. (1995). Children's productive phonological recoding. *Reading Research Quarterly, 30*(3), 464–476.

Moustafa, M. (1997). *Beyond traditional phonics: Research discoveries and reading instruction.* Portsmouth, NH: Heinemann.

Moustafa, M., & Maldonado-Colon, E. (1995). Whole to parts phonics instruction: Building on what children know to help them know more. *The Reading Teacher, 52*(5), 448–458.

Mullis, I., Campbell, J., & Farstrup, A. (1993). *NAEP 1992: Reading report card for the nation and the states.* Washington, DC: National Center for Education Statistics.

Nicholson, T. (1991). Do children read words better in context or in lists? A classic study revisited. *Journal of Educational Psychology, 83,* 444–450.

Nicholson, T., Lillas, C., & Rzoska, M.A. (1988). Have we been misled by miscues? *The Reading Teacher, 42,* 6–10.

Perfetti, C. A. (1985). *Reading ability.* New York: Oxford University Press.

Reutzel, D. R., & Cooter, R.B. (1990). Whole language: Comparative effects on first-grade reading achievement. *Journal of Educational Research, 83,* 252–257.

Rhodes, L.K. (1979). Comprehension and predictability: An analysis of beginning reading materials. In *New perspectives on comprehension* (Monograph in

Language and Reading Studies). Bloomington: Indiana University School of Education.

Ribowsky, H. (1986). *The comparative effects of a code emphasis approach and a whole language approach upon emergent literacy of kindergarten children.* Unpublished doctoral dissertation, New York University.

Richek, M. A., & McTague, B. K. (1988). The "Curious George" strategy for students with reading problems. *The Reading Teacher, 42,* 220–226.

Rosner, J. (1974). Auditory analysis training with prereaders. *The Reading Teacher, 27,* 379–384.

Ruddell, R. B. (1965). The effect of oral and written patterns of language structure on reading comprehension. *The Reading Teacher, 18,* 270–275.

Sacks, C. H., & Mergendoller, J. R. (1997). The relationship between teachers' theoretical orientation toward reading and student outcomes in kindergarten children with different initial reading abilities. *American Educational Research Journal, 34*(4), 721–739.

Scholes, R. J. (1998). The case against phonemic awareness. *Journal of Research in Reading, 21*(3), 177–189.

Slaughter, J. P. (1983). Big books for little kids: Another fad or a new approach for teaching beginning reading? *The Reading Teacher, 36,* 758–761.

Smith, F. (1988). *Understanding reading* (4th ed.) Hillsdale, NJ: Erlbaum.

Smith, N. B. (1965). *American reading instruction: Its development and its significance in gaining a perspective on current practices in reading.* Newark, DE: International Reading Association.

Stanovich, K. E. (1991). Word recognition: Changing perspectives. In R. Barr, M. L. Kamil, P. Mosenthal, & P. D. Pearson (Eds.), *Handbook of reading research* (Vol. 2, pp. 418–452). Hillsdale, NJ: Erlbaum.

Stanovich, K. E. (1994). Romance and reality. *The Reading Teacher, 47,* 280–291.

Stanovich, K. (1986). Mathew effects in reading: Some consequences of individual differences in the acquisition of literacy. *Reading Research Quarterly, 21*(4), 360–406.

Tatham, S. (1970). Reading comprehension of materials written with select oral language patterns: A study at grades two and four. *Reading Research Quarterly, 5,* 402–426.

Taylor, D. (1998). *Beginning to read and the spin doctors of science: The political campaign to change American's mind about how children learn to read.* Urbana, IL: National Council of Teachers of English.

Trachtenburg, P., & Ferruggia, A. (1989). Big books from little voices: Reaching high risk beginning readers. *The Reading Teacher, 42,* 284–289.

Treiman, R. (1983). The structure of spoken syllables: Evidence from novel word games. *Cognition, 15,* 49–74.

Treiman, R. (1985). Onsets and rimes as units of spoken syllables: Evidence from children. *Journal of Experimental Child Psychology, 39,* 161–181.

Treiman, R. (1986). The division between onsets and rimes in English syllables. *Journal of Memory and Language, 25,* 476–491.

Treiman, R., & Baron, J. (1981). Segmental analysis: Development and relation to reading ability. In G. C. MacKinnon & T. G. Waller (Eds.), *Reading research: Advances in theory and practice* (Vol. 3, pp. 159–198). New York: Academic Press.

Troia, G. A. (1999). Phonological awareness intervention research: A critical review of the experimental methodology. *Reading Research Quarterly, 34*(1), 28–52.

Tunmer, W. E., & Nesdale, A. R. (1985). Phonemic segmentation skill and beginning reading. *Journal of Educational Psychology, 77,* 417–427.

Venezky, R. L. (1967). English orthography: Its graphical structure and its relation to sound. *Reading Research Quarterly, 2,* 75–106.

Wylie, R. E., & Durrell, D. D. (1970). Teaching vowels through phonograms. *Elementary English, 47,* 787–791.

CHAPTER ELEVEN

Reading Aloud from Culturally Diverse Literature

Lee Galda and Bernice E. Cullinan

For Reflection and Action: Consider the overwhelming evidence indicating that reading aloud to children is important to their literacy development. Reflect on your own classroom or one with which you are familiar. What kinds of literature are available for children to have read to them or for them to read on their own? Do most of the textbooks and storybooks used reflect the reality of children's lives? List and share some of the things that teachers and parents need to know and do regarding children's literature and reading aloud.

Lee Galda and Bernice Cullinan address the need for literature in the lives of children and its use as a springboard to literacy.

Karen is sitting on a low chair in the front of her room and every single one of her kindergarten children is watching her raptly. If you didn't spot the book in her hand you might think she was a sorceress. How else could one person command the complete attention of 17 energetic bodies and minds? She's reading Jan Brett's *The Mitten*, and the children are following the cumulative plot in the illustrations as Karen reads the words. When she comes to the last page, with the picture of a very puzzled grandmother, they shout with laughter.

> They know something she does not! Several spontaneous dramatic reenactments follow, and then the children move into their own writing time. They know they will hear more stories before the day is through. Karen reads to them frequently, from many different kinds of books. It's difficult to tell if they love her because she reads to them or if they love the books because Karen reads them. Probably both.

When you think back over your school years, which teachers do you remember with the greatest fondness? They are probably the ones who read to you, as read-aloud time is often the most memorable experience for young children in school. As you read aloud to your own students, don't they sit attentively, watching your face and the book, edging ever closer until some are almost sitting on your lap? It's almost as if by reading aloud you're weaving a magic spell, enticing children to enter the world of the book in your hand, putting aside daily concerns for a trip to see the wild things, a chase to catch the gingerbread man, or a quiet moment looking at rain sparkling on a spider's web. You *are* creating magic, with the help of that good book in your hands.

In this chapter we will discuss the following questions:

- Why read aloud?
- What are effective ways to read aloud?
- How do I select books to read aloud?
- How do I select books for a culturally diverse read-aloud program?

Why Read Aloud?

If reading aloud were merely this magically happy experience, it would still be worth the time you took to read aloud every day. The *effect* of reading aloud—having positive experiences with books—is worth the time and effort. From it, children learn that books can bring pleasure, relaxation, excitement, and knowledge. They develop positive attitudes toward books and the people who read them (Hiebert, 1981). The book experience becomes familiar and comfortable. This positive experience can help children approach learning to read with the expectation of pleasure and success. At the same time, children are learning about reading and language (Galda & Cullinan, 1991). Among its many benefits, reading aloud

- provides opportunities for children to hear fluent reading. Often it is only through your reading aloud that children are able to hear what fluent reading sounds like. Your reading aloud can provide your students with models for their own fluent reading.
- increases children's vocabulary (Anderson, Hiebert, Scott, & Wilkinson, 1985; Ninio & Bruner, 1978). As they listen to you read they hear new and interesting words. These words become part of their receptive vocabulary and are then available for use in their reading and writing.
- provides students with models and ideas for their own writing and storytelling (Dressel, 1990; Lancia, 1997). As children listen to books read, they experience a variety of structures and techniques for telling stories and imparting information. Children can use these structures and techniques in their own speaking and writing as they explore ways of saying what they have to say (Harste, Woodward, & Burke, 1984).
- increases children's storehouse of experiences. Books offer children opportunities for experiencing people, places, and events that are not part of their actual lives as well as for gaining knowledge about things that interest them (Cullinan & Galda, 1998). The things they experience and learn through listening to the book you read aloud become part of their repertoire of experiences that allow them to understand new experiences (Anderson et al., 1985). Children learn best when they can relate new ideas to what they already know, and reading aloud increases what it is they know.
- allows children to begin to make connections among books. Hearing many books read aloud provides opportunities for comparing books, for recognizing an author's style, and for noticing what it is that writers do. Children

come to recognize the patterns that mark literature and begin to develop an understanding of what literature is and how it works (Hickman, 1981; Kiefer, 1988).

- whets children's appetites for books and expands their interests. Reading aloud from a planned variety of texts helps nudge children into trying different genres or topics or authors. It piques their interest (Cullinan & Galda, 1998).
- helps children learn how to handle books. As they watch you read they learn how to hold a book and how to turn pages.
- helps children develop many of the concepts about print that they need for their own reading and writing. If they can see the print they come to understand directionality–that one reads from front to back, left to right, and top to bottom in English. They also come to understand that print and pictures work together to tell a story, but the print is what is read. They learn that the words are always the same, no matter how many times a book is read.

Reading aloud introduces new words and presents a variety of forms of language, styles of written language, and sentence patterns. It helps children develop a sense of story, provides ideas for their writing, and enriches their general knowledge. It models the sound of good reading, motivates children to read more, and adds pleasure to the school day. For all of these reasons, reading aloud to children is certainly an important part of the school day. Because it is such an effective way of helping children develop their literacy skills, it is important to think carefully about *how* we read and *what* we read aloud.

What Are Effective Ways to Read Aloud?

One of the important skills that teachers develop is the ability to read aloud well. This is not something that we're born with but something that comes over time, with practice. Reading with the intonation, pacing, and tone that particular books require takes practice. Here are some points to keep in mind as you prepare to read aloud:

- Read the book ahead of time; be familiar with it. If you read ahead of time you have the opportunity to make decisions about how to read. Does the book require a happy, bouncing voice or a more serious, sedate tone? How do the characters sound? What words are important to emphasize? Where might you want to pause for effect? These and other considerations can help you do justice to the book you've selected.
- Develop the quality of your oral interpretation skills. Listen to professionals reading aloud on tape. Read aloud to yourself as an effective way to judge the quality of your oral interpretation. Practice until you can read using a natural voice with inflections and modulations befitting the story. Avoid greatly exaggerated voice changes and overly dramatic gestures. Read slowly, enunciate clearly, and project your voice so that your audience can hear you. This helps them become good listeners.
- If you're reading a picture book, decide whether or not you're going to show the pictures to your students. Sometimes it might be effective to read the text without showing the pictures, to encourage your students to create their own images as they listen. Creating images is an important skill for developing readers, so you might want to do this occasionally, even though the picture book format relies on illustrations and text working together to convey meaning. Some books rely so heavily on the illustrations to convey meaning that reading the text alone would not work, so you have to choose your books carefully.
- If you want to display the pictures as you read, make sure that the illustrations are large enough for all to see. If the children can see the pictures and if they know that you will make the book available to them when you have finished reading aloud, they will be more willing to forgo the close exploration of illustrations that would occur if they were holding the

book themselves. Some teachers show the pictures and read the text simultaneously, holding the book to one side. This means that you have to know the text well and be able to read sideways and upside down. With practice, it's possible, and it's a wonderful skill to have. Others read the text and then show the pictures when they pause at the end of each page.

- As you are reading, look up from the book frequently to make eye contact with your audience. If you never look at your audience you will be sure to lose the attention of those children who are just learning to sit still and listen to a book. At first you might want to plan places where you can pause to glance around the room, but as you get used to reading this will come naturally. When you are reading brief texts it is very easy to scan ahead and read from memory as you are looking at the children.
- Introduce the book to your audience and explore the parts of the book as you do. A very brief comment about why you selected a particular book will serve to capture children's attention. Looking at the cover, end pages, and title page will teach children to notice these things, give them the vocabulary to talk about them, and, again, draw their attention to the book. Reading the dedication aloud is often an effective introduction and will encourage many dedications in the children's own writing as well.
- Begin reading slowly, with frequent pauses to look at your audience, then quicken your pace as they enter the story world.
- Plan your time so that you can read the whole book, or the whole chapter or section, in one sitting.
- Plan your seating. If you have the children stay at their desks, stand as you read to make sure that everyone can see you and the book. And don't allow them to do other work as you read. This devalues the read-aloud experience by implying that it does not deserve full attention. If you have the children move to a special area, make sure that they will be facing away from distractions, such as an open door or bright windows, that might interfere with their ability to see you and the book.

As you read aloud to your students you will become an increasingly skillful oral reader. As your own skill develops, so will the pleasure that you and your students experience.

How Do I Select Books to Read Aloud?

There are several important guidelines to follow when selecting books to read aloud. Most important is to select well-written stories, poems, and nonfiction. There are so many outstanding books for children that it is a waste of time to read something inferior; the benefits of reading aloud are not as great with second-rate texts. Another basic principle to follow is to select books that vary in genre, style, and content. You will want to select books that capture your students' interests, and also books that stretch them as readers. Finally, be sure to select literature that reflects the cultural diversity in our world (Cullinan & Galda, 1998).

Most of the books that teachers of young children select to read aloud are picture books, with some transitional chapter books as well. Picture books can tell stories, elaborate concepts, or impart information—all essential to the learning, growing child. Picture books are unique to children's literature, as they are defined by format rather than content. That is, they are books in which the illustrations are of equal importance as or more important than the text in the creation of meaning. Further, they span the other, more traditional genres. They can be fantasy, folklore, contemporary realistic fiction, historical fiction, biography, science fiction, poetry, or nonfiction about any topic appropriate for children. The wide range of content available means that picture books fit quite nicely into every aspect of the curriculum that you might teach. They are also wonderful examples of visual and verbal artistry at its finest, and with careful selection they can represent many different cultures and experiences.

Selecting Quality: Evaluating Picture Storybooks

Many of the picture books that teachers read aloud are narratives, or books that tell a story. You will base your evaluation of these books on the literary elements of setting, character, plot, theme, and style, in both text and illustrations. Look for the following characteristics as you choose your books:

- Setting, or the time and place of a story, is usually presented quickly through the text and extended through the illustrations. The setting should be appropriate to the story and detailed through the illustrations so that children can clearly identify the where and when. Detailed settings are particularly important in fantasy and historical fiction.
- Characterization, or depicting characters, is a central element in picture storybooks. Characters are usually children or childlike animals, reflecting the actions, thoughts, and emotions of children in the narration, the dialogue, and the art. Central characters should be well-developed, multidimensional characters who actively participate in the story events; they often grow and change over the course of the story. An exception to this is folklore, where characters are usually stock representations of particular types, like the beautiful princess.
- Plot, or the sequence of events, is usually presented in a chronological manner, and rather quickly. It often centers on a problem that children will recognize and understand: being too small, adjusting to a new sibling, and making new friends are some common problems. Good plots are clear in both text and illustration, move forward logically, and contain a recognizable climax and a satisfying resolution.
- Themes, or the major ideas in a story, should reflect children's worlds. Memorable books usually do not blatantly state morals but create rather clear and important ideas for children to explore. We remember a theme long after hearing a story.
- Style, the way in which a book is written, is essential to the quality of a picture storybook. The language should be rich; interesting words should be used in interesting ways to build excitement and thoughtfulness. There should be a melodic quality to the language so that when you read the book aloud, it sounds natural.

Illustrations should enhance and extend the text in setting, characterization, plot, theme, style, and mood. In some books the illustrations verify the text, co-telling the same story. In others they extend the text, adding visual information or meaning not presented in language. Still other illustrations might belie the text, presenting visual information that creates a story within a story. However the illustrations work with the text, they should be appropriate to that particular text and quality art, whatever the medium or technique.

Selecting Quality: Evaluating Nonfiction Picture Books

Just as when you select picture storybooks, when choosing nonfiction picture books you will want to look for books that are wonderful examples of both language and art. They should be interesting, with content that is appropriate to the reader's age and developmental level, accurate, and consistent with current knowledge. As you are choosing nonfiction picture books, keep the following in mind:

- Nonfiction picture books should have intrinsically interesting content, be it spiders, trucks, the alphabet, or farms. Rather than just a dry accounting of a particular concept or body of knowledge, nonfiction picture books should approach the content in unique ways. Interest is often engendered by directly addressing the audience ("Look at a spider's web. What do you see?") and by illustrations that capture interest even while informing.
- Accuracy is essential in nonfiction. It is difficult to be accurate while presenting complex concepts for a young audience, but careful attention to what information is presented and how allows for both accuracy and simplicity. The text should be straightforward, plainly stating the information to be conveyed, and

the illustrations should extend that information, providing a visual representation of what the text is stating. Photographs can serve as authentic and attractive sources of information. Children go to nonfiction to learn, and what they learn should be correct!
- The structure of a nonfiction picture book should support the content being conveyed and enable young readers to build concepts rather than just learn isolated facts.

Far more than an extended encyclopedia entry, nonfiction picture books offer young readers the opportunity to learn about the world around them.

Selecting Quality: Evaluating Picture Books of Poetry and Song

Many memorable picture books present an artist's visual interpretation of a song, poem, or verse. Like other picture books, these should be interesting to and understandable by the intended audience. As you are selecting these books, think about the following:

- A picture book of poetry or song should have interesting ideas presented in beautiful, lyrical language.
- The illustrations should interpret and extend both the text and its emotional content.

Selecting Books to Enhance a Curriculum

One of the wonderful things about books for young readers is that they come in many shapes, sizes, levels, and structures. They also cover almost any content or thematic area that young children might be interested in, and they increasingly reflect the varied cultural heritage that is present in our classrooms and communities. Many teachers routinely select books for reading aloud that reflect the science, social studies, or mathematics material that they are covering in the curriculum; books supplement content curriculum well. They provide more in-depth information, a wider scope, and a greater variability in reading levels because they are many, as opposed to one textbook. Other teachers select picture books that might be good for reading to children in the hope the children will then read the book themselves; thus their selection is based on the words, sentence structures, or linguistic elements that are found in the books. Still other teachers select picture books that supplement their language arts curriculum, looking for books that demonstrate a particular writing style or form, or books that are linked to the thematic units in the basal reading materials. Sometimes teachers decide to study the work of a particular author or illustrator and select books accordingly. There are many ways to organize your read aloud curriculum!

The following brief outline of how a teacher might use picture books to study the environment is but one example of the way picture books can be inserted into the curriculum.

Curriculum-Related Study: The Natural World: Children are interested in the natural world, and eager to know more. If you want to study nature with your students, helping them develop their appreciation for their environment, you could try some of the following activities and books.

Activities

- Take a nature walk. Collect leaves, twigs, flowers, stones, and so on.
- Create a display table to hold your collected signs of nature.
- Plant seeds in paper cups. Record how long it takes them to sprout and grow. Replant in pots to take home.
- Look for places of beauty or interest around you. Draw pictures. Label items.
- Read the following books and discuss them.

Read books, such as those in the following list, that explore different facets of the environment and discuss them.

Booklist for Nature Study

J. Arnosky, *I See Animals Hiding* (Scholastic, 1995)
Betsey Bowen, *Tracks in the Wild* (Little, Brown, 1993)
Eve Bunting, *Flower Garden* (Harcourt, 1994)
Henry Cole, *I Took a Walk* (Greenwillow, 1998)

Margery Facklam, *Creepy, Crawly Caterpillars* (Little, Brown, 1996)
Denise Fleming, *In the Small, Small Pond* (Holt, 1993)
Denise Fleming, *In the Tall, Tall Grass* (Holt, 1991)
Kristine O'Connell George, *The Great Frog Race* (Clarion, 1997)
Kristine O'Connell George, *Old Elms Speaks* (Clarion, 1998)
Patricia Kite, *Down in the Sea: Jellyfish* (Whitman, 1993)
Mary Ling, *Butterfly* (Dorling Kindersley, 1997)
Betsey Maestro, *How Do Apples Grow?* (HarperCollins, 1992)
Joanne Ryder, *My Father's Hands* (Morrow, 1994)
Millicent Selsam and Joyce Hunt, *Keep Looking* (Macmillan, 1988)

Many teachers select books based on how their themes relate to the lives of the children in their classroom. For example, all children are engaged in the process of growing up and moving from home and family into school and community. Many picture storybooks and nonfiction picture books explore this process. By reading books children can relate to, teachers help children realize that *they* are reflected in the books they read. It is important for children to see themselves mirrored in their books. It is also important that children see others. Characters from varied times and places, with beliefs, values, customs, and habits that may be different from those of the reader, can provide windows into the lives of others. Reading about people like and different from themselves helps children to value themselves and others and to appreciate differences and similarities across cultures. This means, of course, that the books you choose to read aloud need to represent the cultural diversity of today's world.

How Do I Select Books for a Culturally Diverse Read-Aloud Program?

When you are selecting books that represent diverse cultures, you will want, first of all, to select quality books, as discussed earlier. You will also want to evaluate the books in terms of the authenticity and honesty of the cultural representation they convey. This isn't always easy, especially since it's hard to judge the authenticity of something you might never have experienced. Although reviews and library purchases are often a good place to begin in determining quality, screening books for cultural authenticity is difficult. It helps to have the opinions of those who are representative of various cultures and practiced in evaluating culturally diverse literature. The Multicultural Booklist Committee of the National Council of Teachers of English prepared an annotated bibliography of multicultural books published between 1990 and 1992 (Sims Bishop, 1994). Their criteria for selection included no stereotyped images in either text or illustration, no demeaning or inaccurate use of language, and no inaccuracies in text or illustration. Their booklist is a good place to start as you begin to select books for your collection.

Look for books that

- avoid stereotypes. Learn to be sensitive to stereotypes as you read.
- portray the cultural group in an authentic manner.
- use natural language that reflects but does not stereotype a particular culture.
- validate the experiences of children from that culture.
- broaden our vision and invite reflection (Cullinan & Galda, 1998).

Following is a list of some authors and illustrators from parallel cultures in America as well as other countries who write for young children. An easy way to increase the diversity of your classroom or school collection is to make sure that these authors and illustrators are well represented.

Culturally Diverse Authors

Alma Flor Ada
John Agard
Elaine Maria Alpin
Rudolfo Anaya
Jeannine Atkins
Olaf Baker
Shonto Begay
John Bierhorst
Pura Belpre
Joseph Bruchac
Maria Cristina Brusca
Ashley Bryan

AN IDEA FROM A TEACHER

A Multicultural "Me Museum"

In my classroom children are encouraged to learn about diversity and appreciate each other's cultural and personal experiences. In addition to reading multicultural literature each Friday for story time, I teach an extensive thematic unit that focuses on the child as the center of relationships. The theme is introduced as "A circle of family, friends, and people in a child's world." The goal in this unit is to teach children that they are surrounded by people who care about them, and to help them appreciate their circle of family, friends, and caregivers. Activities that foster this appreciation include team building in our class, letter writing to distant family members, reading aloud poetry and books about self, friends, and families, and sharing stories from the past during circle time about our families and friends.

Each year the favorite activity related to this unit is the "Me Museum." The Me Museum is a section of the room dedicated to learning about each member of class, one week at a time. Each child is in charge of the museum for a week. At that time, he or she displays items that reflect who the child is personally, socially, ethnically, racially, religiously, and so on. Items featured often include photographs, special books, clothing, and autobiographical items from earlier stages of life. On Friday, the child who has been "on display" is invited to tell about his selections and reads aloud one of his favorite books. This is an extremely rewarding experience for each child, and it helps the class appreciate each other for both differences and similarities.

David Conway, Second-Grade Teacher

Omar S. Castaneda
Sook Nyul Choi
Sandra Cisneros
Lucille Clifton
Floyd Cooper
Martel Cruz
Pat Cummings
Lulu Delacre
Norah Dooley
Arthur Dorros
Michelle Edwards
Valerie Flournoy
Mem Fox
Ina Friedman
Sherry Garland
Jan Spivey Gilchrist
Nikki Giovanni
Eloise Greenfield
Ann Grifalconi
Nikki Grimes
Monica Gunning
Sheila Hamanaka
Rosemarie Hausherr
Gerald Hausman
Juanita Havill
Akiko Hayashi
Daisaku Ikeda
Rachel Isadora
Leland B. Jacobs
Nina Jaffe
Aylette Jenness
Angela Johnson
Hettie Jones
Lynn Joseph
Maria Kalman
Kathleen Drull
Frane Lessac
Riki Levinson
Ted Lewin
E. B. Lewis
Myra Cohn Livingston
Gerald McDermott
Patricia McKissack
Jean Merrill
Lauren Mills
Ken Mochizuki
Tolowa M. Mollel
Pat Mora
Ann Morris
W. Nikola-Lisa
Carmen Santiago Nodar
Isaac Olaleye
Ifeoma Onyefulu
Shulamith Levy Oppenheim
Jose-Luis Orozco
Jerrie Oughton
Argentina Palacios
Brian Pinkney
Gloria Pinkney
Jerry Pinkney
Patricia Polacco
Charlotte Pomerantz
James Ransome
Kristina Rodnas
Eileen Roe
Shelley Rotner
Pam Munoz Ryan
Allen Say
Robert D. San Souci

Culturally Diverse Authors (continued)

David M. Schwartz
Cecile Schoberle
Isabel Schol
Marcia Sewall
Virginia Driving Hawk Sneve
David Soman
John Steptoe
Jenny Stow
Dorothy Strickland
Michael Strickland
Stephanie Stuve-Bodeen
Chief Jake Swamp
Rabindranath Tagore
Luci Tapahonso
Joyce Carol Thomas
Leyla Torres
Martin Waddell
Karen Lynn Williams
Janet Wong
Douglas Wood
Laurence Yep
Jane Yolen
Ed Young

All children need to find themselves and meet new people in the books they read. Affirming past experiences and participating in new ones through literature is one of the most important reasons to read. We need to be sure that our students hear stories, poems, and nonfiction works that present life from multiple perspectives. By reading books about children from diverse cultures engaged in similar processes and facing similar problems, teachers help children realize the bonds that we share as human beings, regardless of culture. And by reading books about children from diverse cultures, teachers also help children realize how they are different, and special. It is crucial to select books that represent well a variety of cultural experiences, and finally there are some wonderful books that do just that. Find them and read them to your students. We *all* need you to do just that.

References

Anderson, R. D., Hiebert, E. H., Scott, J. A., & Wilkinson, I.A. G. (1985). *Becoming a nation of readers: The report of the commission on reading.* Washington, DC: National Institute of Education.

Cullinan, B. E., & Galda, L. (1998). *Literature and the child* (4th ed.). Fort Worth: Harcourt Brace.

Dressel, J. H. (1990). The effects of listening to and discussing different qualities of children's literature on the narrative writing of fifth graders. *Research in the Teaching of English, 24*(11), 397–444.

Galda, L. & Cullinan, B. E. (1991). Literature for literacy: What research says about the benefits of using trade books in the classroom. In J. Flood, J. M. Jensen, D. Lapp, & J. R. Squire (Eds.), *Handbook of research on teaching the English language arts* (pp. 529–535). New York: Macmillan.

Harste, J., Woodward, V., & Burke, C. (1984). *Language stories and literacy lessons.* Portsmouth, NH: Heinemann.

Hickman, J. (1981). A new perspective on response to literature: Research in an elementary school setting. *Research in the Teaching of English, 15*(4), 343–354.

Hiebert, E. (1981). Developmental patterns and interrelationships of preschool children's print awareness. *Reading Research Quarterly, 16,* 236–260.

Kiefer, B. (1988). Picture books as contexts for literary, aesthetic, and real world understandings. *Language Arts, 65*(3), 260–271.

Lancia, P. J. (1997). Literary borrowing: The effects of literature on children's writing. *The Reading Teacher, 50,* 470–475.

Ninio, A., & Bruner, J. (1978). The achievement and antecedents of labeling. *Journal of Child Language, 5,* 5–15.

Sims Bishop, R. (Ed.). (1994). *Kaleidoscope.* Urbana, IL: National Council of Teachers of English.

CHAPTER TWELVE

Fostering Reading Comprehension

Linda B. Gambrell and Ann Dromsky

Linda Gambrell and Ann Dromsky focus on children's acquisition of comprehension skills and strategies as perhaps the most basic and critical component of literacy.

> ***For Reflection and Action:*** Discuss the importance of understanding and making use of what one reads. Collect and share effective strategies for promoting reading comprehension that you have used or know about.

This chapter focuses on ways to foster young children's reading comprehension. The following topics are discussed:

- Using narrative and expository text
- Strategies that foster reading comprehension
  - KWL
  - Retelling
  - Text clues
  - Text frames
- Guidelines for effective comprehension instruction

Young children are natural comprehenders. Perhaps at no other time is the need to generate meaning more fervently experienced than in early childhood. Even before children learn to read, they communicate on many levels and seek to make meaning of their surroundings. This natural curiosity heightens as children learn to read and share literature.

The sophisticated process of gaining meaning from print begins early in literacy development. Educators have moved away from viewing reading comprehension as a set of late-developing, fragmented skills to viewing it as a more interactive and sociocognitive activity. Research has revealed that young children are quite capable of complex thinking, and comprehension is now considered an integral component of early literacy instruction (Applebee, Langer, & Mullis, 1988; Morrow, 1997).

For many years, the literature on the reading process centered on the scope and sequence of skills (Dole, Duffy, Roehler, & Pearson, 1991; Fielding & Pearson, 1994). In general, students were taught *how* to read before being introduced to more cognitively challenging tasks. Common practice included teaching the alphabet and a core set of sight words, and following a prescriptive program of phonics and basal reading series in the primary grades. The emphasis on teaching basic literacy elements before high-level skills such as comprehension sparked great debate over what constituted developmentally appropriate practice. The last two decades, however, have seen a marked increase in research into and knowledge about emergent literacy and developmentally appropriate approaches for young learners. Today, we know that young children are capable of higher-level comprehension and can respond capably to literature in ways that go far beyond mere literal interpretations of text. In fact, engaging children in thinking critically and solving problems prepares them for the challenges of reading more complex text.

Constructivism and Reading Comprehension

Constructivism is a theory about knowledge and learning. Constructivist theory posits that we *construct* our own understanding of the world in which we live. We make sense of our world by synthesizing our prior knowledge with new experiences. With respect to reading comprehension, new learning is generated not by the reader alone or from the text alone, but rather from the unity of the two (Piaget & Inhelder, 1971). According to Brooks and Brooks (1993), our perceptions and understandings "are constantly engaged in a grand dance that shapes our understandings" (p. 4).

Constructivism suggests that for reading comprehension to occur, the learner must actively construct relationships between what is known and the information in the text. This model of learning suggests that teachers can play an important role in fostering reading comprehension by providing strategy instruction that engages readers in actively making connections between their prior knowledge and the text's information.

From the perspective of both constructivism and sociocognitive and interactive learning theories, reading is viewed as an interaction between and among the reader, the text, and other individuals. The dynamic process of this interaction builds children's background knowledge, concepts about books, language facility, and vocabulary through scaffolded experiences with a wide range of reading materials. This active participation in literacy events improves children's language structures and ability to comprehend text (Dole et al., 1991; Morrow, 1997).

Prior knowledge has long been recognized as the most significant predictor of comprehension; consequently, young children who actively participate in literacy experiences are better prepared to comprehend a greater variety of texts. A student's prior knowledge is continuously modified and enhanced through reading. Students who have prior knowledge about a topic are better prepared to read about that topic and determine whether the new information fits or alters existing prior knowledge (Fielding & Pearson, 1994; Morrow, 1997; Pressley, Symons, McGoldrick, & Snyder, 1995). Improved comprehension then leads to more reading, which in turn expands a child's background knowledge. This reciprocal relationship highlights the critical role of comprehension in proficient reading development (Fielding & Pearson, 1994).

Using Narrative and Expository Text

The ultimate goal of reading is to understand a text written by someone else (Pressley et al., 1995). In the primary grades, children typically read narrative texts (Trabasso, 1994). Teachers also choose narrative texts for most teacher read-alouds, and most of the books in primary grade classroom libraries are narrative texts (Chasen & Gambrell, 1992). Although access to many books is important, access to a wide variety of genres also positively influences the literacy development of young readers (Guillaume, 1998).

Length, cohesion, and grammatical structures vary with different texts. It is important in the early years to demonstrate the rich nature of text, as research suggests that even young children are highly interested in and capable of understanding exposition (Moss, 1997). Exposing children only to certain genres limits their interaction and engagement with various text structures (Dreher, 1998/1999). Exposure to a wide variety of texts improves children's comprehension of a broad range of materials and expands their background knowledge. A classroom library with a broad range of genres, teacher read-alouds from different genres, and comprehension instruction using both narrative and informational texts will strengthen and build children's background knowledge and comprehension skills.

Strategies That Foster Reading Comprehension

Strategies are plans that engage the reader in gathering, monitoring, evaluating, and using text information to construct meaning (Reutzel & Cooter, 1993). Teachers can support children in developing and using effective reading strategies in two important ways: through modeling and demonstrating strategy use, and by creating a classroom environment that encourages wide and varied opportunities to read. KWL, retelling, text clues, and text frames, described in the following sections, are examples of techniques that foster increased understanding of text. These four strategic reading activities share some features: they engage children in making personal connections between the text and their prior knowledge, support the development of higher-level thinking skills, and can be used effectively to develop an awareness of narrative and expository text structures.

KWL

KWL is a strategy that encourages children to activate their prior knowledge as they engage in answering the following questions about a particular story or topic: What do I know (K), what do I want to learn (W), and what have I learned (L). This strategy, developed by Ogle (1986), can be used with both narrative and informational text; however, it is particularly effective with informational text. It can by used with whole classes, small groups, or by individual students once they are familiar with the procedure (Tierney, Readence, & Dishner, 1995).

What Do I Know (K): The first step of the KWL strategy, what do I know, is a prereading activity in which the students engage in two levels of accessing prior knowledge: (1) brainstorming what they already know, and (2) categorizing information. Before the students read the text, the teacher prompts the children to brainstorm what they already know about the story (based on title and pictures) or the topic of the informational text. For example, the teacher might ask the children, "What do you already know about spiders?" Then the teacher creates a simple chart, and a list is made in the "What I Know" column as children contribute their ideas (see Figure 12.1). To stimulate higher-order thinking, Ogle (1986) suggests asking children where or how they got their information.

In the next phase of the "what do I know" step, the teacher helps students identify ways in which the ideas on the list can be reorganized into categories of information. For example, the list in Figure 12.1 shows three items related to things that spiders eat. These items could be reorganized under the heading of "Spider Food" or "Things Spiders Eat." The remaining items on the list, "have 8 legs" and "use spinnerets to make webs," might be listed under the heading "Spider Body Parts." This step involves complex thinking and may initially be difficult for young children. The teacher may need to scaffold instruction by modeling how categories are developed and may need to provide categories during the initial teaching of this phase of KWL.

AN EXAMPLE OF A KWL CHART

Topic: ____________________

K What I Know	W What Do I Want To Learn	L What Have I Learned
Spiders: • eat flies • eat bugs • eat moths • have 8 legs • use spinnerets to make webs		

Figure 12.1

What Do I Want To Learn (W): During the *W* step of the KWL strategy, the students are encouraged to identify gaps, inaccuracies, and inconsistencies in their prior knowledge of the topic. This step provides children with a purpose or reason for reading as they develop questions about what they want to learn. The teacher can play an important role by pointing out gaps in knowledge and helping children pose questions about things they would like to know. Reutzel and Cooter (1993) suggest having young students use the question stem, "I wonder." After group questions have been generated, children can write down any personal questions for which they would like answers.

What Have I Learned (L): This step takes place as a postreading activity. After reading the text, the students can discuss or write down what they learned. This activity can take a variety of forms. For example, the student might write answers to the questions posed during the *W* phase of KWL, or they might tell or write a concise summary of their learning. The questions and answers might be shared as a group, or children might share their ideas with a partner. Sharing knowledge learned is important because it allows children to learn from their peers as well as assess their own learning.

KWL is a highly motivating strategy that supports students in making personal connections between their prior knowledge and the text. As a result, students are prepared to think at higher levels as well as to organize many of the facts and ideas represented in the text. Research suggests that KWL increases reading comprehension and helps students learn to activate and organize their prior knowledge (Carr & Ogle, 1987; Dewitz & Carr, 1987).

Retelling

Another approach to fostering reading comprehension is to have children engage in retelling stories or information they have either listened to or read. Retelling is an effective comprehension strategy because children use their prior knowledge of story and information structures for remembering text. Retelling also helps students focus on the most relevant information, supporting details, and sequence of events.

Early studies revealed that having children retell a story after teacher read-aloud events facilitated story recall (Zimiles & Kuhns, 1976). Morrow (1984) expanded this research to analyze how retelling affected comprehension and related skills. Results suggested that some young children (kindergartners) did not seem to understand how to approach the task of retelling. Teachers in Morrow's study provided scaffolded instruction to support kindergartners in retelling stories, resulting in a dramatic improvement in young children's ability to retell stories independently. Similar results were reported in a study that provided scaffolded instruction to support children in retelling expository text (Gambrell, Kaskinen, & Kapinus, 1985). These findings are consistent with the current view that consistent, frequent scaffolded practice leads to appropriate and effective strategy application.

Research also indicates that having children retell what they have read enhances reading comprehension, as measured by literal and interpretive questions (Gambrell, Pfeiffer, & Wilson, 1985). In addition, retelling appears to enhance reading comprehension for both proficient and less proficient readers (Gambrell, Koskinen, & Kapinus, 1991). The research of Gambrell, Pfeiffer, and Wilson (1985) suggested that retelling improves reading comprehension

RETELLING PROMPTS FOR STORIES

Tell about:

- the main characters
- where the story took place
- when the story took place
- the important event that started the story (initiating event)
- the other important events in the story
- how the story ended

Figure 12.2

because students engage in rehearsing the structure and content of the text.

Some tips for helping students retell a text successfully include the following:

- Model retelling by taking a few minutes to retell a portion of a story. The modeling should include a good beginning, middle, and ending for stories, accurate sequencing for narrative text, and main ideas and supporting details for informational text.
- Retell a portion of a text that children have listened to or read and have them finish retelling the story.
- Ask students to tell what they thought was the most important or interesting event or episode in a text they have listened to or read.
- Pair students for retelling text. One partner can retell from the beginning to a specified event and the other partner can pick up the retelling at that point and retell to the end.
- During individual reading conferences, teachers can ask students to retell what they have read as an assessment of reading comprehension. Retellings can be scored for major ideas (informational text) or story grammar elements (narrative text), such as setting, initiating event, attempts, resolution, and so on.

Retelling with Partners: A typical retelling activity involves having children work together after reading a story. Students first silently read a story or portion of text, and then work with a partner in retelling the text. One partner becomes the "storyteller," who tries to retell everything that is important about the story, while the other partner is the "listener." Partners can take turns being storyteller and listener. A chart or handout with retelling prompts can support children in being successful (see Figures 12.2 and 12.3).

RETELLING PROMPTS FOR INFORMATIONAL TEXT

Tell about:

- the topic
- most important idea
- supporting ideas

Figure 12.3

Students also benefit from receiving feedback from a listener about their retelling. Providing feedback gives the student who is serving as the listener an important purpose for listening. An active listening role not only provides a purpose for listening, it helps the listener stay on task. In addition, the listeners learn to notice feature of retelling that can enhance their own retelling, and retellers get to hear compliments about their work (Koskinen, Gambrell, Kapinus, & Heathington, 1988). Using a reaction sheet like the one in Figure 12.4 can provide students with guidance in giving positive feedback to their peers.

RETELLING REACTION SHEET

Name: ______________________

Date: ______________________

I listened to ______________________

retell the story ______________________

written by ______________________.

One thing ______________ did well was:

_____ tell about the characters

_____ tell about the setting

_____ tell a good beginning

_____ tell about the events in the story

_____ tell a good ending

Figure 12.4

Retelling is grounded in an understanding of the crucial role that oral language plays in both the formation and sharing of meaning. Having the opportunity to talk about what they have read appears to facilitate children's reading and listening comprehension (Gambrell, Koskinen, & Kapinus, 1991; Gambrell, Pfeiffer, et al., 1985). It provides students with practice in comprehension as they relate one part of the text to another, draw on their prior knowledge in order to determine what is worth retelling, and begin and end with logical chunks of information.

Using Text Clues to Support Struggling Readers

Although many children come to school with excellent retelling skills, some children, particularly those who have difficulty remembering, find retelling difficult and frustrating. Using text clues is one way to support struggling readers in their efforts at retelling. Text clues are words and phrases selected from the text that "give away" or reveal the gist of the story or the most important aspects of an informational text. Teachers can prepare text clues for stories or informational text that children have either listened to or read.

After students have read a story, such as "Something from Nothing" (Gilman, 1992), the teacher prepares and then presents the students with a list of text clues. In the first part of this story a grandfather makes a baby blanket for his grandson, Joseph. The blanket gets old and worn, so Joseph's mother says, "It's time to throw it out." Joseph says, "Grandpa can fix it." The grandfather then makes his grandson a wonderful jacket out of the old blanket. When the jacket gets too small for Joseph, his mother says, "It's time to throw it out." Joseph says, "Grandpa can fix it." The grandfather then makes his grandson a vest from the old jacket. Finally, the grandfather makes a tiny button for Joseph's pants, but the button is soon lost. Joseph's mother tells him, "Even your grandfather can't make something from nothing." Joseph then goes to school, where he writes a story about his wonderful grandfather and the blanket.

After the children have listened to or read "Something from Nothing," the teacher provides a list of text clues like the ones below to support children in retelling the story:

Joseph
Grandfather
blanket
throw it out
fix it
jacket
vest
tie
handkerchief
button
gone
story

Children are asked to use the text clues to retell the story to a partner. The list of text clues can be divided in half, with child 1 retelling the first part of the story and child 2 retelling the second half. Children can also take the list of text clues home to retell the story to a family member. The scaffolding provided by the text clues supports children in being successful in retelling text and promotes the development of text structure awareness.

It is best to begin using text clues with short, simple stories and informational text. Key words and phrases that reveal significant information are selected as text clues. The text clues help children reconstruct and sequence the events in stories and the information in expository text. This technique is especially effective for children who do not have well-developed story or expository text structure awareness or do not have good memory skills.

Text Frames

Text frames can be used to develop comprehension and have been found to be effective with children as young as 5 and 6 years (Cudd & Roberts, 1987; Fowler, 1982). Text frames consist of key language structures. The key language structures or elements that are provided are often transitional and reflect a particular line of thought. Text frames can be used effectively with both narrative and expository text to help children develop a sense of text structure.

Most basic text frames can be used in both prereading and postreading activities to promote comprehension. As a prereading activity, text frames can be used to activate prior knowledge and engage children in making predictions. After reading, children use the frame to reconstruct the text. As a postreading activity text frames are especially useful as a scaffold for retelling. After children have completed a text frame, they enjoy reading and sharing their work with peers, using the frame to support their retelling.

Narrative Text Frames: Although many children come to school with a well-developed sense of story, some children have great difficulty reconstructing stories they have listened to or read. Children develop an awareness of story structure by hearing stories read aloud and by reading stories with more advanced readers. Through such exposure children develop an awareness of characters and how they relate to plot and story outcomes. According to Ruddell and Ruddell (1995), basic to awareness of story structure are

- an awareness that stories have characters, settings, an initiating event, plot episodes, and a resolution;
- a sense of sequence of events as the story unfolds;
- the ability to make simple inferences and predictions about the story events and outcomes; and
- the ability to retell and create stories in a variety of ways, such as by drawing, writing, and orally sharing these stories with other children.

Teachers who decide to use narrative text frames as a prereading activity should select appropriate stories. Stories should have a title, pictures, words, or charts that would stimulate prediction. The narrative text frame shown in Figure 12.5 is useful with stories that reflect the basic story elements of character, setting, initiating event, episodes, and resolution.

As a prereading activity children might be introduced to a story such as "The Three Little Pigs. The teacher would provide the story title and then introduce some words from the story, such as *three, pigs, wolf, huff, puff, straw, twigs,* and *bricks.* In the prereading activity, children might make predictions, as a group or individually, about what they think will happen in the story. The children would be encouraged to use as many of the words as possible in their "prediction" story.

NARRATIVE TEXT FRAME

Title: ______________________

In this story the problem begins when ________
______________________.

After that, ______________________
______________________.

Next, ______________________
______________________.

Then, ______________________
______________________.

The problem is solved when ________
______________________.

The story ends when ______________________
______________________.

Figure 12.5

After reading the story, children could fill in the narrative text frame, using their own words or referring to the text for clues. When used in postreading activities, the narrative frame focuses student attention on the major elements of basic stories and facilitates the recall of major story parts. This results in increased knowledge of story structure, which in turn helps students process text more productively and with improved comprehension. Reutzel and Cooter (1993) suggest that the greatest benefit associated with using text frames is that students begin to read more like writers because they pay more attention to structure, sequence, and meaning making.

There are a variety of narrative text frames that are useful as both pre- and postreading activities. Following are just two examples.

Someone/Wants/But/So Frame: This frame is particularly useful for problem-solution narrative stories. Figure 12.6 shows how this frame was used with the folktale, "The Turnip."

Story-Specific Frames: These frames can be developed by the teacher to provide more structure and scaffolding for the student (Cudd &

EXAMPLE OF A SOMEONE/WANTS/BUT/SO FRAME

Title: *The Turnip*

Someone	Wants	But	So
The old man	to pull the turnip up	it won't budge	he calls his whole family and all the animals to help him pull up the turnip!

Figure 12.6

Roberts, 1987). The development of these text frames requires more time and effort on the part of the teacher; however, they provide additional support for the struggling learner. An example of a story-specific frame for "The City Mouse Comes to Visit" is shown in Figure 12.7.

Expository Text Frames: Young children typically have more experience with narrative text than with expository text. Using expository text frames can support children in developing an awareness of the variety of expository text structures. Expository text frames support children's activating prior knowledge, making predictions, and determining important ideas and supporting facts.

Expository text frames help children understand and react to what they have learned. Figures 12.8 and 12.9 show two frames that are especially appropriate for activities requiring students to have read specific texts or to have studied a particular topic using a range of books and resources. Using expository text frames helps students activate their prior knowledge and attend to new information as well as the most important or most interesting information. The expository frame shown in Figure 12.8 is appropriate for younger readers, while the frame in Figure 12.9 is more advanced and requires elaboration of facts and details.

EXAMPLE OF A STORY-SPECIFIC FRAME

Title: *The City Mouse Comes to Visit*

The city mouse missed his brother. He decided to go to the ________________ to visit his brother. He loved the green ____________. But he did not like the ________________. They scared him. They had a loud ________ _________. They ________________ him and he had to run very fast to get away. The squirrels hit him with ________________. The chickens _______________ him. The city mouse could not understand why his brother loved living in the ________________. He decided that he was a ________________ mouse and his brother was a ____________ _________ mouse. He was so glad to get back to the ______________________.

Figure 12.7

EXAMPLE OF A BASIC I KNEW/I LEARNED FRAME

Topic: Snails

I learned many things about snails. I already knew that they are slimy and slow, but I learned the snails eat their shells. I also learned that they leave a slimy trail. I would like to learn more about how snails move along on the slimy trail they make.

Figure 12.8

AN IDEA FROM A TEACHER

Extending Learning by Retelling Stories

After my second graders have become familiar with the process of retelling stories, I invite them to retell the stories they have read into a tape recorder. The children listen to their recordings and assess the quality of their own retellings. In the beginning, the children follow a simple checklist of story elements on a worksheet. The worksheet has spaces for their name, the date, the title, and author of the story being told. There is the statement, "In my retelling I told about," followed by a checklist for the main characters, setting, beginning, middle, and end of the story. The children check off which parts of the story they remembered to retell. At the end of the worksheet, a space is provided for them to say what they liked best about their retelling and how they could improve. They complete the statements "One thing I did well was . . ." and "The next time I retell a story I will work on . . ." with our ideas.

Involving students in self-evaluation increases metacognition and awareness of important attributes in retelling. I even had one student tally the number of times he said "uhmm" and "and then." This student was learning to monitor and assess his retelling ability. This activity will help develop good oral speaking, listening, and learning skills.

Ann Dromsky, Second-Grade Teacher

Guidelines for Effective Comprehension Instruction

Comprehension is a complex topic for classroom teachers and researchers to address, in part because strategic readers do not use single approaches but orchestrate a number of approaches (e.g., activating prior knowledge, predicting, verbally rehearsing or retelling) when reading. Thus, instruction to aid in comprehension development is not a simple task. Although there are multiple comprehension strategies that span developmental levels, the teaching of reading comprehension entails much more than simply teaching a few strategies. The following guidelines are associated with effective instruction across a wide range of comprehension strategies and teaching techniques, such as KWL, retelling, text clues, and text frames.

EXAMPLE OF AN ELABORATED I KNEW/I LEARNED FRAME

Topic: Stars

Although I already knew that stars are hot, I learned some new things about stars. I learned that the coolest star is red, the warmest star is yellow, and the very, very hot stars are blue. I also learned that seven stars make the shape of a dipper. However, the most interesting thing I learned was that the North Star stays in its place. That's why it's called the Pole Star.

Figure 12.9

1. Teach a limited number of strategies. Focus on one strategy at a time until children are able to use and understand the approach (Pressley et al., 1995).
2. As students construct meaning, scaffold instruction to support acquisition of the strategy. Modeling is extremely important to the young child just beginning to develop more

complex interactions with text (Fielding & Pearson, 1994).

3. Be explicit in explanations of when and where to use strategies. It is important that young children develop metacognitive awareness of strategy use (Durkin, 1978/1979; Pressley et al., 1995).
4. Practice, practice, practice. Here is where literacy experts strongly agree. Proficiency in comprehension strategy use requires that students have ample opportunity to read and practice strategies (Fielding & Pearson, 1994; Pressley et al., 1995).
5. Provide children with opportunities to choose reading materials. Choice fosters motivation and gives students a chance to practice strategies with meaningful texts (Fielding & Pearson, 1994; Gambrell, 1996; Gambrell, Pfeiffer, et al., 1985).
6. Allow students to read, share, and actively discuss narrative and informational text. Encourage them to discuss their strategy use as well. Peers can reinforce strategy use and comprehension monitoring (Gambrell & Almasi, 1996).

These guidelines only begin to tap the complexity of teaching comprehension. There is a plethora of comprehension approaches and strategies that improve young children's cognition and reading. For teachers, this creates a depth versus breadth dilemma. What type of comprehension strategy instruction is most appropriate for young children? How does this instruction occur in the classroom? Clearly, effective comprehension instruction is not the same as teaching a predetermined list or number of strategies. Rather, informed teachers are familiar with a range of theory- and research-based strategies and are able to determine which strategies are most appropriate for their students.

References

Applebee, A., Langer, J., & Mullis, M. (1988). *Who reads best? Factors related to reading achievement in grades 3, 7, and 11.* Princeton, NJ: Educational Testing Service.

Brooks, J. G., & Brooks, M. (1993). *The case for constructivist classrooms.* Alexandria, VA: Association for Supervision and Curriculum Development.

Carr, E., & Ogle, D. (1987). K-W-L plus: A strategy for comprehension and summarization. *Journal of Reading, 30,* 626–631.

Chasen, S. P., & Gambrell, L. B. (1992). A comparison of teacher read aloud practices and attitudes: 1980–1990. *Literacy: Issues and Practices,* 9, 29–32.

Cudd, E. T., & Roberts, L. L. (1987). Using story frames to develop reading comprehension in a 1st grade classroom. *The Reading Teacher, 41*(1), 74–81.

Dewitz, P., & Carr, E. M. (1987, December). *Teaching comprehension as a student directed process.* Paper presented at a meeting of the National Reading Conference, St. Petersburg, FL.

Dole, J. A., Duffy, G. G., Roehler, L. R., & Pearson, P. D. (1991). Moving from the old to the new: Research on reading comprehension instruction. *Review of Educational Research, 61*(2), 239–264.

Dreher, M. J. (1998/1999). Motivating children to read more nonfiction. *The Reading Teacher, 52*(4), 414–417.

Durkin, D. (1978/1979). What classroom observations reveal about reading comprehension instruction. *Reading Research Quarterly, 15,* 481–533.

Fielding, L., & Pearson, P. D. (1994). Reading comprehension: What works. *Educational Leadership, 51*(5), 62–68.

Fowler, G. L. (1982). Developing comprehension skills in primary students through the use of story frames. *The Reading Teacher, 36*(2), 176–179.

Gambrell, L. B. (1996). Creating classroom cultures that foster reading motivation. *The Reading Teacher, 50,* 14–25.

Gambrell, L. B., & Almasi, J. F. (Eds.). (1996). *Lively discussions! Fostering engaged reading.* Newark, DE: International Reading Association.

Gambrell, L. B., Koskinen, P. S., & Kapinus, B. A. (1985, December). *A comparison of retelling and questioning as reading comprehension strategies.* Paper presented at a meeting of the National Reading Conference, San Diego.

Gambrell, L. B., Koskinen, P. S., & Kapinus, B. A. (1991). Retelling and the reading comprehension of proficient and less proficient readers. *Journal of Educational Research, 6,* 356–362.

Gambrell, L. B., Pfeiffer, W. R., & Wilson, R. M. (1985). The effects of retelling upon reading comprehension and recall of text information. *Journal of Educational Research, 78*(4), 216–220.

Gilman, P. (1992). *Something from nothing.* New York: Scholastic.

Guillaume, A. M. (1998). Learning with text in the primary grades. *The Reading Teacher, 51*(6), 476–486.

Koskinen, P. S., Gambrell, L. B., Kapinus, B. A., & Heathington, B. S. (1988). Retelling: A strategy for enhancing students' reading comprehension. *The Reading Teacher, 41*(9), 892–896.

Morrow, L. M. (1984). Effects of story retelling on young children's comprehension and sense of story structure. In J. A. Niles & L. A. Harris (Eds.), *Changing perspectives on research in reading/language processing and instruction* (pp. 95–100). Thirty-third yearbook of the National Reading Conference. Rochester, NY: National Reading Conference.

Morrow, L. M. (1997). Literacy development in the early years. Needham Heights, MA: Allyn & Bacon.

Moss, B. (1997). A qualitative assessment of first grader's retelling of expository text. *Reading Research and Instruction, 37*(1), 1–13.

Ogle, D. (1986). A teaching model that develops active reading of expository text. *The Reading Teacher, 39,* 564–570.

Piaget, J., & Inhelder, B. (1971). *The psychology of the child.* New York: Norton.

Pressley, M., Symons, S., McGoldrick, J. A., & Snyder, B. L. (1995). Reading comprehension strategies. In M. Pressley & W. Woloshyn (Eds.), *Cognitive strategy instruction that really improves children's academic performance* (pp. 57–100). Cambridge, MA: Brookline Books.

Reutzel, R. E., & Cooter, R. B. (1993). *Teaching children to read: From basals to books.* New York: Macmillan.

Ruddell, R. B., & Ruddell, M. R. (1995). Teaching children to read and write. Boston: Allyn & Bacon.

Tierney, R., Readence, J. E., & Dishner, E. K. (1995). *Reading strategies and practices: A compendium.* Needham Heights, MA: Allyn & Bacon.

Trabasso, T. (1994). The power of the narrative. In F. Lehr & J. Osborne (Eds.), *Reading, language, and literacy: Instruction for the twenty-first century* (pp. 187–200). Hillsdale, NJ: Erlbaum.

Walker, B. (1996). *Diagnostic teaching of reading: Techniques for instruction and assessment.* Englewood Cliffs, NJ: Merrill.

Zimiles, H., & Kuhns, M. (1976). *A developmental study in the retention of narrative material.* Final Report (Research Report 134), Banks Street College of Education. Washington, DC: National Institute of Education.

CHAPTER THIRTEEN

Assessing Reading and Writing in the Early Years

Bill Harp and Jo Ann Brewer

For Reflection and Action: Investigate and share what you learn about the major methods now used to assess literacy in your school or a school with which you are familiar. What is measured by each of these assessments? How is the information used?

Bill Harp and Jo Ann Brewer offer an abundance of practical suggestions as they stress the need for classrooms where instruction and assessment are highly interrelated.

The year 1998 saw remarkable consensus around important issues in bringing young children to literacy. The National Research Council (NRC) issued a landmark report entitled *Preventing Reading Difficulties in Young Children.* The International Reading Association (IRA) and the National Association for the Education of Young Children (NAEYC) issued a joint position statement entitled "Learning To Read and Write: Developmentally Appropriate Practices for Young Children." Both of these important documents drew on years of research in early literacy to make significant recommendations (some controversial) for programs and practices.

We begin this chapter by looking at the recommendations in these reports that have implications for assessment and evaluation with young readers and writers. By the end, we will have addressed all of the following topics:

- The assessment goals drawn from the NRC study and the IRA/NAEYC position statement
- How to use anecdotal records, checklists, and rating scales to record growth in literacy
- How to organize a literacy portfolio for a young child
- How attitude and interest surveys can be used in planning effective literacy instruction
- How to assess a child's knowledge of print features
- How to assess phonemic awareness
- How to assess a child's reading behavior and individualize instruction
- How to assess a child's writing behavior
- How to use reading and writing interviews as assessment procedures
- How to use a developmental continuum for assessing performance

The NRC Report

The NRC report recommends that attention be paid in every primary grade classroom to the full array of early reading accomplishments that children must make in order to be successful readers. These accomplishments are the development of phonemic awareness, understanding the alphabetic principle, developing a sight vocabulary, reading words by mapping speech sounds to parts of words, achieving fluency, and comprehension. The report further recommends that comprehension be enhanced by instruction aimed at developing background knowledge, concept and vocabulary growth, and knowledge about the syntax and rhetorical structures of written language. The 17-member committee that developed the NRC report also recommends direct instruction in comprehension strategies such as summarizing, predicting, and monitoring. With regard to spelling and writing, the committee points out that instruction should be designed with the understanding that the use of invented spelling is not in conflict with teaching correct spelling. The writers note that beginning writing with invented spelling can actually be helpful in developing an understanding of segmentation in speech sounds and of phonics. However, the report states that correct spelling should be developed through careful instruction and practice, with final writing products correctly spelled.

Before we examine the assessment and evaluation implications of the NRC report, we shall look at the recommendations in the IRA/NAEYC joint position statement.

IRA/NAEYC Joint Position Statement

The instructional recommendations contained in the IRA/NAEYC joint statement are remarkably like those in the NRC report. Like the NRC report, the joint statement underscores the value of children developing phonemic awareness and understanding the alphabetic principle, the temporary use of invented spelling, the development of vocabulary and comprehension, and systematic code instruction, along with the reading of meaningful texts. But unlike the NRC report, the joint statement offers specific recommendations for assessment and evaluation. The joint statement calls for accurate assessment of children's knowledge, skills, and dispositions in reading and writing. It cautions that reading and writing cannot simply be measured as a set of narrowly defined skills on standardized tests.

The joint report makes the following statement about assessment:

> [S]ound assessment should be anchored in real-life writing and reading tasks and continuously chronicle a wide range of children's literacy activities in different situations. Good assessment is essential to help teachers tailor appropriate instruction to young children and to know when and how much intensive instruction on any particular skill or strategy might be needed (p. 206).

The joint report calls for teachers to understand a developmental continuum of reading and writing and to be skilled in a variety of strategies to assess and support each child's development and learning across the continuum. In addition to tracking children's progress across a developmental continuum, teachers are urged to regularly and systematically use multiple assessments of reading and writing growth, such as observation of children's oral language, evaluation of children's work, and evaluation of performance on authentic reading and writing tasks.

The use of multiple-choice, standardized tests of reading and writing before third grade, and preferably before fourth grade, is strongly discouraged by the IRA and NAEYC. The joint statement offers the following argument against such practice:

> The younger the child, the more difficult it is to obtain valid and reliable indices of his or her development and learning using one-time test administrations. Standardized testing has a legitimate function, but on its own it tends to lead to standardized teaching—one approach fits all—the opposite of the kind of individualized diagnosis and teaching that is needed to help young children continue to progress in reading and writing (p. 210).

We can draw on both the NRC report and the IRA/NAEYC joint statement to guide us in planning assessment and evaluation activities in kindergarten through second grade.

Report Implications for Assessment and Evaluation in Kindergarten Through Grade 2

When we examine the instructional recommendations in both reports and the assessment recommendations in the joint report, we are able to list important areas in which kindergarten through grade 2 teachers should assess and evaluate children's performance. By *assess* we mean collect data. By *evaluate* we mean interpret that data to make instructional decisions. Figure 13.1 lists the assessment and evaluation goals for reading and writing in kindergarten through second grade culled from these reports.

With the assessment and evaluation goals identified, we now turn our attention to the tools we can use to meet these goals. Fortunately, several of the goals can be met through the use of a single tool. We will not need to use 15 tools to meet our 15 goals. However, we must keep one recommendation of the joint report in mind: Sound assessment should be anchored in real-life writing and reading tasks and should continuously chronicle a wide range of children's literacy activities in different situations.

The Power of Observation

We begin with a focus on observation because of the power it holds for us in understanding the behavior, attitudes, and understandings of our learners, both as readers and as writers. One of our most important goals in working with children is to deepen and extend our knowledge base so that we can become increasingly more careful and analytical observers of children.

When taken with care, informal observations can be enormously helpful to teachers in planning appropriate instruction for each young child. Learning to be a close observer of children is a skill that is valuable, and one that can be learned.

In addition to being an informed observer of children, we need to develop efficient ways to record our observations and analyze them for instructional purposes. Observational recording systems include anecdotal records, checklists, and rating scales. Different kinds of observations are recorded using each of these devices.

When making observations, you must first decide what kind of information is needed and what form of observation would be most efficient in obtaining that information. Anecdotal records have the advantage of providing more detail for later use, while checklists and rating scales are much quicker to use and do not require as much skill on the part of the observer. In comparison with anecdotal records, however, checklists and rating scales provide only limited information.

GOALS FOR READING AND WRITING ASSESSMENT AND EVALUATION, K–2

1. Continually expands oral vocabulary
2. Has phonemic awareness
3. Has knowledge of letter names
4. Knows conventions of print (i.e., we read from right to left and from top to bottom)
5. Has knowledge of the alphabetic principle
6. Matches spoken words to written ones
7. Increasingly develops sight vocabulary
8. Uses invented spellings, moving toward conventional spellings
9. Decodes and blends sounds in words
10. Reads with increasing fluency
11. Writes with increasing fluency
12. Writes across genres and for varying audiences
13. Uses graphophonic, semantic, and syntactic cues with increasing efficiency
14. Uses strategies (predicting, confirming, summarizing, monitoring) when comprehension breaks down
15. Reads with increasing comprehension

Figure 13.1

Anecdotal Records

An anecdotal record is a recording of factual information. Most anecdotal records are short and record only one incident. Anecdotal records can be used to document behavior or social interactions as well as academic goals. Teachers choosing to use anecdotal records must consider the limitations and possible biases that can be involved in teacher records. Bias may exist on the part of the teacher or the child being observed. Teachers tend to see what they are looking for in children. For example, if the teacher feels that a child is not learning, then he or she might be more likely to record incidents focusing on the child's needs and ignore incidents that might indicate strengths. We also know that children are likely to change their behavior if they know they are being observed. We know that one anecdotal record is not very helpful, but a collection gathered over time may reveal meaningful patterns that can guide the teacher's planning. Teachers who are aware of the possible limitations or biases of anecdotal records will take records frequently and interpret these records with care.

An anecdotal record should be as objective as we can make it. We try to record only what we observe, and if we make interpretations of those observations, we will make those interpretations clear in the record. For example, if we see a child slap a book down on a table, we could record that the child slapped the book on the table, but if we decide that the slapping behavior was a result of frustration on the child's part, that is an interpretation. Only if the child tells us that he "cannot read that awful book" do we have assurance that the feeling was frustration. Perhaps it was triumph over having finished his first book that led to slapping the book on the table.

We shall focus on the goals listed in Figure 13.1 and describe some possibilities for making useful anecdotal records related to those goals. For example, phonemic awareness means that a child knows that words are made up of a series of sounds. Phonemic awareness can be observed as children attempt to sound out the words they encounter in print. Children who have developed phonemic awareness can also participate easily in rhyming games or in activities in which they combine onsets with a variety of different rimes and determine which ones can be words.

Children's knowledge of letter names can be observed as a child plays with magnetic letters or selects letters from a box as a teacher requests them. Children frequently comment on their own knowledge by pointing out letters that are in their names or the names of their friends. While the teacher is reading a big book, some children will comment on the letters they are seeing.

As we observe children writing, we can easily record whether the child knows the principles of directionality in written English. Children can also make their knowledge of these principles clear as they use the pointer to lead the reading of a big book, a poster, or a song chart.

Children who are writing letters to record their messages have obviously learned the alphabetic nature of English and that sounds are recorded with letters. Even children who are in the random letter stage of spelling development know that it takes letters to record words and that words are not written with one letter used over and over.

Children who can follow along with their fingers in a small book while the teacher reads the print from a big book or who can follow the words in a small song book while the class sings the song are able to match spoken words to written ones. Children can also be observed trying to match the print to the words they know. For example, they may have memorized the text of a simple book, but when they read it themselves, they may make no effort to match what they are saying to the print. As children become more aware of the print, they can be observed matching the print with the words they say or becoming confused if they are unable to make the print and their spoken words match.

As we observe children demonstrating various literacy abilities, we should date the record and record briefly what was observed and under what circumstances. For example, a record might read as follows:

> 11/1/99 Juan was using the pointer to lead the group in singing "Row, Row, Row Your Boat." He pointed to the correct word with 100% accuracy.

Or a record might read:

> 10/2/99 Susie was playing with the alphabet letters and naming them as she placed them on the magnetic board. She named all of the letters accurately except Q.

Because teachers make many observations in the course of a day, there will never be time to rewrite them in another form after school, so we suggest that teachers keep anecdotal records on computer labels or some other self-sticking material that can be placed directly in the child's record. A loose-leaf binder with a page for each child is one way to store these records. If you complete more formal observation tasks, these records can also be placed in the binder. Such records need to be reviewed on a regular basis and evaluated. These observations guide daily planning as teachers think about what a child or children need to be better readers or writers. A summary statement of all observations and indications for instruction can be made every grading period or every month.

Anecdotal records can also be extremely useful in recording the child's attitudes toward reading and writing. For example, when choices are allowed in the classroom, how often does the child choose to read or write? How excited is the child to find a word that she recognizes in the newspaper? Do the children bring to school drawings or writing they have done at home? How often does the child bring a book to school that she is reading at home? Does the child choose to participate in story sessions? Does the child initiate literacy activities, such as making signs in the block areas or writing a prescription for a patient in the doctor's office? It is important for us to know whether the child's interests in reading and writing are being strengthened or weakened.

Anecdotal records can provide information that we cannot access in other ways, but for some information, a quick check to show who can or cannot complete some tasks may be enough to aid classroom planning. One alternative to the anecdotal record is a checklist.

Checklists

A checklist is a list on which the teacher records an observation of a task being completed. Usually a checklist is dated whenever a certain task is observed, but the checklist does not indicate how many trials were necessary or with what level of skill the task was completed. For example, a checklist might have an item labeled "chooses a book," meaning that the child chooses a book for sustained silent reading. It is dated whenever the child is able to go to the bookshelves and choose a book without prompting from the teacher.

A checklist might also be used to record such observations as the use of various strategies when the child is reading. For example, the checklist might be labeled "reads on," "checks illustrations," or "asks a friend," and when the child is observed using these strategies, it can be recorded on a checklist. Checklists might be more formal, such as the list in Figure 13.2, which helps teachers record reading behaviors that are important as children develop as readers.

READING CHECKLIST

Emergent Reader Behaviors

- Enjoys listening to stories, rhymes, songs and poems
- Eagerly participates in group stories, rhymes, songs, and poems
- Approaches books with enthusiasm
- Revisits some books
- Knows that his or her language can be written and then read
- Understands how to handle books for reading
- Is able to make predictions and follow plot
- Knows some print conventions (period, question mark)
- Knows some book conventions (front cover, back cover, title page)
- Uses reading in play activities
- Uses pictures to help create meaning
- Is developing finger, print, and voice matching
- Identifies some words
- Is beginning to use graphophonic cues
- Is beginning to develop strategies to use when meaning fails

Developing Reader Behaviors

- Eagerly attends to long books in reading and listening
- Shows an interest in meeting challenges of texts
- Displays confidence as a reader; is willing to take risks and make predictions
- Is eager to share ideas with others
- Has increasing knowledge of book and print conventions
- Understands how background knowledge contributes to meaning
- Appreciates the value of predicting, confirming, and integrating
- Has several strategies to invoke when meaning fails
- Increasingly makes more accurate predictions
- Reads increasingly more complicated texts across a range of genre
- Chooses to read independently

Fluent Reader Behaviors

- Expects books to offer a variety of meanings, some satisfying, some not
- Is confident as a reader
- Eagerly participates in book discussions, author studies, and other forms of response to literature
- Appreciates the power of reading
- Uses the cueing systems that best meet the reading needs and demands of the text
- Understands the role of purpose in reading
- Knows how to use the library to get information and meet needs
- Knows how to use electronic media to get information and meet needs
- Demonstrates increasing sophistication in prediction, sampling, confirming, and integrating as a reader
- Is developing study skills and can use textbook features
- Is able to summarize, outline and retell in detail (Harp, 1996)

Figure 13.2

You may find it useful to add columns to the checklist so that you can record the dates of your observations or add qualifiers to your observations. For example, if the checklist called for observing whether a child chose a book that was appropriate for independent reading, then a rating scale might add "not yet," "some of the time," or "most of the time."

All of the observations you make and the materials you select to illustrate those observations can be stored in a portfolio. Portfolios can be invaluable to a teacher in planning instruction and conferencing with parents and learners.

Portfolios

Portfolios can be described as a systematic means of collecting information that will document the child's progress in the development of literacy and inform the planning for instruction. Examples of a child's work can be collected that specifically demonstrate a given skill or ability. For example, running records made on a regular basis provide the teacher with knowledge of the child's sight vocabulary, his ability to decode unknown words, and his ability to apply reading strategies. These records can also indicate the fluency with which the child reads and the richness of retellings. As children write, many of the other objectives of a good literacy program can be observed. The writing piece through which the ability is demonstrated can be placed in the portfolio. For example, a child may leave a space between words in her writing for the first time. This piece can be dated and placed in the portfolio with a short note explaining why it has been saved. As children write more accurately (employ more of the conventions of print), samples of their writing are placed in their portfolios.

The danger of a portfolio is that it can easily become so unwieldy that the teacher cannot organize it or make sense of it. One way to avoid that pitfall is to keep a list of the objectives on the front of the portfolio and mark each entry to match the objective. If the entry does not match any of the objectives, perhaps it should be eliminated. On the objective list, you can record a tally mark when you have included a sample to illustrate one of the objectives. Objectives without tally marks should be readily apparent, and teachers can then pay attention to collecting samples for those objectives.

The portfolio should be evaluated every few weeks so that old examples can be removed and new, up-to-date examples of abilities added. A short summary of the child's growth (with specific references to pieces in the portfolio) can be written every few weeks and new goals set for the child. Even very young children should participate in setting the new learning goals. For example, with a kindergarten child, it would be appropriate to review with the child what he has learned and talk about what he can learn next. If Raymond has learned the directional principles of print, then the teacher might help him plan to learn to match spoken words to print. Older children can see that they are using more conventional writing and set a goal to learn to write in a new genre or for a new audience.

All anecdotal records and checklist information can be placed in a portfolio. The goal of keeping all of these observations is to form an accurate picture of the child and the child's growth in literacy. Keeping careful records for each child will help teachers know more about the child's progress and ensure that no child slips through the cracks and fails to make progress.

A final component of an effective portfolio is the child's self-assessment. Children can either write or dictate what they have learned and what they are interested in learning. Such self-evaluations can be linked to attitude or interest surveys, which can be revisited so that the child can make comments on any changes in them or link an interest to an area of growth.

Attitude and Interest Surveys

Attitude surveys are sets of questions used by teachers to assess children's feelings toward particular subjects. A number of attitude surveys have been published. Surveys that assess attitude typically make statements to which children respond indicating the strength of their feelings in response to given statements. Statements on reading attitude surveys typically include: I like to read at home; Reading is fun at school; I like reading more than watching TV; I enjoy going to the library; I like to get books as gifts. Writing attitude surveys typically include such statements as "I am a good writer," "I like to write," "I like it when other people read my writing," "I like to get help when I am writing," "I like to write at home." Other surveys include open-ended questions to which children are asked to respond. They might ask "What do you like to read most?" or "What kinds of writing do you like to do?"

Interest inventories are questionnaires aimed at tapping into each child's interests so that the teacher can choose materials or activities that would engage the child. Interest inventories in reading and writing could ask "What are your favorite books?" "Where do you like to read?" "What do you think you should do to become a better reader?" "What do you like to write?" "Where do you like to write?" "What should you do to become a better writer?" Such inventories could also ask what the child likes to read about, what parts of school he or she likes best, and any other questions that might aid the planning of instruction. If the child likes books about dogs or fantasy books, then the teacher makes such books available. If the child likes to write at home more than at school, then the teacher might try to determine how to make the school environment more conducive to writing.

Putting Research Into Practice: Assessing and Evaluating Reading

In this section we offer suggestions about how to meet some of the assessment goals listed in Figure 13.1. Each assessment strategy or tool is linked to specific goals.

Concepts About Print (Goals 4 and 6 in Figure 13.1)

Children come to us in kindergarten and first grade with widely varying experiences and understandings about print and how it works. Some have benefited from many hours of being read to at home and have had many experiences with paper and writing instruments. Others, unfortunately, have had very limited experiences with print. One early assessment and evaluation task is to learn what these children understand about print and how it functions.

One way to assess children's concepts about print is to perform a series of tasks designed by Marie Clay, using either of two small paperback books, *Stones* (Clay, 1979) or *Sand* (Clay, 1972). The tasks, done one-on-one with a child, take about 10 minutes to complete. The purpose of the tasks is to help you understand what the child knows about print and how it is used in books. You hand the child the book and then observe his or her behavior as you ask a series of questions. You will be able to determine what the child knows about how to hold books, whether the child knows that print, not pictures, carries the meaning, what the child knows about directionality with print, and the child's concepts of letters and words, as well as other important information. Complete instructions for administration and scoring are found in Marie Clay's *An Observation Survey of Early Literacy Achievement* (1993).

This assessment and evaluation tool is only one in an array of tools you can use to learn more about children as readers. In New Zealand, Clay's surveys on print tasks are used as one way to obtain information about each 5-year-old as he or she enters school. When you discover that a child does not know how to orient a book for reading, does not know that we read from left to right and from top to bottom, or does not know the difference between words and letters, you can use this information to structure lessons using big books and shared reading. After introducing these understandings in shared reading, you can then reinforce them when working one-on-one with children.

Phonemic Awareness (Goal 2 in Figure 13.1)

In addition to children's concepts about print, research supports the importance of phonemic awareness in beginning reading. We must carefully assess and evaluate children's growth in this important aspect of learning to read. Both the NRC report and the IRA/NAEYC joint statement underscore the importance of phonemic awareness in learning to read. The NRC report (1998) defines phonemic awareness as "the insight that every spoken word can be conceived as a sequence of phonemes. Because phonemes are the units of sound that are represented by the letters of an alphabet, an awareness of phonemes is key to understanding the logic of the alphabetic principles and thus to the learnability of phonics and spelling" (p. 52). Cunningham (1988) defined phonemic awareness as the ability to manipulate the sounds of language independent of meaning. Phonemic awareness is not one skill that a child has or does not have; it is a cluster of skills. For example, a child may be able to recognize rhyming words, then be able to manipulate the beginning sounds of words, and finally to segment all the phonemes in a given word. The research evidence suggests that phonemic awareness is strongly related to success in reading and spelling acquisition.

Hallie Kay Yopp has developed the Yopp-Singer Test of Phoneme Segmentation, first introduced in the September 1995 issue of *The Reading Teacher* (pp. 20–29). It measures a child's ability to separately articulate the sounds of a spoken word in order. For example, when you pronounce the word *dig,* the child should respond with three separate sounds: /d/-/i/-/g/. To get credit for the item the child must produce the individual sounds, not the letter names. The test has 22 items and takes about 10 minutes to administer. The items are shown in Figure 13.3.

The Yopp-Singer Test of Phoneme Segmentation may be used to give you an idea of how phonemically aware your learners have become. Performance on this test will likely vary greatly across a group of 5- or 6-year-olds. A child who correctly responds to all or nearly all of the items is demonstrating considerable phonemic awareness. The child who correctly segments some of the items is demonstrating emerging phonemic awareness. There are many instructional activities you can provide for children who need to develop phonemic awareness. Following are some examples.

YOPP-SINGER TEST OF PHONEME SEGMENTATION

Student's Name: ______________________

Date: ______________________

Score (number correct): ______________________

Directions: Today we're going to play a word game. I'm going to say a word and I want you to break the word apart. You are going to tell me each sound in the word in order. For example, if I say "old," you should say "/o/ - /l/ - /d/." (Administrator: Be sure to say the sounds, not the letters in the word.) Let's try a few together.

Practice items: (Assist the child in segmenting these items as necessary.) ride, go, man

Test items: (Circle those items that the student correctly segments; incorrect responses may be recorded on the blank line following the item.)

1. dog	________	12. lay	________
2. keep	________	13. race	________
3. fine	________	14. zoo	________
4. no	________	15. three	________
5. she	________	16. job	________
6. wave	________	17. in	________
7. grew	________	18. ice	________
8. that	________	19. at	________
9. red	________	20. top	________
10. me	________	21. by	________
11. sat	________	22. do	________

Figure 13.3

Song Charts: Children learn to sing a song by rote and then to follow the lyrics as they are presented on a chart and subsequently in individual copies. Once the children have mastered the one-to-one matching of words to print, the teacher can manipulate the print by changing the beginning sounds to create new words to sing. If the children learned "Row, row, row your boat," then the manipulation might be to sing *float, coat, moat, goat,* and so on (emphasizing the fact that some inventions are nonsense).

Rhyming Books: After reading books with rhyming texts, the children can fill in the rhyming words as teachers read the book, stopping before the rhyming words. A chart of other words that rhyme with each of the words in the story could be created. For example, after reading *In the Tall, Tall Grass* (Fleming, 1991), a chart of the words to rhyme with lunch, sip, hum, flap, and so on could be created. As the teacher reads the lists of rhyming words, the children can be asked to identify the beginnings of the words as well as the rhymes.

Environmental Print: Children can bring labels from items they eat or use at home and a large bulletin board can be created with a section for each letter of the alphabet. The words can be reviewed whenever a new label is brought to school so that the children can decide where it should be placed. Children who indicate that they understand the first letters could be asked to arrange items into sections that end with the same sound (not all 26 letters, since English words do not end in vowels except silent *e* and *y* or *w* when they represent vowel sounds, nor do they end with the consonants *q, v,* or *j*).

Taking Dictation: As teachers record words or sentences dictated by the children, they emphasize each of the phonemes as they are recorded. Because it takes a few seconds to write each word, this exercise provides an opportunity for stretching out the sounds in a more authentic use of language than drills conceived for this purpose.

Running Records (Goals 5, 6, 7, 9, 10, and 14, in Figure 13.1)

When children begin reading connected text, we need to carefully monitor their progress. We find running records a very useful tool for this purpose.

Marie Clay (1993) invented running records as a method for closely observing and recording children's reading behavior. Running records are observations of a child's oral reading behavior. The markings follow a standard set of conventions so that any teacher familiar with running records would be able to reconstruct exactly what the child did while reading. Running records are not tests in the usual sense of the word; they are used to plan instruction and to communicate to the child (and others) goals for an individual child. The analysis will record what the child can do and what cueing systems are used; evaluative words such as good and bad are not part of the running record.

Space limitations prevent us from offering a detailed discussion of how to make and analyze running records. However, we view running records and their careful interpretation as a critical part of good primary grade assessment and evaluation in reading. We refer teachers to *An Observation Survey of Early Literacy Behavior,* by Marie Clay, for a detailed discussion of running records.

For young children (kindergarten through second grade), running records should be made every 3 to 4 weeks. The child at this age is typically making such rapid progress that a running record is out-of-date in a short time.

Putting Research Into Practice: Strategies for Assessing and Evaluating Writing

As young children begin writing, the scribbles they produce reflect their attempts to gain control of the form—to make the writing instrument make a line where they want it to mark. Most children then begin to scribble in forms that look like the writing of their communities. When a child is an English language community, the writing often resembles wavy lines going across the page. Next the child will begin to add letters, numerals, or symbols to his writing. With a little more experience, the child begins to write mostly letters and believes that the letters can be read. This stage, called random letter writing, leads to phonetic writing, in which the child records sounds with specific letters. In the next stage, the child spells some words conventionally and some words phonetically. Finally, the child spells most words conventionally. As the young child is learning about how words are recorded, he is also learning other writing rules. For example, children learn that English is written from left to right and top to bottom and that sentences begin with capital letters and end with periods. They continue to learn about the functions of print as they leave messages, write explanations, compose stories, and make lists.

In assessing children's writing, the goal is to uncover the child's knowledge about written language, which will guide the teacher in planning instruction for the child. Clay (1975, 1993) recommends that writing be evaluated in terms of the language the child uses, the concepts about the purposes of writing that are displayed, and the directional principles that are evident. In terms of language, the rater determines whether the child used letters, a word, a word group, a sentence, a punctuated story, or a paragraphed story. In trying to determine the child's concept about the functions of print, the rater determines if the child: conveys a message, copies a message, uses a sentence pattern repetitively, attempts to write a message, or produces a complete composition. In examining directional principles, the child is rated as exhibiting no evidence of directional knowledge, some knowledge of directional principles, correct use of directional principles, correct use of directional principles and spacing between words, or having no difficulties arranging text on a page.

For more experienced first-grade writers and most second-grade writers, we suggest that teachers examine samples of the child's writing on three dimensions—meaning, structure, and conventions. In meaning, we look for ideas, clarity, and relevance to form and the purposes of writing. In assessing structure, we look at organization, unity, and sequence. As we look at conventions, we focus on spelling, vocabulary, usage, and punctuation. Teachers can determine which system of assessment best meets the needs of their students. Each of the assessments suggested will provide the teacher with specific information about the child's developing skill as a writer and will guide instructional planning. For example, if the child is using capital letters at the beginning of sentences and periods at the end of the sentence, but not using the apostrophe of possession, you can help the child learn to use that mark. If the child is not aware of directional principles, you can model these principles while reading aloud and while demonstrating writing. If the child does not sequence the elements of his story properly, you could put the story on sentence strips which are then cut apart, and ask the child to reorganize the sentences. Good assessment leads to good instruction that is useful to the learner.

Putting Research Into Practice: Strategies for Assessing and Evaluating Both Reading and Writing

There are some assessment and evaluation strategies that apply equally well to both reading and writing. There is no point in discussing their applications in these two areas separately. Here we look at the power of reading and writing interviews and a developmental continuum in reading and writing.

Reading and Writing Interviews (Goals 4, 5, 6, 7, and 14 in Figure 13.1)

Reading interviews are question-and-answer sessions conducted one-on-one between you and your students. The purpose of the interview is to learn how children view reading and to gain insight into their understanding of the reading process and how it operates. We suggest conducting these interviews as early in the school year as possible and with each child who comes new to your room during the year. Some teachers find it helpful to conduct reading interviews periodically throughout the year to track children's changing views as they learn more about reading and the reading process.

When interviewing children about reading, you may wish to ask some of the following questions:

What is reading?
What do you do when you read?
If you wanted to help someone be a better reader, how would you help that person?

For children who are beyond the emergent reader stage, you may wish to ask additional questions, such as:

What parts of the text you read were difficult for you?

What made them difficult?
When you come to a difficult part, what do you do?
When you don't understand what you are reading, what do you do?

Children's responses to questions like the above can give you valuable insight into what beginning readers know or anticipate reading to be, and what kinds of instruction developing readers may have previously experienced. For example, if a beginning reader responds to "What is reading?" by saying, "Reading is saying words," you will know that you need to work on helping that child appreciate reading as a meaning-making process as you read to children and as you do shared reading. If a child new to your second-grade room responds to the same questions with "Reading is sounding out words," you may suspect that he or she has had intensive phonics instruction but does not appreciate the role phonics plays in helping readers create meaning with text.

Interviewing children about the views of writing is easily done during writing conferences. Questions you may wish to ask about writing include:

What are you doing well as a writer?
What is something new you have learned to do as a writer?
What would you like to be able to do better as a writer?
When you have trouble with your writing, what do you do?
If you were going to help someone become a better writer, how would you do it? (Harp, 1996)

A Developmental Continuum (All Goals Listed in Figure 13.1)

Learning to read and learning to write are both highly developmental processes. The use of a developmental continuum helps us maintain a developmental perspective and track the progress our learners are making.

Developmental continua specify indicators at various stages of development that guide our assessment and evaluation of children's progress in reading and writing. Developmental continua are a resource to help us look at what children can do as readers and how they do it. In this way we are able to look at accomplishments and plan for instruction that carries children further along the path toward fluency. Some school systems have developed their own continua as part of curriculum frameworks. There are commercially available continua such as those in the Australian program, *Reading Developmental Continuum* and *Writing Developmental Continuum* (Education Department of Western Australia, 1997).

Space limitations preclude the inclusion of a developmental continuum in this chapter. However, we recommend that you consider the continuum presented in the IRA/NAEYC's 1998 joint position statement, "Learning to Read and Write." We recommend this particular continuum because for each phase, examples of what children can do are offered, as well as examples of what teachers can do and what parents and family members can do. This view of reading and writing instruction as a collaboration between learner, teacher, and family is also consistent with the recommendations of the NRC.

We recommend that you make copies of the continuum so that you have one per student. You can then develop a schedule that will allow you to carefully observe each of your learners as readers and writers for the purpose of placing them on the continuum. For example, at the beginning of the year, you should make judgments as quickly as possible (in the first 2 weeks) about each learner. As you observe a behavior, note the date on the continuum when you are confident that behavior is consistently exhibited. After you have placed each child on his or her continuum, create a schedule so that you deliberately reconsider each child in light of the continuum. If you have 24 students, you might identify which six that you will carefully attend to—in terms of the continuum—each week. That way, every 4 weeks you will have reviewed each child's placement on the continuum. Of course, whenever you see a "breakthrough," you will want to record it. The items on the continuum are not intended to be inclusive. You may find that you want to add

AN IDEA FROM A TEACHER

Portfolio Friday

It is important to me to be consistent in collecting samples of students' work for evaluation. To maintain an accurate view of improvement in writing and reading, I set aside time each week for assessment. Every Friday is Portfolio Friday. My students know that they will be assessed for learning during the course of the day, and that their work should be as neat and creative as always. The students first receive a creative writing assignment and work independently, both writing and illustrating their work. During this time, I call up children to make running records of their reading. When the children have finished working and I have completed the running records, they place their work in a writing portfolio and I place their running records in a separate folder for each of them. Then I read a passage from a book and ask comprehension questions. Children write their responses on a piece of paper that I collect. This paper goes into yet another folder for each child. This routine is consistent and well received. The children come to expect the portfolio performance challenge and enjoy reflecting on their improvement at the end of each marking period. At the same time, I am able to take these folders home and browse each weekend to identify where children are struggling in writing, reading, and comprehension, to target my instruction for the following week. The folders are also a wonderful resource for conferences throughout the year.

Alyson Crane, Second-Grade Teacher

items that fit your learners or that bring the continuum in line with your curriculum.

We have presented an array of assessment and evaluation tools useful for monitoring the reading and writing achievement of young children. The most important use of this information is, of course, in planning instruction that meets the individual needs of each learner. A second, highly important use of these data is in communicating with significant audiences.

Communicating with Parents, Administrators, and the Public in the Age of Accountability

In the not too distant past, our methods of communicating children's progress in reading to parents, administrators, and the public were archaic compared to the kind of information we can share using today's assessment and evaluation tools. Instead of reporting that Nathan is reading "at the primer level" or that Estelle is "reading at the 2.1 level," we can be very specific about how children are applying skills and strategies to maximize the use of the reading process. We can share children's perceptions of reading and writing from information gained through interviews, and we can report which of the cueing systems the child is using from annotations in running records. We can be very specific about the reading and writing behavior the child is exhibiting since our last report by using a developmental continuum. It is possible to confidently report a child's instructional reading level using the accuracy rate and retellings identified in running records.

Although you will use the information you collect on a daily basis to plan instruction, it is

SUMMARY OF READING AND WRITING DEVELOPMENT

Name: ______________________________

Date: ______________________________

Concepts About Print

___ Orientation of book	___ Reordered letters
___ Print carries meaning	___ Question mark
___ Directional rules	___ Punctuation
___ First and last	___ Rev. words
___ Picture inversion	___ Letter concept
___ Print inversion	___ Word concept
___ Line sequence	___ First, last letter
___ Left before right	___ Capital letter
___ Letter order	

Impressions drawn from reading interview:

Impressions drawn from writing interview:

Running Record

Accuracy rate: ______________________________

Error ratio: ______________________________

Self-correction rate: ______________________________

Current independent level: ______________________________

Current instructional level: ______________________________

Adequacy of retellings:

Use of cueing systems:

Reading and Writing Developmental Continuum

Current phase: ______________________________

Key indicators of placement in phase:

Writing Development

Major strengths:

Current goals:

Figure 13.4

important to organize the data in such a way that it can be easily presented to parents and other audiences. Figure 13.4 shows an example of a summary sheet you might develop to organize the information you have collected across an array of assessment and evaluation strategies. We hope you will modify it in ways that make it especially useful to you and your learners, and we wish you the greatest success in coming to know your students as readers and writers!

References

Clay, M. M. (1972). *Sand.* Auckland, New Zealand: Heinemann.

Clay, M. M. (1975). *What did I write? Beginning writing behaviour.* Portsmouth, NH: Heinemann.

Clay, M. M. (1979). *Stones.* Auckland, New Zealand: Heinemann.

Clay, M. M. (1993). *An observation survey of early literacy achievement.* Portsmouth, NH: Heinemann.

Cunningham, A. E. (1988). *A developmental study of instruction in phonemic awareness.* Paper presented at a meeting of the American Educational Research Association. New Orleans.

Education Department of Western Australia. (1997). *Reading Developmental Continuum.* Port Melbourne, Victoria, Australia.

Education Department of Western Australia. (1997). *Writing Developmental Continuum.* Port Melbourne, Victoria, Australia.

Fleming, D. (1991). *In the tall, tall grass.* New York: Henry Holt.

Harp, B. (1996). *The handbook of literacy assessment and evaluation.* Norwood, MA: Christopher-Gordon.

International Reading Association & National Association for the Education of Young Children. (1998). Learning to read and write: Developmentally appropriate practices for young children. *The Reading Teacher, 52,* 193–216.

National Research Council. (1998). *Preventing reading difficulties in young children.* Washington, DC: National Academy Press.

Yopp, H. K. (1995). A test for assessing phonemic awareness in young children. *The Reading Teacher, 49,* 20–29.

CHAPTER FOURTEEN

Sign of the Times: Technology and Early Literacy Learning

Shelley B. Wepner and Lucinda C. Ray

For Reflection and Action: Reflect on the use of technology in your school or one you know about. How much access do children have to the available technology, and how is it integrated into the curriculum? How have the teachers been trained to use these resources?

Shelley B. Wepner and Lucinda C. Ray provide useful information for classroom teachers on the role of technology in the classroom and its potential as a powerful tool for literacy development.

Remy is a freshman at a prestigious university in the United States. Atop her rather small wooden desk in her dorm room sits a brand new computer that her university required her to purchase before she began her first year. The first thing Remy does each day is turn on her computer, because it is her way of communicating to her immediate world that she is available for a quick note or a brief conversation. Throughout the day, she lets the important people in her life know that she is "in class," "exercising," "taking a shower," or simply "unavailable to talk." She rarely uses the telephone anymore. Rather, she uses her instant messaging system or e-mail to talk to her peers, her professors, and her family in the United States and Australia. She conducts all university business electronically, from registering for classes to accessing her grades after each examination. She does this through her self-created home page, which links her automatically to the university's web site. When she is concerned about any of her classes, she contacts the professor, who invariably gets back to her electronically within hours.

Remy, who has been quite proficient at using the keyboard, the Internet, and a multitude of software programs since her high school years, uses the computer for studying, for research, and for all of her written communication. Never compelled to become technically proficient with the computer's infrastructure, she has been a bona fide end user since her earliest memories. How and where did Remy begin to use computers?

Remy was one of those fortunate children who live in homes where they can "play" and learn with computers during the preschool years, and who go to schools where the teachers use computers for instruction. Remy used the computer to develop her reading vocabulary, to practice reading, to learn about the solar system, and to learn about insects. She remembers vividly some of the World War II atrocities she viewed on laser disk, which helped clarify her heritage. She also remembers a high school science teacher who embraced the computer's ability to demonstrate concepts that he could not explain as well with words alone as with the graphic images on the screen.

Remy began to acquire basic desktop publishing skills in her primary years because of her teachers' and parents' willingness to help her "dress up" her reports. She learned to keyboard officially in upper elementary school, learned how to use a database and spreadsheet in middle school, and learned a bit of programming during high school.

Why do we introduce this chapter with a college student's experiences with technology? Remy is one of the lucky students whose teachers were early adopters of technology. Their interest in technology meant she was exposed to its possibilities during her early literacy acquisition. All children deserve this opportunity. Even though schools and teachers cannot control what happens at home, we can influence what our children experience in the classroom. Integrating technology with learning early in children's literacy development enables students to develop a sense of how it can be used for learning, discovering, and communicating.

Included in this chapter are the following:

- A rationale for using technology
- Types of instructional software for skill development, reading development, and writing development
- Ideas for selecting and using software
- Ideas and examples for using web sites as instructional resources
- Two instructional plans that use technology

Rationale for Using Technology for Early Literacy Development

We have come a long way since Remy first began to use computers. Whereas Remy worked on mouseless computers with 48K that used 5.25-inch disks and synthesized speech, children today are using computers with 640 MB or more of hard disk storage, CD-ROM drives, digitized speech, and Internet connections. Within the next decade, young children will have access to even faster computers equipped with writable DVD-ROM drives and digital camera devices that allow visual "phone calls" to be made over the Internet (E. Balajthy, personal communication, January 15, 1999).

Research into the usefulness of technology for literacy development has grown apace with the rapid changes in technology in the past two decades. We have learned that technology provides opportunities for developing literacy that typically are unavailable through other means.

Technology offers young children the opportunity to engage in independent explorations, to socially co-construct knowledge about symbol making and about literacy, to take part in integrated language arts experiences, and to engage in a variety of electronic symbol-making experiences (Labbo, 1996; Labbo & Ash, 1998; Labbo, Reinking, McKenna, Kuhn, & Phillips, 1996; Reinking & Watkins, 1996).

Technology also serves as an effective means of engaging and motivating children to want to succeed (Casey, 1997, 1998; Fogarty, 1998; Kirkpatrick & Cuban, 1998). Children at the primary grade level have shown achievement gains in word attack skills (Charles, 1991). Electronic books in particular strengthen reading skills and reading development (Fernandez, 1999; Matthew, 1995; McKenna, Reinking, Labbo, & Watkins, 1996; Stine, 1993). They improve sight vocabulary, concepts about print, and knowledge about story language and genre (Kinzer & McKenna, 1999; Stine, 1993). Children who use electronic books and spend time interacting with the animated features demonstrate an ability to recount story events (Underwood & Underwood, 1996).

Technology is valuable for literacy development because it offers (1) icons that can be activated and animated to help a student more clearly visualize a concept; (2) infinite patience, which allows children to take time figuring out a concept; (3) the possibility, with hypermedia, of the user's navigating at will and gaining access to layers of information that typically are not available with other text; (4) access to huge databases of information; and (5) the opportunity to communicate with people across the world. With its multisensory, multidimensional, and multipersonal characteristics, technology offers young children an important communication medium for using their receptive and expressive skills to develop as literacy learners. In sum, technology offers teachers unanticipated opportunities for motivating and sustaining productive learning.

Recommendations for Three Types of Instructional Software

Instructional technology's potential for early literacy learning owes in part to the extensive research and development that goes into software production. Some of the best software programs represent years of research by educators before publishers bring in their teams to design and develop the concept. Children can only benefit from the flow of talent into a medium that is becoming such an important part of their world.

This section describes some software programs that develop, reinforce, and extend children's skill development, reading development, or writing development. The programs discussed require potential users to have at least one computer with CD-ROM and floppy drives, a printer, an LCD projector or TV monitor for large-group use, and possibly Internet access.

Software for Skill Development

Well-designed software for skill development is characterized by unique features that aid children's skill development. Among these features are the following:

- *Immediacy and predictability of visual and auditory cues.* The child does not have to wait for the reinforcement or response of a teacher who may have been distracted by another child's question or who may have misunderstood his or her attempt.
- *Focused individual feedback.* The child does not have to wait in a group to take a turn. Each attempt, action, or input is reinforced.
- *Opportunity for multiple repetitions.* Children need different amounts of practice to achieve mastery of specific skills. Software programs allows repetition as needed and can motivate children to stay engaged through multiple repetitions.
- *Introduction of skills in a predictable sequence.* Children can continue to learn skills as needed, regardless of absence from school because of illness, religious observances, or other unanticipated events.
- *Development of concepts through visual, auditory, and kinesthetic modalities.* Children with different learning styles can respond in a variety of modes.

Developing children's phonemic awareness (the understanding that spoken language consists of words, rhymes, syllables, and sounds) and phonics skills (an understanding of the relationship between the sounds of spoken words and the letters of written words) (Fox, 2000) is a critical and ongoing responsibility for classroom teachers. Wall charts, songs, rhymes, chants, books, flash cards, and manipulatives are some of the resources and techniques good teachers use. Software designed especially by educators with experience in the classroom is an ideal complement to existing resources.

Skill development software usually is created to teach children new information and principles through tutorial activities or to reinforce skills already taught through drill and practice activities. Often these activities have gamelike formats to capture children's interest. Some products provide a comprehensive and sequenced array of skill development activities that can take months to complete. Others offer a more limited set of activities that are clustered to develop several different skill areas rather than a whole curriculum and can be completed in a few sessions. Teachers should study the available products carefully before purchasing them to ensure they match the students' needs.

The *Let's Go Read!* series (Edmark, 1998) is a comprehensive and sequenced program that uses the story motif of a squirrel-and-raccoon team traveling across an island and an ocean to develop phonemic awareness and phonics skills, respectively, in *Let's Go Read!1 An Island Adventure* and *Let's Go Read!2 An Ocean Adventure.* The island adventure focuses on letter recognition and letter sounds in isolation and in words. The ocean adventure concentrates on phonics skills, such as short and long vowel sounds, consonant digraphs, and consonant blends. Each program uses a sequenced series of tutorial and drill and practice activities to develop children's success with each skill. Original interactive books accompany each product so that children can practice their acquired skills in context. The speech recognition technology allows children to interact vocally with each of the activities.

The *Reader Rabbit* series, and particularly *Reader Rabbit's Learn to Read* (The Learning Company, 1999), is another carefully sequenced program that introduces and provides practice with phonemes, blends, word families, and a core vocabulary to aid the development of both phonemic awareness and phonics skills. The sounds and simple vocabulary are always presented in a rich context, reinforced with visual and auditory cues, and then cumulatively re-presented in a series of specially designed electronic storybooks in which the sounds and words occur in context. Because children are prompted to respond orally to the program and can record and listen to their own voices as they read, they are actively involved in both identifying and producing sounds and words.

Read, Write & Type! (The Learning Company, 1995) is a comprehensive program for building phonics skills that is particularly effective for children who learn best through tactile or kinesthetic modes. Letter-sound correspondences are presented and reinforced through letter locations on the keyboard. As children progress through the 10 levels of the program, they identify the appropriate sounds and select the corresponding letters by typing their responses to program prompts, rather than merely clicking the mouse. A careful sequence of activities presents initial sounds, final sounds, word families, and simple stories built from these combinations. This program combines the development of receptive skills through phonics practice with the development of expressive skills through writing at the keyboard. Sullivan and Sharp (2000) have proposed that letter position on the keyboard should be the emphasis in primary grades, with touch typing introduced in the intermediate grades as students develop the needed dexterity and finger span.

Bailey's Book House (Edmark, 1995) includes a wide range of activities that can be randomly selected to explore letters, words, sentences, rhyming, and stories. Each of the seven different activities has a different primary purpose for emerging literacy. Examples include Letter Machine for recognizing upper- and lowercase letters, Three-Letter Carnival for spelling and sounding out three-letter words, Read-A-Rhyme for completing rhymes illustrated with animation by choosing words, and Make-A-Story for creating stories by choosing characters, settings, and actions.

Phonics programs use a variety of techniques such as songs, games, and adventures to engage students' interest. Examples include *Curious*

George Learns Phonics (Houghton Mifflin Interactive, 1979), *Kid Phonics* and *Kid Phonics 2* (Davidson/Knowledge Adventure, 1994, 1996), *Reading Mansion* (Great Wave Software, 1998), *Madeline 1st and 2nd Grade Reading* (The Learning Company, 1998), and *Reading Who? Reading You!* (Sunburst, 1996). Fox and Mitchell (2000) give especially high marks to *Reading Mansion* because of the broad spectrum of skills developed as children go on a scavenger hunt through the rooms of a mansion.

Software for Reading Development

Software for reading development uses books and passages to encourage children to read and interact with both narrative and expository text. Questions and activities often are used to promote and assess children's text comprehension. Two types of software—electronic books and reading passages and reading systems—are described.

Electronic Books: Electronic books use popular children's trade titles in a multimedia format with original illustrations. Sometimes referred to as a variation of lap reading, electronic books are a powerful tool for introducing children to the rich array of literature available and to the imaginative pleasure embedded in the reading process. Children can hear the book read aloud, have the text and graphics animated with sound and voice, and receive on-line help to enhance comprehension and recall. Electronic books usually focus on narrative text for emerging and developing readers and on expository text for developing and independent readers (grades 3 and beyond). As animated versions of *narrative* texts, electronic books heighten attention to plot, setting, and character. As narrated examples of *expository* text, electronic books broaden children's exposure to content with the layers of information accessed from each screen. Electronic books can be used for recreational reading, thematic units, author studies, and topical studies with instructional frameworks such as KWL, directed reading activity, and directed reading-thinking activity (Wepner & Ray, 2000).

There are many variations of electronic books, ranging from those that simply put the book on the screen with minimal animation to those that expand the book with an extensive array of animated features. An example of the latter is Marc Brown's *Arthur's Teacher Trouble* (Broderbund/The Learning Company, 1993) with its 24 screen pages of the storybook. The story follows the main character, Arthur, through a school spelling competition. Underwood and Underwood (1996) describe this program as follows: Each screen page has part of the text of the story displayed and read aloud. A rich illustration from the text also is displayed. The user may then interact with both words and illustrations with a mouse click. Clicking on a word results in its pronunciation. Clicking on a feature of the illustration results in some type of animation. Characters may provide additional dialogue or perform actions, and objects such as toys and cookies come alive, adding songs or actions.

Other examples with a similar interface include Mercer Mayer's *Just Grandma and Me Deluxe* and *Little Monster at School*, Marc Brown's *Arthur's Reading Race* and *Arthur's Birthday Deluxe*, Dr. Seuss's *The Cat in the Hat* and *Dr. Seuss's ABC*, Janell Cannon's *Stellaluna*, and Kevin Henkes' *Sheila Rae, the Brave* (all from Broderbund/The Learning Company).

Another electronic book format is *The Art Lesson* (MECC/The Learning Company, 1996). Containing a storybook, 14 art activities, and video interviews, this software program showcases the life of Tomie dePaola. In the interactive storybook, children learn about the young artist Tomie at home and at school. With video interviews, children learn about Tomie's life today, and his work as a writer and an illustrator of books.

Inside Stories, produced by Mimosa Technology, in Australia, offers eight fairy tales, such as *Cinderella, The Three Little Pigs*, and *Goldilocks and the Three Bears*. These stories are told through puppetry, storytellers, a play, and a song. Different activities accompany each story title to develop children's comprehension, grammatical awareness, and word recognition skills.

Troll Associates produces a series of CD-ROM electronic books that includes biographies for young children. Even with its minimal animation, this line of software defines highlighted words, asks questions about each page, creates a photo album for a sequencing activity, offers a time line of events, and enables children to write their own version of each page. Among the 10 titles available are *Young Harriet Tubman: Freedom Fighter, Young Orville & Wilbur Wright: First to Fly, Young Abraham Lincoln: Log-Cabin President*, and *Young Jackie Robinson: Baseball Hero.*

Reading Passages and Reading Systems: A balanced reading program includes focused skill development and immersion in whole works of literature. This category of reading software helps children develop their literacy skills as a supplement to existing reading programs. These programs typically have children read material and answer questions or engage in activities related to the reading passages. Management systems often accompany these programs to monitor children's progress.

Some examples of this genre were so popular in classrooms in the 1980s that their instructional frameworks were upgraded technologically for CD-ROM versions. An example is *Tiger's Tales* (Sunburst), which was originally published in 1986 and then revised in 1995. This program is a collection of seven stories about the adventures of a cat named Tiger and his animal friends. Children make decisions throughout the stories. The stories then adjust to the child's choices. Children actively participate in the story development while focusing on reading as a problem-solving activity.

Software developers also have designed more comprehensive reading systems. Two examples are *WiggleWorks Plus* (Scholastic) and the Little Planet's *The Ribbit Collection* (Houghton Mifflin Interactive). These programs go beyond enrichment or supplementary activities and move toward a central place in a teacher's reading curriculum.

WiggleWorks Plus is designed as a comprehensive early literacy system for kindergarten second grade. Two types of reading material are used: (1) electronic storybooks, called WiggleWorks books, which are written specifically for the program, and (2) printed trade books available in electronic form from the publisher's anthology. Children hear the story text read aloud, record themselves reading the same text, enter their own text, hear their own text read aloud, develop word lists from the reading, and color and print their own versions of the stories. Complete lesson plans and an assessment module for the teacher are also part of the system.

The Ribbit Collection, part of the Little Planet Literacy Series (Houghton Mifflin Interactive), offers a more multimedia-intensive approach to a comprehensive literacy system for kindergarten through grade 2. This research-based program, developed in cooperation with Vanderbilt University, presents a series of video-style stories. Children are asked to sequence story segments and then retell the stories in their own words, both orally and in writing. Word attack activities also are an integral part of the system, proving a balanced "anchored reading" approach. Children's own retellings of the stories are added to the electronic "library" within the program, where their retellings can be shared electronically and can be printed in book format. A web site enables children to post letters about characters and stories.

Software for Writing Development

Electronic writing tools offer several advantages for emergent writers that are not available with the traditional paper-and-pencil approach:

- *Combination of drawing and text.* Because children gradually make a transition from drawing to a combination of drawing and writing, good software for writing development enables students to work with multiple drawing tools and text at the same time. In addition, the wide variety of graphics can inspire students to generate additional ideas and write about them.
- *Support of student-generated text through text-to-speech capabilities.* Most programs now include a text-to-speech feature that enables children to hear their text read back to them, reinforcing the meaning they are striving to communicate.

- *Encouragement for students to expand, revise, and edit their work.* Electronic text is much easier for students to rearrange, add to, and revise than the painstaking process of recopying or rewriting by hand. Tools such as dictionaries and spell checkers empower developing writers to edit and prepare their pieces for publication. As Kim Montano, a first-grade teacher in Lakeview Elementary School, says, "Children who don't like to write will write on their computer. Children in general will write more, and write stories that have more to them. They like to play [a story] back, and as they hear it read to them, they correct their writing."

Standard features of children's writing programs include an ability to draw or manipulate graphics and create text. Each program described below combines these features in a unique way. The programs are presented according by stage of writing fluency.

Paint, Write & Play! (The Learning Company, 1996) is designed for emergent writers. Drawing tools, a collection of words and illustrations that act as a simple picture dictionary, and inviting backgrounds all provide support for early literacy. Children can create text by clicking on words rather than typing from the keyboard. These words are accompanied by appropriate pictures and are also read aloud, assisting children in the beginning stages of composing. Children can draw their own pictures or choose from a series of illustrated background scenes. Objects in the background scenes, such as a ball, an elephant, a playground slide, or a tree, say their names aloud, encouraging children to incorporate these items into a story. Both the pictures and text print in storybook format, with the picture at the top of the page and the text at the bottom.

The *Kid Pix* family of products, including *Kid Pix Studio Deluxe* and *Kid Pix Studio 3rd Edition* (Broderbund/The Learning Company) are drawing and creativity programs that are also widely used by teachers for early literacy activities and for writing projects throughout the primary and elementary grades. The Talking Alphabet Stamp tool enables children to hear the name of each letter of the alphabet as they select it to construct a word. The text-to-speech feature reads aloud all text entered from the keyboard. Both features are available in both Spanish and English. The extensive Rubber Stamp collection provides easy-to-use graphics for rebus activities and for the creation of picture dictionaries. The program also allows children to record their own voices to accompany their pictures and text. Pages can be printed or presented as electronic storybooks with the program's SlideShow component.

Fred Wellington, a first-grade teacher in the Wallingford-Swarthmore School District, Pennsylvania, has children design an ABC slide show with *Kid Pix Studio* (Broderbund/The Learning Company, 1993). His children design a card for a letter of the alphabet. They add graphics, animation, and sound for each letter. They also add their own voices to read the card. Once all children have created their cards, he works with them to create a slide show that he copies onto videotape for presentations.

Sunbuddy Writer (Sunburst, 1996) is a word processor designed for primary grade children. Features typically found in fully equipped word processors are included, along with an ability to record sounds or children's voices. A word finder provides words and rebus pictures that are organized alphabetically, topically, and in surprise order.

Storybook Weaver Deluxe (MECC/The Learning Company, 1996) is a writing program that supports children's imaginations and storytelling. A rich array of graphics and backgrounds invites story writing in a variety of subject areas, from castles, knights, princesses, and dragons to contemporary city neighborhoods and sports. Text appears at the bottom of each page, following the journal paper model so common in the primary grades. The same CD-ROM offers a complete version of the program in Spanish, including a dictionary and the text-to-speech feature.

Easybook Deluxe (Sunburst, 1998) is a program for writing, illustrating, and printing children's work in book form. Features include eight possible page layouts, eight categories of stamps, six categories of backgrounds, and a magic wand to sprinkle the art work with a selected shape. Pages can be printed to become big books, back-to-back full-page books (8 × 11 inches), greeting card–size books, or minibooks.

Ultimate Writing & Creativity Center (The Learning Company, 1995) offers special help with the writing process through oral and written prompts that are appropriate for the specific kind of writing activity in which the child is engaged. Children who use one of the four Writing Lands to gather ideas are given prewriting suggestions and tips. They can collect their ideas in a special notebook that they keep and add to throughout a writing project. In the drafting area, Post-it notes can be placed on a student draft by the teacher or by peer readers, asking questions or commenting on the emerging piece of writing. An extensive collection of animations, sounds, music, photographs, and graphics is available to enhance students' texts. A dictionary, spelling-check program, and thesaurus are available when students are ready to edit. When students prepare to publish, they can format their writing as reports, stories, or newsletters, or they can even present them in a multimedia theater that reads their text aloud.

The Amazing Writing Machine (Broderbund/The Learning Company, 1995) focuses on creative writing with five genre and page formats: story, poetry, journal, letter, and essay. A Bright Ideas feature provides hundreds of story starters, quotations, sayings, and even jokes, to spark students' imaginations for writing. A rhyming dictionary, text-to-speech feature, and a spelling-check feature are also available. The *Kid Pix* (Broderbund/The Learning Company, 1993) drawing tools enable students to illustrate their writing projects, which can be printed in a variety of sizes.

Matching Software with Your Instructional Needs

Like other media—trade books, basal readers, big books, worksheets, cassette tapes, daily newspapers—software is an instructional tool and a resource. Software is valuable only when it fits within the larger context of the curriculum and when it provides an experience or a way of learning or interacting that is not already available in other media.

Selecting Software

In selecting software, consider your teaching and learning goals, which might include introducing a concept or skill, assessing children's understanding of a concept or skill, or providing enrichment activities. Then consider your personal philosophy of teaching and the needs of the children who will be interacting with the software. Any software you select should have a philosophy in its design that is comfortable for you. Some fo the children in your classroom may need minimal distractions and a highly structured learning environment. You may want children to respond to their reading activities by writing. Or you may be looking for a way to increase children's motivation during sustained silent reading time.

Figure 14.1 provides a checklist of software design features to consider in determining whether software fits your goals for its use. It represents what we have observed and learned from others about software design features (Bliss, 1998; Matthew, 1995, 1996).

Certain assumptions accompany this checklist:

- The software offers something special that you cannot achieve with traditional means of instruction.
- The software accomplishes what it purports to accomplish.
- The concepts and content are accurate, developmentally appropriate, and considerate of race, age, sex, ethnicity, and disabilities.

Certain thought processes also need to go into evaluating a software program's value for your unique teaching environment. Look at both the content load and the skills needed to use the software. Even though students can read the content, they may still find it difficult to process the concepts or perform the tasks. Alternatively, if the children cannot read the content, there may be enough reading assistance in the program (text that is read aloud, "help" characters that give prompts, an intuitive interface design) that they can process the content. Software programs also may serve one type of population (urban children learning about farm animals) and not

SOFTWARE FEATURES TO CONSIDER

- The activities and tasks within the program are compelling enough to hold the students' interest.
- The instructions to children are clear, concise, and easy to follow without significant adult help.
- The graphics and sound are of high quality, are an integral part of the concepts and content taught, and are appropriate for the age level intended.
- The content fits into or expands beyond what children are supposed to be learning.
- The text is narrated so that children can read the material independently, and the text is highlighted as it is read so that children can follow along.
- The program provides enough practice on important concepts, especially if you are looking for a program that builds skills.
- The publisher provides a teacher's guide with lessons, ways to introduce the program to your children, and supplementary materials to assist you.
- Record keeping or assessment features are built into the program, especially if this is an important issue providing accountability for your use of technology.

Figure 14.1

another. Parts of the program may be useful for all children, or different parts may be useful for different types of children. The best way to determine a program's usefulness is to watch your own students' responses to and involvement with the program.

Using Software

As with other instructional resources, plan and manage your use of software. Develop your own skills and confidence in using the software so that you know what you want to accomplish and can answer children's questions confidently. Use the manual and the publisher's web site to get assistance, ideas, and specific lesson plans. Once you are comfortable with the software, model ways in which children can use different parts of the program to get maximum use of its features. Make sure children are able to control the mouse. Fred Wellington's first-grade children use a mouse practice program first so that they learn how to navigate with the mouse before they actually work with software. Create rules and a computer schedule to assist with equitable and appropriate use. Pair children appropriately so that at least one of the children is computer literate. Monitor software use so that children do not overaccess animated graphics and underaccess print (Kinzer & McKenna, 1999). Provide time for discussion of the software so that children can articulate what they are experiencing.

Using Web Sites as Instructional Resources

The Internet, especially the World Wide Web, provides a number of new resource opportunities for your own preparation and for direct use by children. Publishers' sites and distribution sites, such as Amazon.com, provide opportunities for visitors to review the books they offer. Children can read reviews submitted by other readers, and they can upload and post their own reviews. Naturally, you will want to protect children's anonymity by posting reviews under the school name.

Recommended Web Sites

The web sites identified below can be used to get assistance, to enrich instruction, and to share ideas. This list is by no means exhaustive. In fact, web sites are proliferating so rapidly that many new and better sites will likely be available by the time this book is published.

Sites to Review Software Programs: Four sites that review software and rate software by content area and/or grade level are The Review Zone (www.thereviewzone.com/reading-writing-index.html), the California Instructional Technology Clearinghouse (www.clearinghouse.k12.ca.us), The BrainPlay (www.brainplay.com), and the SuperKids Educational Software Review (www.superkids.com).

Sites That Contain Electronic Books: Although they do not yet offer the high level of interactivity that most CD-ROM versions do, these sites nevertheless offer animated graphics, music, and sound. One site with electronic books (www.candlelightstories.com) offers stories such as *Thumbelina* and *Rumpelstiltskin*. This site links to additional storybooks with titles such as *The Lion King* (disney.go.com/Kids/lkstory/) and *Pocahontas* (disney.go.com/Kids/pocastory/). Children's stories from books by both well-known authors and newcomers to children's literature are available at www.acs.ucalgary.ca/~dkbrown/storcont.html. Storybook listings of nursery rhymes, fairy tales, adventures, fables, and spooky tales are available at www.bconnex.net/~mbuchana/realms/page1/index.html. A directory of sites for children up to age 12 that includes some stories already published is available at Berit's Best Sites for Children (www.cochran.com/theodore/beritsbest). For quality control, we recommend that you use sites that have stories that have already been published, are current, and are created and maintained by known publishers, authors, or academic institutions.

WEB SITE FEATURES TO CONSIDER

- The entire web site loads quickly.
- The title page provides you with an overview of the content.
- The graphics and sound (when available) are of high quality, are an integral part of the concepts and content presented, and are appropriate for the web site.
- The content fits with the web site's overall purpose and your overall purpose.
- Icons exist to link you to another page, and when you do link to another page, you can return easily to the first page.
- Language usage and spelling are correct.
- The author's or publisher's name and the date of the page's creation or update are included.

Figure 14.2

Sites for Specific Authors: A number of author sites exist, among them Dr. Seuss (www.randomhouse.com/seussville), Marc Brown (www.pbs.org/wgbh/arthur), and Jean Craighead George (www.jeancraigheadgeorge.com). These sites provide additional author information, book summaries, photographs, or regular updates about book-related activities or the author's speaking engagements. Children engaged in an author study may find these helpful sources of information.

Teacher Sites: Teachers from around the country are using the Internet to locate resources for planning units and specific lesson plans. Connecting Students Through Literacy (www.connectingstudents.com) provides resources and lesson plans. Sites such as the Scholastic Network (www.ScholasticNetwork.com) provide a wealth of language arts lessons, activities, and resources. For example, there are regular guest appearances by authors, who answer questions submitted by students. In addition, some sites act as matchmaking areas for teachers who wish to set up key pals or class exchanges for their children. Classroom Connect (www.classroomconnect.com) hosts a popular site that many educators use to exchange lessons and contact one another to set up collaborative projects and classroom exchanges. Web66 (web66.coled.umn.edu) is a site open to any school in the United States that wants to post a school web site. Visiting this web site may help you locate a school and classroom with which you could set up an e-mail relationship for your children or an exchange of lessons and projects with a teacher.

Many communities, cities, and states host web sites that are rich with local photographs, maps, and historical information. All of these resources can be printed or downloaded to enrich the context for a particular reading activity or to support children's projects and presentations. As with software, evaluate a web site for its overall purpose, content, design, and features before deciding on its usefulness for your classroom. Figure 14.2 provides a checklist for evaluating a web site.

Examples of Teachers' Uses of Web Sites

Diane Wenger, a first-grade inclusion teacher in Chichester, Pennsylvania, uses a checklist like the one in Figure 14.2 to assess sites for her 4-week unit, "How Can We Help the Ocean Community?" This unit helps children compare their own community with the ocean community and learn about different animals and ways to save them. Ms. Wenger found two web sites that complement her collection of books, magazines, and audio- and videotapes. The first site offers information about different seals and sea lions (www.yahooligans.com/Science_and_Oddities/Animals/). After she and her children visit this site together, she has children complete a framed paragraph to check their understanding of sea lions. The second site provides information about coral and coral reefs and how they are being destroyed (www.blacktop.com/coralforest/). After she and her children visit this site together, she asks a number of higher-level questions about coral reefs to check for understanding. With both web sites, Ms. Wenger follows a similar pattern for whole-class instruction. Before the lesson, she calls up the web site to be sure she can gain access. She uses a large television monitor so that children can see the screen from their seats. She then explains the purpose of visiting each site and reviews various areas of the sites with her children before giving them a follow-up activity. This type of activity is an important first step in integrating the Internet into the classroom (Kinzer & McKenna, 1999).

Reading consultant Maya Eagleton has her children retell stories by creating student-designed web pages. One of her second-grade children uses Halloween graphics to retell *Goodnight, Moon* as "Nicholas's Scary Page" (www.azstarnet.com/~khalsa1/nicholas.html). Second-grade teacher Susan Silverman (www.kids-learn.org/), from Port Jefferson Station, New York, created a web site that includes and welcomes examples of students' projects from around the world about different thematic literary projects (Valmont, 2000). Tim Lauer, in Portland, Oregon, created a web site (buckman.pps.k12.or.us/room100/room100.html) for his kindergarten through second grade students that includes literacy projects across content areas. For instance, his children created an alphabet book with a space theme to support their learning about space and the nine planets.

A great book for learning more about using the Internet and for identifying web sites specifically created for young children is *101 Best Web Sites for Kids* (Meers, 1999). It provides descriptions of web sites that are written "by kids, for kids," as well as web sites for exploring such places as museums, zoos, safaris, volcanoes, rain forests, and oceans.

Instructional Plans

We offer two sample instructional plans that use the software we described earlier in the chapter. In the first plan, software technology is used to develop phonics skills, while in the second plan technology is used to develop reading and writing within a thematic framework.

Plan for Developing Phonics Skills

This instructional plan provides multiple ways for kindergarten and beginning first-grade students to strengthen their phonics skills. It combines phonics activities with writing tools to create word family charts and stories (see Figure 14.3 for plan).

As a beginning motivational activity, teachers could ask children to identify objects in the room that have a certain letter sound, such as *a* (as in *alphabet, tablet,* and *basket).* For a whole-class, you could work with the "a" page of *Dr. Seuss's ABC* (Broderbund/The Learning Company, 1995). Ask several children to click on the page and hear the many different words that begin with *a.* You might also use flash cards, pictures, or other resources to provide additional practice. Conclude this part of the lesson by having children practice saying the sounds and writing the letter *a.*

Provide time for children to use *Reader Rabbit's Learn to Read* (The Learning Company, 1999). Instruct them to take paper and pencil with them to the computer. Instruct them choose the Pick and Play mode, which enables them to select a specific practice area of the program: Letters and Sounds. Then have them choose the letter *a,* and explore. Have them draw at least four things that have the *a* sound. Then, have them use the Sorter Magic or Music Labeler activities, which provide practice with the *a* sound in words, particularly at Level 1.

PLAN FOR DEVELOPING PHONICS SKILLS

Objectives

To provide multiple ways for students to strengthen their phonics skills

Materials

Reader Rabbit's Learn to Read, Dr. Seuss's ABC, Kid Pix Studio Deluxe, paper

Activities

Motivational activity with classroom objects: use *Dr. Seuss's ABC* to reinforce letter-sound relationships; use *Reader Rabbit's Learn to Read* to practice letter-sound relationships; use *Kid Pix Studio Deluxe* to draw or locate stamps representing words that fit in with word families with specified letter-sound relationship

Assessment

Mastery of activities, as indicated on individual students' progress charts in *Reader Rabbit's Learn to Read,* and writing samples from *Kid Pix Studio Deluxe*

Figure 14.3

Finally, direct the children to use *Kid Pix Studio Deluxe* (Broderbund/The Learning Company, 1998). Have them use the Talking Alphabet Stamp tool to create words using *a.* They can use the drawings they made while working with *Reader Rabbit's Learn to Read* as a reference. They can illustrate these words by drawing or by selecting a Rubber Stamp that illustrates the word. They also can create word family lists that contain *a,* such as *-at, -ap,* and *-an,* illustrating each of the words they create with an appropriate drawing or Rubber Stamp. These activities can be printed out, so that students can share their words and illustrations. They also can create stories using as many words as possible with the *a* sound.

Thematic Plan About Tolerance for Reading and Writing

This unit helps children develop basic literacy skills while exploring the theme of tolerance. Unit concepts about tolerance provide the framework for working with the unit activities and materials (see Figure 14.4 for plan). Two of the concepts include "Each person has the opportunity to find and appreciate the specialness in others" and "The more accepting we are of others, the more accepting we are of ourselves."

As a beginning motivational activity, have children work as partners to interview each other about reasons why they might agree or disagree with their siblings or other family members. Use children's ideas to help them think about ways to handle their differences to be more tolerant of the unique qualities of others. Introduce to the entire class the software program, *Arthur's Teacher Trouble* (Broderbund/The Learning Company, 1993), by prompting children to look for three things that Arthur needs to learn to tolerate. (Marc Brown's web site can be shown to introduce the author.) Ask follow-up questions

PLAN FOR DEVELOPING READING AND WRITING SKILLS

Theme

Tolerance of individual differences

Objectives

To use theme of tolerance to promote text comprehension, sight vocabulary acquisition, spelling, and self-expression through art activities and writing; to help students understand the concepts of hard work and respect for others through guided discussion and critical thinking activities

Materials

Arthur's Teacher Trouble, The Art Lesson, Sunbuddy Writer, comparison charts, tolerance awards, paper for drawing

Activities

Motivational activity about tolerance, whole-group reading and individual exploration of *The Art Lesson,* follow-up questions and activities related to both stories, writing assignment

Assessment

Responses to follow-up questions and comparison charts, written paragraph on tolerance

Figure 14.4

AN IDEA FROM A TEACHER

All My Children's Stories Are Fit to Print

My classroom has five computers, one large screen monitor, and two printers, one with color. Each year, to facilitate interest in writing and promote computer literacy, I create a writing disk for each student. I introduce children to the typing program *KidKeys*. I have the children use this program at least twice, so that they can find the letters and know the location of the punctuation keys. Then I introduce children to *The Amazing Writing Machine*. I tell the students that they can collect as many stories on their writing disks as they can. I first have students start their writing collection by writing a story about themselves. Then I have them write a science story about the signs of fall, and a holiday story about Halloween. As the year progresses, the themes reflect what we are learning in class and children's personal choices. I set up flexible weekly grouping schedules so that children know when they might have free time for writing on the computer. Children may choose to work independently or in pairs. Most children choose to write during their free time and to add stories to their story collection. I have found that children who don't like to write will write using the computer. These children, in general, will write more, and write stories that have more substance, when they are allowed to do their writing assignments on the computer. They like to look back through and correct their writing, too. As a culminating activity, for the end of the year, I print out every story that the children have written and illustrated, and they take the stories home in booklet form.

Kim Montano, First-Grade Teacher

such as "Describe how Arthur feels now that he learned to tolerate these things" or "Name three things that you learned to tolerate this week." Create a Toleration Oscar award for children who have shown tolerance for others.

Before introducing the second electronic book, *The Art Lesson* (MECC/The Learning Company, 1996), have children draw a picture of someone they would like to tolerate more. Introduce *The Art Lesson.* Have children think about three things that Tomie had to learn to tolerate at home and at school. Follow up with questions such as, "If you were Tomie, what would you have done?" and "What did you learn from Tomie's experience?" Have children work with two comparison charts to compare Arthur's and Tomie's tolerance at the beginning, middle, and end of the stories and to compare their experiences with tolerance at home, at school, and with themselves. Have them share their favorite character, and tell reasons for their selections. Allow time for children to work independently or in pairs with each electronic book in your learning center or in a lab. Have children write independently or in pairs with *Sunbuddy Writer* (Sunburst, 1996) or another electronic writing tool.

Concluding Remarks

Technology in the primary grade classroom is a sign of the times. It offers important opportunities for emergent readers and writers. With the advent of the World Wide Web and the development of software products representing millions of dollars in research and development, children now can learn by means heretofore unavailable to them. Adjusting our instructional schemas to include these technological enhancements is not always easy, but the reward for that adjustment is the knowledge that we are helping children to develop literacy with today's tools for tomorrow's future.

Computer Programs Cited in Text

The Amazing Writing Machine [Computer software]. (1995). Cambridge, MA: Broderbund/The Learning Company.

The Art Lesson [Computer software]. (1996). MECC/The Learning Company.

Arthur's Birthday Deluxe [Computer software]. (1997). Cambridge, MA: Broderbund/The Learning Company.

Arthur's Reading Race [Computer software]. (1996). Cambridge, MA: Broderbund/The Learning Company.

Arthur's Teacher Trouble [Computer software]. (1993). Cambridge, MA: Broderbund/The Learning Company.

Bailey's Book House [Computer software]. (1995). Redmond, VA: Edmark.

The Cat in the Hat [Computer software]. (1997). Cambridge, MA: Broderbund/The Learning Company.

Cinderella [Computer software]. (1998). Trophy Club, TX: Mimosa Technology.

Curious George Learns Phonics [Computer software]. (1997). Somerville, MA: Houghton Mifflin Interactive.

Dr. Seuss's ABC [Computer software]. (1995). Cambridge, MA: Broderbund/The Learning Company.

EasyBook Deluxe [Computer software]. (1998). Pleasantville, NY: Sunburst.

Goldilocks and the Three Bears [Computer software]. (1998). Trophy Club, TX: Mimosa Technology.

Just Grandma and Me Deluxe [Computer software]. (1997). Cambridge, MA: Broderbund/The Learning Company.

Kid Phonics [Computer software]. (1994). Torrance, CA: Davidson & Associates/Knowledge Adventure.

Kid Phonics 2 [Computer software]. (1996). Torrance, CA: Davidson & Associates/Knowledge Adventure.

Kid Pix Studio [Computer software]. (1993). Cambridge, MA: Broderbund/The Learning Company.

Kid Pix Studio Deluxe [Computer software]. (1998). Cambridge, MA: Broderbund/The Learning Company.

Kid Pix Studio (3rd ed.) [Computer software]. (2000). Cambridge, MA: Broderbund/The Learning Company.

Let's Go Read!1 An Island Adventure [Computer software]. (1998). Redmond, VA: Edmark.

Let's Go Read!2 An Ocean Adventure [Computer software]. (1998). Redmond, VA: Edmark.

Little Monster at School [Computer software]. (1995). Cambridge, MA: Broderbund/The Learning Company.

Madeline 1st and 2nd Grade Reading [Computer software]. (1998). Cambridge, MA: The Learning Company.

Paint, Write & Play! [Computer software]. (1996). Cambridge, MA: The Learning Company.

Reader Rabbit's Learn to Read [Computer software]. (1999). Cambridge, MA: The Learning Company.

Reading Mansion [Computer software]. (1998). Scotts Valley, CA: Great Wave Software.

Reading Who? Reading You![Computer software]. (1996). Pleasantville, NY: Sunburst.

Read, Write & Type! [Computer software]. (1995). Cambridge, MA: The Learning Company.

Sheila Rae, the Brave [Computer software]. (1996). Cambridge, MA: Broderbund/The Learning Company.

Stellaluna [Computer software]. (1996). Cambridge, MA: Broderbund/The Learning Company.

Storybook Weaver Deluxe [Computer software]. (1996). MECC/The Learning Company.

Sunbuddy Writer [Computer software]. (1996). Pleasantville, NY: Sunburst.

The Ribbit Collection [Computer software]. (1996). Somerville, MA: Houghton Mifflin Interactive.

The Three Little Pigs [Computer software]. (1998). Trophy Club, TX: Mimosa Technology.

Tiger's Tales [Computer software]. (1986/1995). Pleasantville, NY: Sunburst.

Ultimate Writing & Creativity Center [Computer software]. (1995). Cambridge, MA: The Learning Company.

Young Abraham Lincoln: Log-Cabin President [Computer software]. (1996). Mahwah, NJ: Troll.

Young Harriet Tubman: Freedom Fighter [Computer software]. (1996). Mahwah, NJ: Troll.

Young Jackie Robinson: Baseball Hero [Computer software]. (1996). Mahwah, NJ: Troll.

Young Orville & Wilbur Wright: First to Fly [Computer software]. (1996). Mahwah, NJ: Troll.

WiggleWorks Plus [Computer software]. (1999). New York: Scholastic.

References

Bliss, J. (1998, August). Getting the most from software. *Technology & Learning*, p. 16.

Casey, J. (1997). *Early literacy: The empowerment of technology.* Englewood, CO: Teachers Ideas Press.

Casey, J. (1998). Early literacy: The empowerment of technology, the end of the reading wars. *California Professors of Reading, 32*(1), 25–27.

Charles, D. F. (1991). *Implementing a program using a zoological treasure hunt to enhance word attack skills of low performing first grade students.* Practicum report, Nova University, Fort Lauderdale, FL. (ERIC Document Reproduction Service No. ED 338 584)

Fernandez, M. (1999). Electronic versus paper. *Learning and Leading with Technology, 26*(8), 33–34.

Fogarty, R. (1998). The intelligence-friendly classroom: It just makes sense. *Phi Delta Kappan, 79*(9), 655–657.

Fox, B. (2000). *Word identification strategies: Phonics from a new perspective* (2nd ed.). Columbus, OH: Merrill.

Fox, B., & Mitchell, M. J. (2000). Using technology to support word recognition, spelling, and vocabulary acquisition. In S. B. Wepner, W. Valmont, & R. Thurlow (Eds.), *Linking literacy and technology: A guide for K–8 classrooms.* Newark, DE: International Reading Association.

Kinzer, C. K., & McKenna, M. C. (1999, May). *Using technology in your classroom literacy program: Current and future possibilities.* Paper presented at a meeting of the International Reading Association, San Diego.

Kirkpatrick, H., & Cuban, L. (1998, Summer). Computers make kids smarter—right? *Technos Quarterly for Education and Technology, 7*(2), 1–10 [On-line]. Available: www.TECHNOS.NET/journal/volume7/2cuban.htm

Labbo, L. D. (1996). A semiotic analysis of young children's symbol making in a classroom computer center. *Reading Research Quarterly, 31,* 356–385.

Labbo, L. D., & Ash, G. E. (1998). What is the role of computer related technology in early literacy? In S. B. Neuman & K. A. Roskos (Eds.), *Children achieving: Best practices in early literacy* (pp. 180–197). Newark, DE: International Reading Association.

Labbo, L. D., Reinking, D. R., McKenna, M., Kuhn, M., & Phillips, M. (1996). *Computers real and make-believe: Providing opportunities for literacy development in an early childhood sociodramatic play center* (Instructional Resource No. 26). Athens, Georgia: University of Georgia, National Reading Research Center. (ERIC Document Reproduction Service No. ED 396 254)

Matthew, K. I. (1995). *A comparison of the influence of CD-ROM interactive storybooks and traditional print storybooks on reading comprehension and attitude.* Unpublished doctoral dissertation, University of Houston.

Matthew, K. I. (1996, March). The promise and potential of CD-ROM books. In B. Robin, J. D. Price, J. Willis, & D. A. Willis (Eds.), *Technology and teacher education annual, 1996: Proceedings of Seventh International Conference of the Society for Information Technology and Teacher Education,* Phoenix, AZ [On-line]. Available: www/coe.uh.edu/insite/elec_pub/html1996/03readin.htm

McKenna, M. C., Reinking, D., Labbo, L. D., & Watkins, J. H. (1996). *Using electronic storybooks and beginning readers* (Instructional Resource No. 39). Athens: University of Georgia, National Reading Research Center. (ERIC Document Reproduction Service No. ED 400 521)

Meers, T. B. (1999). *101 Best Web Sites for Kids.* Lincolnwood, IL: Publications International.

Reinking, D., & Watkins, J. (1996). *A formative experiment investigating the use of multimedia book reviews to increase elementary students' independent reading* (Reading Research Report No. 55). Athens, GA: National Reading Research Center. (ERIC Document Reproduction Service No. ED 398 570)

Stine, H. A. (1993). *The effects of CD-ROM interactive software in reading skills instruction with second grade Chapter 1 students.* Unpublished doctoral dissertation, George Washington University.

Sullivan, J., & Sharp, J. (2000). Using technology for writing development. In S. B. Wepner, W. Valmont, & R. Thurlow (Eds.), *Linking literacy and technology: A guide for K–8 classrooms* Newark, DE: International Reading Association.

Underwood, G., & Underwood, J. (1996, March). Gender differences in children's learning from interactive books. In B. Robin, J. D. Price, J. Willis, & D. A. Willis (Eds.), *Technology and teacher education annual, 1996: Proceedings of Seventh International Conference of the Society for Information Technology and Teacher Education,* Phoenix, AZ [On-line]. Available: www/coe.uh.edu/insite/elec_pub/html1996/03readin.htm

Valmont, W. J. (2000). What do teachers do in technology-rich classrooms? In S. B. Wepner, W. Valmont, & R. Thurlow (Eds.), *Linking literacy and technology: A guide for K–8 classrooms.* Newark, DE: International Reading Association.

Wepner, S. B., & Ray, L. (2000). Using technology for reading development. In S. B. Wepner, W. Valmont, & R. Thurlow (Eds.), *Linking literacy and technology: A guide for K–8 classrooms.* Newark, DE: International Reading Association.

CHAPTER FIFTEEN

Still Standing: Timeless Strategies for Teaching the Language Arts

Diane Lapp, James Flood, and Nancy Roser

For Reflection and Action: As you complete this book, take time to look both backward and forward. If you are a practicing teacher or administrator, list some of the most significant changes you will make to your work. Organize them in three columns: practices you will add, practices you will discard, and practices you will alter in some way. Keep in mind that teaching and learning are lifelong pursuits. We wish you well.

Diane Lapp, James Flood, and Nancy Roser provide a wrap-up of the entire book with an extraordinary collection of strategies and useful ideas that reflect the thinking set forth in the preceding chapters.

People often look at the limitations within classrooms—the lack of resources, equipment, and so on. But as long as you have children, you have everything you need.

Kentucky teacher on Nightline, *July 6, 1999*

With students as the focus, each of the strands of the language arts—reading, writing, speaking, listening, and viewing—has been thoughtfully addressed in this book. In this summary chapter we reiterate five instructional strategies, each grounded in research, that reflect and underpin effective language arts teaching for young children. Although we separate the language arts for the sake of organizing our discussion, we recognize that the arts of language are mutually enhancing, interwoven, interactive processes that students and teachers use in logically connected ways as they explore and make meaning (Flood, Jensen, Lapp, & Squire, 1991). Our purpose, then, is to highlight the recurring themes in this book by describing practices, listed in Figure 15.1, that have both a past and a future in teaching the language arts to young children.

Focus on Reading

Strategy: Providing More Opportunities

Some of the most reassuring research (to educators and parents) is the significant evidence of the value of time spent reading. For example, Cunningham and Stanovich (1990, 1991, 1997) showed that children who read just 15 minutes each day at home consistently scored at the 80th percentile or higher on standardized reading tests. In addition, these children scored higher than their counterparts who did not read at home, both on literacy tests and on measures of general knowledge. The researchers suggest, for example, that children who read more outside of school are exposed to and learn more vocabulary words than children who read less frequently at home.

Because Cunningham and Stanovich focused on adults and older children, they did not examine the relationship between reading at home and the reading ability of young children. In a recent study, we and our colleagues modified and replicated the study with kindergarten and first-grade children (Flood, Lapp, Goss, LeTourneau, Moore, & Fisher, 1999). Our results showed the same patterns Cunningham and Stanovich had found: The most able readers read more at home and scored higher than their counterparts on all six measures of literacy and general knowledge.

More than two decades ago, Allington's (1977) findings on the dearth of opportunities for low achievers to read led him to ask, "If they don't read much, how they ever gonna get good?" Earlier, Dolores Durkin (1966) had shown that children who read early were those who had opportunities to read. Among the most frequently cited studies linking self-initiated reading and gains in reading achievement are those of Anderson, Wilson, and Fielding (1988) and Taylor, Frye, and Maruyama (1990), both of which support the importance of opportunity to read. More pointedly, through classroom accounts of what happens when reading is valued and made time for, teacher researchers, whose voices are represented and referenced in this volume, provide addi-

LANGUAGE ARTS FOCUS: INSTRUCTIONAL STRATEGIES

Reading

Providing increased opportunities to read (at home and at school)

Writing

Establishing classroom writing centers and writing clubs to encourage collaborative writing

Providing guidance on how the written language system works, including instruction in phonemic awareness

Speaking

Supporting oral language development

Encouraging thoughtful, precise, and expressive book talk

Listening

Guiding active, purposeful listening during sharing time

Viewing

Providing opportunities to comprehend and represent understanding through multiple means

Figure 15.1

tional evidence of the homely truth that practice makes (almost) perfect.

Application: How the Strategy Looks

In the closing decades of the twentieth century, classrooms of young children offered more opportunities than ever before for independent "just reading" of self-selected materials (cf. Austin & Morrison, 1963; Baumann, Hoffman, Moon, & Duffy-Hester, 1998). Despite widespread pressure for higher test scores, more test practice, and more direct instruction, it appears that informed school leaders are protecting time for sustained reading. In addition, teachers of young children marshal resources to ensure that books sit ever ready in baskets, stand invitingly on open shelves, are read aloud during story time, and travel home in plastic bags and on audiotape, providing invitations to read (Morrow, 1993).

Some of the most successful books-to-home approaches invite parents to listen in and talk over what children are reading in school, or to marvel at their child's command of texts that are new but within reach. Still other teachers send books home with the expectation that parents will read to their children. In yet other family reading programs, parents agree to set aside specific times of the afternoon or evening for "just reading" at home (Morrow, Tracey, & Maxwell, 1995; Richgels & Wold, 1998). To monitor children's reading and keep in touch with home, some teachers ask parents to sign off on what is read or to write in a traveling journal what they and their child thought about the story. In that way, parents, children, and teachers converse in a triangulated fashion.

Library programs have also been a force in developing independent reading, both at home and at school. Library programs provide access to books that all children need. We found that students whose teachers ensured they had a valid library card and who took them to the local public libraries at least once a week were more successful readers than students who did not visit the library regularly (Lapp, Flood, Fisher, & VanDyke, 1999). We also discovered that the staff of the local library were eager to establish programs with neighborhood schools. Many had already designed programs that matched children with appropriately leveled books and provided encouragement for wider reading.

When other researchers have looked at classroom libraries, the results have again tended to point to access. Morrow and Weinstein (1982) described the design features of classroom libraries that encourage voluntary reading. Martinez and Teale (1988) found that the books children selected most frequently from classroom libraries were those that had been read aloud to them. It seems important that young children have choice in their reading. Early readers need access to a wide variety of materials that provide for both support practice and provide challenge (Fountas & Pinnell, 1996; Lysacker, 1997). When we examined the free-reading book selections of four second-grade classes, we found that regardless of the classroom library's organization, the children chose what they could manage (Martinez, Roser, Worthy, Strecker, & Gough, 1997).

In some ways, this is indeed a new age for beginning readers and writers. There is increased interest in early literacy and greater pressure on teachers of young children to produce readers (Snow, Burns, & Griffin, 1998), as well as widespread anxiety that children have not been getting what they need in reading instruction recently (Strickland, 1998). When these concerns for the rigor of the literacy curriculum are added to the time demands of busy homes and even the demands of beginners' books on some less skilled parent readers (Edwards, 1989, 1996), we can only hope that time set aside for "just reading" is a practice still standing in the decades to come.

Focus on Writing

Strategy: Making Writing a Daily, Collaborative, Purposeful Act

For nearly two decades, researchers and teachers have noted the importance of frequent writing throughout the school day (Graves, 1994; Morrow, 1997; Pierce, 1996). One first-grade teacher who was asked to keep track of all of the forms of writing his students engaged in in one day and the reasons for the writing, surprised even himself with the following list (Roser, 1995):

- Journal
- Attendance slip
- Weather chart
- Temperature graph
- Missing library books
- Blackboard sentences—"news" words
- Word-processed stories with self-selected topics, such as Ninja Turtles, rats, horses, pets, and "scaries"
- Drawing and writing—art center
- Word work—erasable words/sentences
- Graphs of eye colors—labels for columns
- Paired writing of word problems
- Number sentences
- Word and number puzzles
- Responses to a story on group chart
- Free writing time
- Answers to questions in centers
- Labels for land forms
- Self-evaluations

Dahl and Farnan (1998), summarizing the literature on writing development among elementary schoolchildren, reported that the craft and content improved in direct proportion to the frequency with which the children wrote during the school day. Dyson (e.g., 1989) demonstrated some of the ways children work to make sense of their world through their writing. Many kindergarten and first-grade teachers have instituted innovative instruction practices, such as the traveling suitcase that Kimberly Miller-Rodriguez (1998) uses to get children writing and parents involved in the children's writing, or the gentle scaffolding that Karen Bromley proposes in this book.

Strategy: Using Writing to Give Children Insights Into Phonemic Awareness

The work of Read (1971), Chomsky (1971), and Henderson and his colleagues (1972, 1980) stresses the value of children's writing as a route toward understanding the alphabetic principle on which written language is based. These educators early gave voice to the concept that phonemic awareness—the understanding that spoken words are composed of sounds—develops not just in the periods and times devoted to its instruction, but also as children work to encode their language through writing.

The development of phonemic awareness skills in young children has been demonstrated to be related to later reading achievement (e.g., Foorman, Francis, Fletcher, Schatschneider, & Mehta, 1998). Cunningham and Stanovich (1997) argue that children who have little phonological awareness will have great difficulty acquiring alphabetic coding skills. Even as debate continues over what kinds of instruction in phonemic awareness will help which children accomplish what (Strickland, 1998), teachers with writing centers and writing clubs are helping children acquire the pieces of the literacy puzzle as they write.

Application: How the Strategy Looks

In the same way that an everyday classroom activity is elevated to special status by virtue of its label, timing, and accorded significance, so the notion of book clubs gave students and teachers license to explore meaning together. The first two authors have been involved in a project installing writing clubs in kindergarten and first-grade classrooms. In this project, thematic units provide the context for the purposeful, all-day use of oral and written language. For example, in a unit called "All About Me," children were encouraged to think about what made them special. As they read and discussed what made other people important—both those inside and those outside the classroom—they were introduced to the concept of autobiography, a word they relished saying over and over. They were invited to think about their own lives as a potential topic for their writing.

The children brainstormed ideas that they wanted to include in their own autobiographies: when and where they were born, what kind of day it was, where they fit in their families, what they were interested in, and what and how they expected to change as they grew. They spent time talking about audiences, including what others might want to hear about and how to make sure that others would understand their ideas. They called their first attempts "sloppy copy"—a label that allowed for getting ideas out and down on paper, for approximate spellings, and for understanding that both forgetting and including too much were both fixable.

Like the first graders in Carol Avery's (1993) writing workshops, these young members of the writing club talked seriously about their writing in conferences with peers and adults, so that second drafts were constructed collaboratively as well. By the time some children were at work on a third draft, many wanted to share their life stories with some invited guests. A flurry of decision making produced the format (a punch party) and the special guest list (including both the "boss" of the schools—the superintendent—and their favorite student teacher from the previous semester). Some children worked on a large-scale public proclamation to be mounted on construction paper and posted in the hall to announce a benchmark day. Others, working in small groups, painstakingly prepared invitations ("I'm writing 'dear.' I say it real slow—/d/—I hear **d**; deehr; I hear **e**; d-eeh-er, I hear **r**. D-e-r. Dear"). As Bear and Templeton (1998) caution, "Beginning writers make speed and accuracy trade-offs as they write. If they write too fast they miss so many letters that the text is hard to reread; if they write too slowly . . . they may lose track of what they want to say" (p. 227).

Until the big day arrived, there was practice on producing "audience-ready" drafts of public work ("Yes, we have to get a quiet **a** into the spelling of "der", but the pattern [-ear] will help write hear, fear, near, and even year") (Lapp, Flood, & Goss, in press). In this classroom and in many others, writing serves important purposes, feeds an understanding of how written language works, and delights audiences when read aloud (Martinez, Cheyney, McBroom, Hemmeter, & Teale, 1989). The notion of a writers' club within the language arts program establishes writing as a priority rather than just an activity to do at a given time of day.

We have found that purposeful writing tasks give children a reason to focus on the phonemes of spoken language. Further, children who are helped to accomplish writing tasks that make sense to them have the impetus for successfully decoding other people's writing on charts, signs, messages, and in songs and books.

Focus on Speaking

Strategy: Encouraging Expressive Language Through Book Conversations

Young children have enormous capacity for language learning. They delight in the sounds and meanings of new words, rolling the names of dinosaurs off their tongues, for example (Baker, 1995). But oral language development is more than facility with labels: it is coming to understand the need for precision, purpose, and audience in using language. One of the best opportunities for hearing language worth talking about—and for using language to say exactly what one means—comes with sitting on the story rug and talking about children's books (Strickland, Morrow, Feitelson, & Iraqi, 1990). We found first-language Spanish-speaking children in South Texas eager to talk about related sets of books and to see their ideas recorded on "language charts" (Roser, Hoffman, & Farest, 1990). Eeds and Wells (1989) refer to the best of book talk as "grand conversations," and Lea McGee (1992) found that even first graders were capable of reflecting on stories from their own perspectives while they shared personal experiences, made connections to other stories, speculated about events, and used text evidence to support ideas—all activities requiring thought and language. When Jennifer Battle (1995) worked with kindergarten teacher Cris Contreras, they found that bilingual 5-year-olds, too, had "so much to notice and so much to say" on the story rug:

> [T]hey talk about book features . . . and even the book's publication dates; they talk about book language—its rhyme, lilt, and meanings; they talk about illustrations; and they talk about literary elements—characters, setting, and plot (p. 160).

Perhaps most important of all, these kindergarten children worked together to untangle stories, providing living testament to meanings "socially constructed" (Lindfors, 1999; Vygotsky, 1978).

Application: How the Strategy Looks

It is no secret that children want to talk with one another about books (Morrow, 1988). As a mother of a kindergarten child wrote to us recently, "Naomi doesn't understand her computer teacher, and doesn't know which buttons to push. No wonder children talk to each other at school. They are like natives of the same land in a foreign country."

Aiden Chambers (1985) offers help for getting all of us talking together about books. Chambers proposes a general framework for guiding story discussion, and teachers have found it useful for encouraging children's thought and talk (see, e.g., Martinez, Roser, Hoffman, & Battle, 1992). Chambers refers to the scheme as "the three sharings." Children are invited to share their observations or "noticings" about books, their "puzzlements," or wonderings, and their "connections" with the story. When we work with children in literature study, they are often invited to prepare for talking by writing down one or two ideas they would most like to talk about. The invitation to talk often begins with "What do you most want to say?" "What did you notice?" or "What are you thinking or feeling about this story?"

In San Antonio, Ronnie Gonzalez's second graders are familiar with the framework, use it to shape the columns on their language charts, and "save" important parts of their discussion under these categories. The three sharings creep into their talk about books, as in the following excerpt from a discussion of *The Quicksand Book*, by Tomie dePaola:

> *C:* It reminds me of *The Cloud Book.*
>
> *C:* It gets you information of how you can fall into quicksand.
>
> *C:* I wonder why the jungle boy told the jungle girl to float on her back and the jungle boy didn't float on his back.
>
> *T:* Ummm. Good wondering. What do you think? Just come on into the conversation.
>
> *C:* I think he did that because maybe he didn't really know how to float on his back.
>
> *T:* Ahhh! Maybe he told her, "This is what you should do," but maybe he himself didn't do it.
>
> *C:* He didn't know *how* to do it.
>
> *C:* It was all sticky on his back.
>
> *C:* But he slipped too fast on his back and he *couldn't* turn over.
>
> *T:* He couldn't turn over fast enough to float.
>
> *C:* I didn't even know where the quicksand was 'til she fell in. I would never go in quicksand in my whole life.
>
> *C:* We stopped to have a picnic and I stepped in it, and I started to sink in it. It wasn't a very big patch. It was a little patch.
>
> *C:* I wonder why the girl didn't look where she was going. You should always look where you're swinging. You just might end up in quicksand.
>
> *C:* She might have just slipped off the rope.
>
> *C:* It did. It said the girl was swinging on the rope and—
>
> *C:* —the vine broke!
>
> *C:* I know, but she didn't slip off.
>
> *C:* She should have used a stronger rope. . . .
>
> *C:* I wonder how Tomie dePaola knew how to make quicksand. He must be smart.
>
> *T:* Any comment on what Kelly mentioned?
>
> *C:* He probably looked it up in the encyclopedia or something like that. He probably just didn't *think* if that would be correct.
>
> *C:* I think he got it from his friends.
>
> *T:* What do you mean, Ben?
>
> *C:* He put most of his friends in books that we have read . . . well, one of his friends might be like Encyclopedia Brown!

The conversation continued for another 10 minutes, and the book was consulted to support points. The author's rationale for making Jungle Boy the authority on quicksand was discussed ("He [dePaola] could have made the girl [know] because he was the one that wrote the story. He could make the girl know it if he wanted to"). There was evidence of reasoning, literature comparison, and awareness of the author as a crafter of material—one who makes decisions in his writing and acts on them. These second graders have an open invitation to notice, to wonder, and to connect. As discussion leader, Ms. Gonzalez knows she has a role to play, but the use of language to express thought is becoming well established. She asks fewer questions now; she doesn't need to prompt as frequently as she once did; she waits her turn to talk. The three sharings have become embedded, and talk takes center stage.

Focus on Listening

Strategy: Guiding Active, Purposeful Listening During Sharing Time

When language arts specialists talk about listening, they often refer to it as the neglected language art. It is, many contend, what children are asked to do most and taught to do least (Devine, 1978). Funk and Funk (1989) maintain that there are a number of reasons for the neglect. Some teachers believe that listening develops naturally and so does not need to be taught. Others believe it cannot be taught or evaluated. (For example, the new "essential knowledge and skills" for language arts in Texas include "listening," leaving many teachers speculating whether there may eventually be a state "basic skills" test for listening.) And some teachers may not have been taught to teach listening and so feel diffident about teaching it.

Yet if we borrowed from the well-accepted guidelines for teaching the other language arts, we could speculate that good listening instruction would be meaningful to children, would occur throughout the day, would sometimes be brought to a conscious level with strategy help ("What are some good ways we can show Felipe we're listening?"), and would be varied in purposes, setting, and tasks. We can assume it involves more than simply telling someone to do it (Watson, 1985). And, contrary to the tables of contents in the newest books on early literacy, the skills of listening are far more demanding than hearing the separate sounds in spoken words. Children may be phonemically aware and still not be good listeners.

Application: How the Strategy Looks

Researcher Pat Edwards (1996) asked two kindergarten teachers in a school serving working-class families of varied income, ethnic, and educational backgrounds what they were least satisfied with in their instructional program. Both teachers had the same immediate answer: sharing time. Sharing time in these classrooms, as in many classrooms across the country, had come to mean one child holding up yet another Barbie or a new pair of tennis shoes while 17 others lay comatose on the rug. Edwards worked with the teachers and the children's parents to make sharing time a better language experience. As children became more aware of the audience for their speech, the listeners became more aware of what the speaker was trying to do. For example, as speakers learned to make more interesting choices about what to talk about and how to capture attention, use eye contact, and make sure that listeners could see and hear, the listeners were also learning to have expectations from speakers—a step toward active listening.

> "I can't hear what she is saying," piped a 5-year-old voice. "She does need to talk louder," Mrs. Bowker agreed, "but remember, you need to watch her very carefully" (p. 348).

In fact, both teachers came to believe that kindergartners "learned far more about listening in sharing time now that their classmates had something interesting to say" (p. 347). Each week the teachers saw evidence of learning by listening. And, although the teachers did not focus on listening instruction, they melded speaking and listening instruction in sharing time. It is possible to imagine the next steps: preparation for purposefully listening to a visiting veterinarian, a demonstration of pinata making, a grandmother's story, or a video on the water cycle.

Focus on Viewing

Strategy: Providing Opportunities to Comprehend, Interpret and Represent Understandings

Recently, literacy educators have been expanding their definitions of "ways of knowing" to include a wider variety of acceptable texts and sign systems that are not necessarily print or even language-based (Leland & Harste, 1994). Including "viewing" as a language art

AN IDEA FROM A TEACHER

Using Buddies to Increase Voluntary Reading

I have a class of children with special needs. The children in my class are often discouraged when it comes to reading and have low self-esteem in regard to making friends. To increase voluntary reading both at home and during the school day and to build my students' self-esteem, I invite children from other classes in the school to buddy read with my class. Twice each week the buddy readers come to the room and bring their favorite easy reader books from their home. (I tell the buddies ahead of time to select simpler texts, to facilitate sharing.) Then the buddies lend the book they read to the children in my class. (I tell the buddies to select books that could be replaced in case of damage or loss, although this has never been necessary.) My students are then able to read the buddy's book during their free time and at home. Each student is motivated to read because there is a sense of pride attached to having been lent a book from a peer or older admired person. They share the books with each other, and because they are familiar with the story, they can read or retell the story to their classmates and families at home.

Maria Ramos, First/Second-Grade Teacher

acknowledges that multiple sign systems and tools are available both to interpret and to represent our understandings and perspectives. Viewing does not equate with technical prowess, even though media in many forms (computers, video, television, film) have come to be accepted as appropriate vehicles for literacy instruction (Flood, Heath, & Lapp, 1997; Labbo, Reinking, & McKenna, 1999). Nor does viewing equate just with visual appreciation, although, for example, the potential of picture books to increase visual literacy has not been fully exploited (Kiefer, 1995). Children at very young ages understand, interpret, and represent their interpretations of meanings in a variety of ways. Hubbard (1989), for example, studied children's meaning making with drawings before and as they wrote. Saul (1989) prepares teachers to reach for the essence of the literature they will share with children by representing its meanings visually before they introduce and discuss it. Students who move, dance, compose, paint, film, draw, tape, graph, or map their interpretations or understandings—or interpret others' representations—are demonstrating viewing and representing.

Application: How the Strategy Looks

Ms. Frizzle of Joanna Cole's *The Magic School Bus* series renown is not the only teacher who provides hands-on learning opportunities and encourages her students to develop and show their understanding in myriad ways. Leland and Harste (1994) describe a study by Berghoff of first graders at work:

> In the inquiry into Colonial America, children were invited to be museum curators, inhabit an Indian wigwam, make quilts, read poetry rhythmically to the beat of drums, hear Indian legends, tell math stories using the flannel board cutouts of Pilgrims and the Mayflower, view art of the era, draw portraits of themselves and their friends, and paint with dyes made from squash and berries (Berghoff, as cited by Leland & Harste, 1994, p. 341).

Whether children make character webs to extend understanding of a story (Bromley, 1995) or produce images of Sylvester and the Magic Pebble from the vantage point of a mathematician or artist (Leland & Harste, 1994) or compare a story with a video (Lapp, Flood, & Fisher, 1999), they are engaged in viewing and representing. Children view when they interpret the graphics in their texts and newspapers; they represent when they choose music and images to match the mood of a story or historical event. Critics fear that viewing means more television or video rolled into the classroom; instead, it may mean more movement, tools of expression, and openings for students with particular strengths.

Putting It All Together

A wealth of instructional recommendations for teaching young children have been offered in this book. Our intent was to focus on just a few time-honored and research-supported activities that enrich and enliven language arts instruction. As was clearly pointed out by the International Reading Association in its 1998 position statement on beginning reading, "There is no single method or single combination of methods that can successfully teach all children to read. Therefore, teachers must have a strong knowledge of multiple methods . . . and a strong knowledge of children." The same current flows through listening, speaking, writing, and viewing.

Although each section of this chapter has highlighted just one of the language arts, each practice still standing requires that children use *all* of their language facility productively and purposefully. And, within each seemingly straightforward practice, there are implications for resources, teacher preparation, community involvement, and for both change and refusal to change. The common thread linking successful teaching is trust in the capacity of children and the infinite creativity of teachers to ensure that beginning reading and writing are just that—the beginning.

References

Allington, R. (1977). If they don't read much, how they ever gonna get good? *Journal of Reading, 21,* 57–61.

Anderson, R. C., Wilson, P. T., & Fielding, L. G. (1988). Growth in reading and how children spend their time outside of school. *Reading Research Quarterly, 23,* 285–303.

Austin, M. C., & Morrison, C. (1963). *The first R: The Harvard report on reading in elementary schools.* New York: Macmillan.

Avery, C. (1993). *And with a light touch: Learning about reading, writing, and teaching with first graders.* Portsmouth, NH: Heinemann.

Baker, S. (1995). *Vocabulary acquisition: Curricular and instructional implications for diverse learners.* Bloomington: Indiana University, National Center to Improve the Tools for Educators. (ERIC Document Reproduction Service No. 386861)

Battle, J. (1995). Collaborative story talk in a bilingual kindergarten. In N. L. Roser & M. G. Martinez (Eds.), *Book talk and beyond: Children and teachers respond to literature* (pp. 157–167). Newark, DE: International Reading Association.

Baumann, J. F., Hoffman, J. V., Moon, J., & Duffy-Hester, A. M. (1998). Where are teachers' voices in the phonics/whole language debate? Results from a survey of U.S. elementary classroom teachers. *The Reading Teacher, 51,* 636–650.

Bear, D. R., & Templeton, S. (1998). Explorations in developmental spelling: Foundations for learning and teaching phonics, spelling, and vocabulary. *The Reading Teacher, 52,* 222–242.

Bromley, K. (1995). Enriching response to literature with webbing. In N. L. Roser & M. G. Martinez (Eds.), *Book talk and beyond: Children and teachers respond to literature.* Newark, DE: International Reading Association.

Chambers, A. (1985). *Booktalk: Occasional writing on literature and children.* New York: Harper & Row.

Chomsky, C. (1971). Write now, read later. *Childhood Education, 47,* 296–299.

Cole, J. (1987). *The magic school bus: Inside the earth.* New York: Scholastic.

Cunningham, P., & Stanovich, K. (1990). Assessing print exposure and orthographic processing skill in children: A quick measure of reading experience. *Journal of Educational Psychology, 82,*733–740.

Cunningham, P., & Stanovich, K. (1991) Tracking the unique effects of print exposure in children: Associations with vocabulary, general knowledge, and spelling. *Journal of Educational Psychology, 83,* 264–274.

Cunningham, P., & Stanovich, K. (1997). Early reading acquisition and its relation to reading experience and ability ten years later. *Development Psychology 33*(6), 934–945.

Dahl, K., & Farnan, N. (1998). *Children's writing: Perspectives from research.* Newark, DE: International Reading Association.

dePaola, T. (1984). *The quicksand book.* New York: Holiday House.

Devine, T. G. (1978) Listening: What do we know after fifty years of research and theorizing? *Journal of Reading, 21,* 296–304.

Durkin, D. (1966). *Children who read early: Two longitudinal studies.* New York: Teachers College Press.

Dyson, A. H. (1989). *Multiple world of child writers: Friends learning to write.* New York: Teachers College Press.

Edwards, P. A. (1989). Supporting lower SES mothers' attempts to provide scaffolding for book reading. In J. Allen & J. Mason (Eds.), *Risk makers, risk takers, risk breakers: Reducing the risks for young literacy learners.* Portsmouth, NH: Heinemann.

Edwards, P. A. (1996). Creating sharing time conversations: Parents and teachers work together. *Language Arts, 73,* 344–349.

Eeds, M., & Wells, D. (1989). Grand conversations: An exploration of meaning construction in literature study groups. *Research in the Teaching of English, 23,* 4–29.

Flood, J., Heath, S. B., & Lapp, D. (Eds.). (1997). *Handbook of research on teaching literacy through the communication and visual arts.* New York: Macmillan.

Flood, J., Jensen, J. M., Lapp, D., & Squire, J. (Eds.). (1991). *Handbook of research on teaching the English language arts.* New York: Macmillan.

Flood, J., Lapp, D., Goss, K., LeTourneau, M., Moore, J., & Fisher, D. (1999). *An investigation of the relationship between literary and world knowledge and reading ability of kindergartners and first graders.* Paper presented at a meeting of the International Reading Association, San Diego.

Foorman, B. R., Francis, D. J., Fletcher, J. M., Schatschneider, C., & Mehta, P. (1998). The role of instruction in learning to read: Preventing reading failure in at-risk children. *Journal of Educational Psychology, 90,* 37–55.

Fountas, I. C., & Pinnell, G. S. (1996). *Guided reading: Good first teaching for all children.* Portsmouth, NH: Heinemann.

Funk, H. D., & Funk, G. D. (1989). Guidelines for developing listening skills. *The Reading Teacher, 42,* 660–663.

Graves, D. H. (1994). *A fresh look at writing.* Portsmouth, NH: Heinemann.

Henderson, E. H., Estes, T., & Stonecash, S. (1972). An exploratory study of word acquisition among first graders at midyear in a language experience approach. *Journal of Reading Behavior, 4,* 21–30.

Henderson, E. H., & Beers, J. W. (Eds.). (1980). *Developmental and cognitive aspects of learning to spell: A reflection of word knowledge.* Newark, DE: International Reading Association.

Hubbard, R. (1989). *Authors of pictures, draughtsmen of words.* Portsmouth, NH: Heinemann.

International Reading Association. (1998). Learning to read and write: Developmentally appropriate practices for young children. A joint position statement of the International Reading Association (IRA) and National Association for the Education of Young Children (NAEYC). *Young Children, 53,* 30–46.

Kiefer, B. Z. (1995). *The potential of picturebooks: From visual literacy to aesthetic understanding.* Englewood Cliffs, NJ: Merrill.

Labbo, L. D., Reinking, D., & McKenna, M. C. (1999). The use of technology in literacy programs. In L. B. Gambrell, L. M. Morrow, S. B. Neuman, & M. Pressley (Eds.), *Best practices in literacy instruction* (pp. 311–327). New York: Guilford.

Lapp, D., Flood, J., & Fisher, D. (1999). Intermediality: How the use of multiple media enhances learning [Column]. *The Reading Teacher, 52,* 776–780.

Lapp, D., Flood, J, Fisher, D., & VanDyke, J. (1999). *The effects of access to print through use of the community library on the reading fluency, attitudes and performance of students from diverse ages, cultures, and socioeconomic groups.* Paper presented at the 49th Annual National Reading Conference, Orlando, FL.

Lapp, D., Flood, J., & Goss K. (in press). Desks don't move—students do: Ineffective classroom environments. *The Reading Teacher.*

Leland, C. H., & Harste, C. H. (1994). Multiple ways of knowing: Curriculum in a new way. *Language Arts, 71,* 337–345.

Lindfors, J. (1999). *Children's inquiry: Using language to make sense of the world.* Language and Literacy Series. New York: Teachers College Press.

Lysacker, J. (1997). Learning to read from self-selected texts: The book choices of six first graders. In C. K. Kinzer, K. A. Hinchman, & D. J. Leu (Eds.), *Inquiries in literacy: Theory and practice* (pp. 273–282). Chicago: National Reading Conference.

Martinez, M., & Teale, W. (1988). Reading in a kindergarten classroom library. *The Reading Teacher, 41,* 568-573.

Martinez, M., Cheyney, M., McBroom, C., Hemmeter, A., & Teale, W. H. (1989). No-risk kindergarten literacy environments for at-risk children. In J. Allen & J. Mason (Eds.), *Risk makers, risk takers, risk breakers: Reducing the risks for young literacy learners* (pp. 93–124). Portsmouth, NH: Heinemann.

Martinez, M., Roser, N., Hoffman, J., & Battle, J. (1992). Fostering better book discussions through response logs and a response framework: A case description. In C. K. Kinzer & D. J. Leu (Eds.), *Literacy research, theory, and practice: Views from many perspectives.* Forty-first yearbook of the National Reading Conference (pp. 303–311). Chicago: National Reading Conference.

Martinez, M., Roser, N., Worthy, J., Strecker, S., & Gough, P. (1997). Classroom libraries and children's book selections: Redefining "access" in self-selected reading. In C. K. Kinzer, K. A. Hinchman, & D. J. Leu (Eds.), *Inquiries in literacy: Theory and practice* (pp. 265–272). Chicago: National Reading Conference.

McGee, L. M. (1992). An exploration of meaning construction in first graders' grand conversations. In C. K. Kinzer & D. J. Leu (Eds.), *Literacy research, theory, and practice: Views from many perspectives.* Forty-first yearbook of the National Reading Conference (pp. 177–186). Chicago: National Reading Conference.

Miller-Rodriguez, K. (1998). Home writing activities: The writing briefcase and the traveling suitcase. In R. Allington (Ed.), *Teaching struggling readers: Advice for helping children with reading/learning disabilities* (pp. 300–301). Newark, DE: International Reading Association.

Morrow, L. M. (1988). Young children's responses to one-to-one readings in school settings. *Reading Research Quarterly, 23,* 89–107.

Morrow, L. M. (1993). *Literacy development in the early years: Helping children read and write* (2nd ed.). Boston: Allyn & Bacon.

Morrow, L. M. (1997). *The literacy center: Contexts for reading and writing.* York, ME: Stenhouse.

Morrow, L. M., Tracey, D. H., & Maxwell, C. M. (Eds.). (1995). *A survey of family literacy in the United States.* Newark, DE: International Reading Association.

Morrow, L. M., & Weinstein, C. (1982). Increasing children's use of literature through program and physical design changes. *Elementary School Journal, 83,* 131–137.

Pierce, K. M. (1996). Getting started: Establishing a reading/writing classroom. In K. G. Short, J. C. Harste, & C. Burke (Eds.), *Creating classrooms for authors and inquirers* (2nd ed., pp. 151–167). Portsmouth, NH: Heinemann.

Read, C. (1971). Pre-school children's knowledge of English phonology. *Harvard Educational Review, 41,* 1–34.

Richgels, D. J., & Wold, L. S. (1998). Literacy on the road: Backpacking partnerships between school and home. *The Reading Teacher, 52,* 18–29.

Roser, N. (1995). Writing all say in first grade. In *Write idea* (Vol. 1, p. 26). New York: Macmillan/McGraw-Hill.

Roser, N. L., Hoffman, J. V., & Farest, C. (1990). Language, literature, and at-risk children. *The Reading Teacher, 43,* 554–559.

Saul, E. W. (1989). "What did Leo feed the turtle?" and other nonliterary questions. *Language Arts, 66,* 295–303.

Snow, C. E., Burns, M. S., & Griffin, P. (Eds.). (1998). *Preventing reading difficulties in young children.* Washington, DC: National Academy Press.

Steig, W. (1979). *Sylvester and the magic pebble.* New York: Windmill.

Strickland, D. S. (1998). What's basic in beginning reading? Finding common ground. *Educational Leadership, 55,* 6–10.

Strickland, D. S., Morrow, L. M., Feitelson, D., & Iraqi, J. (1990). Storybook reading: A bridge to literary language. *The Reading Teacher, 44,* 264–265.

Taylor, B. M., Frye, B. J., & Maruyama, G. M. (1990). Time spent reading and reading growth. *American Educational Research Journal, 27,* 351–362.

Vygotsky, L. S. (1978). *Mind in society.* Cambridge: Harvard University Press.

Watson, E. D. (1985). Sit up, pay attention and clear your desks! *Early Years, 15,* 58–59.

ABOUT THE EDITORS AND CONTRIBUTORS

Kathryn H. Au is a professor of education at the University of Hawaii. She has taught kindergarten through grade 2. Her research interest focuses on the school literacy development of students of diverse cultural and linguistic backgrounds, and she has published numerous articles in this field. She serves on the board of directors of the International Reading Association and is a past president of the National Reading Conference. She is a recipient of the Oscar S. Causey Award for outstanding contributions to reading research and is a member of the Reading Hall of Fame.

Sue Bredekamp is director of research of the Council for Early Childhood Professional Recognition and a senior consultant to the Head Start Bureau. Between 1984 and 1998, she served as director of professional development and accreditation of the National Association for the Education of Young Children (NAEYC). She coauthored the 1998 joint position statement of the International Reading Association and the NAEYC. She is also the primary author of the NAEYC's *Developmentally Appropriate Practice in Early Childhood Programs* (1987 and 1997 editions). Dr. Bredekamp holds a doctorate in early childhood education from the University of Maryland.

Jo Ann Brewer is associate professor of education at Salem State College, Salem, Massachusetts. She teaches courses in reading, early childhood education, and children's literature. She was a kindergarten teacher for many years before earning a doctorate in early childhood education from Texas Tech University. She has held several administrative positions in higher education and served as an assistant superintendent for curriculum for a school system. Her university experience includes positions at Oregon State University and Northern Arizona University.

Karen Bromley is a professor at the State University of New York at Binghamton. Formerly she taught third grade and was a K–6 reading specialist in New York and Maryland. She obtained her doctorate from the University of Maryland. Her research interests are classroom literacy instruction and the writing process. She has written several books for teachers.

Bernice E. Cullinan is a professor of early childhood and elementary education at New York University, where she specializes in children's literature, language arts, and reading. She is a member of the editorial board of *The New Advocate* and a book reviewer for *The Horn Book Guide*. Dr. Cullinan taught elementary school for 15 years before receiving her doctorate from Ohio State University. She is past president of both the International Reading Association and the IRA Reading Hall of Fame. She is a recipient of the Arbuthnot Award for Outstanding Teacher of Children's Literature.

Ann Dromsky is a doctoral student and fellow at the University of Maryland at College Park. She has held both elementary and middle school teaching positions. Her research interests center on the use of expository reading texts in primary grades and early literacy comprehension. In addition to her academic work, she is a consultant to the program Reading Is Fundamental, in Washington, D.C., on literacy intervention projects. She has published several chapters and contributes to the *Maryland State Journal* of the International Reading Association.

James Flood, a professor of reading and language development at San Diego State University, has taught in preschool, elementary, and secondary schools and has been a language arts supervisor and vice principal. He has also been a Fulbright scholar at the University of Lisbon in Portugal and president of the National Reading Conference. Dr. Flood has chaired and co-chaired many IRA, NCTE, NCRE, and NRC committees. Currently he teaches preservice and graduate courses at SDSU. He has co-authored and edited many articles, columns, texts, and handbooks on reading and language arts issues. His many educational awards include being named Outstanding Teacher Educator in the Department of Teacher Education at SDSU, Distinguished Research Lecturer in SDSU's Graduate Division of Research, and a member of the California Reading Hall of Fame.

Lee Galda is a professor of children's literature at the University of Minnesota. After receiving her doctorate from New York University, she taught for many years at the University of Georgia. She has co-authored a book of literature for children and published numerous articles on reading. She also served as the children's books column editor for *The Reading Teacher* from 1989 to 1993 and as co-editor of the "Professional Resources" column for *The New Advocate* from 1996 to 1998. Dr. Galda has served on a number of committees involving research and children's literature.

Linda B. Gambrell is professor and director of the School of Education at Clemson University. She received her doctorate from the University of Maryland in curriculum and instruction, reading education. Before assuming her position at Clemson University she was associate dean of research in the College of Education at the University of Maryland. She began her career as an elementary classroom teacher and reading specialist. She has co-authored books on reading instruction and published numerous articles in research and practitioner journals. In 1998 she was the recipient of the International Reading Association's Outstanding Teacher Educator in Reading award. In 1999 she served as president of the National Reading Conference. Her current interests are in the areas of reading comprehension strategy instruction, literacy motivation, and the role of discussion in teaching and learning.

Celia Genishi is a professor of education in the Department of Curriculum and Teaching, Teachers College, Columbia University. She is a former secondary Spanish and preschool teacher and now teaches courses in early childhood education and qualitative research methods. Previously she was on the faculty at the University of Texas at Austin and Ohio State University. She has co-authored and edited books on the assessment of children's work. Her main interests include collaborative research with teachers on alternative assessment, childhood bilingualism, and language use in classrooms.

Bill Harp is a professor of language arts and literacy in the Graduate School of Education at the University of Massachusetts–Lowell, where he teaches in the graduate program. His elementary school teaching experience ranges from Head Start through sixth grade, and he has served as an elementary school principal and director of programs for the gifted. Dr. Harp earned his doctorate in curriculum and instruction, with an emphasis on reading, at the University of Oregon, Eugene. His university experience includes positions at the University of Delaware, Oregon State University, and Northern Arizona University.

Diane Lapp, professor of reading and language in the Department of Education at San Diego State University, has taught in elementary and middle schools. Dr. Lapp, who co-directs and teaches field-based preservice and graduate courses, spent her recent sabbatical leave team teaching in a public school first-grade classroom.

Although her leave has been completed, she continues to team teach in a first-grade classroom every morning. Dr. Lapp has co-authored or edited many articles and books on reading and language arts issues. She has also chaired and co-chaired several IRA and NRC committees. Her many educational awards include being named Outstanding Teacher Educator and Faculty Member in the Department of Teacher Education at SDSU, Distinguished Research Lecturer in SDSU's Graduate Division of Research, a member of the California Reading Hall of Fame, and IRA's 1996 Outstanding Teacher Educator of the Year.

Lesley Mandel Morrow is a professor in Rutgers University's Graduate School of Education and coordinator of the graduate literacy programs. She began her career as a classroom teacher, became a reading specialist, and received her doctorate from Fordham University in New York City. She has done extensive research in the area of early literacy development and has published numerous books and journal articles. She has received awards for excellence in teaching and research from Rutgers University. She was an elected member of the board of directors of the International Reading Association and received the IRA's Outstanding Teacher Educator of Reading award. She has also served as a principal research investigator for the National Reading Research Center. Dr. Morrow is presently serving as an elected member of the board of directors of the National Reading Conference. She received Fordham University's Alumni Award for Outstanding Achievement.

Margaret Moustafa received her doctorate in education from the University of Southern California and is a professor of education at California State University, Los Angeles. She is an experienced elementary-grade teacher and teacher educator. Her publications include articles and books about the role of phonics in reading instruction. The teacher portraits in Chapter 10 reflect her experiences as a researcher, teacher, and teacher educator working to create instruction in letter-sound correspondences compatible with children's cognitive and linguistic processes.

Susan B. Neuman is a professor in the Educational Studies Department in the School of Education at the University of Michigan, Ann Arbor. She is Director of the Center for the Improvement of Early Reading Achievement (CIERA). Her interests include beginning reading and writing, family literacy, and parental involvement. Dr. Neuman has been co-editor of the *Journal of Literacy Research* and currently serves on seven editorial boards. She is chair of the Publications Committee and a board member of the National Reading Conference, and president of the Literacy Development for Young Children Special Interest Group of the International Reading Association.

Anthony D. Pellegrini is a professor of educational psychology at the University of Minnesota. He received his doctorate in 1978 from Ohio State University. He has co-authored a book about school literacy and play. His teaching and research interests are observational methods and play.

Lucinda C. Ray is the director of curriculum development at IntelliTools, Inc., in Petaluma, California. Previously she was group product marketing manager of The Learning Company's School Division and education product manager at Broderbund Software. She was an English teacher and drama director at the middle school, high school, and college levels in Massachusetts, Vermont, and Iowa; her master's degree is from the Bread Loaf School of English. Her research interests include multimedia in literacy development and instructional design in electronic learning tools. Her publications include teacher's guides for software and several book chapters on literacy and technology.

Nancy Roser is a professor of language and literacy studies and the Flawn professor of early childhood education in the College of Education at the University of Texas at Austin. A former elementary schoolteacher, Dr. Roser now teaches preservice and graduate classes in elementary reading and language arts. She is co-editor of two books as well as chapters and articles related to the teaching of reading and language arts. She is a member of the IRA's Research Committee and the Committee Against Censorship of the National Council of Teachers of English. She served as co-director of the project that helped to produce the standards for the English language arts in Texas. She received the Texas Outstanding College/University English Language Arts Award from the Texas Council of Teachers of English for 2000.

Susan Stires taught for 30 years in rural and urban elementary schools, most recently as a primary grade teacher at the Center for Teaching and Learning, a demonstration school in Maine. She now works as a consultant in literacy acquisition and development while pursuing an advanced degree at Teachers College, Columbia University. Her publications are about teaching reading and writing to elementary and special students. She recently finished a book on teacher research in reading and writing with the support of a Spencer grant.

Dorothy S. Strickland is the State of New Jersey Professor of Reading at Rutgers University. She is past president of both the International Reading Association and the IRA Reading Hall of Fame. Her publications include many books. She received the 1994 NCTE Rewey Belle Inglis Award as Outstanding Woman in the Teaching of English, the National Council of Teachers of English 1998 Award as Outstanding Educator in the Language Arts, and the IRA's Outstanding Teacher Educator of Reading award.

William H. Teale is a professor of education at the University of Illinois at Chicago, where he also serves as director of the UIC Reading Clinic. His research has focused mainly on early reading and writing development. His publications include chapters in many books and articles in a variety of reading, language arts, and early childhood education journals; and he is coeditor of a book on emergent literacy that has become a standard reference in the field.

Diane H. Tracey is an associate professor at Kean University, Union, New Jersey, where she teaches graduate and undergraduate courses in literacy education. Her research interests include family literacy and the role of technology in literacy education. Diane is a co-editor of a survey of family literacy and is a former member of the International Reading Association's Family Literacy Commission. Prior to her tenure at Kean University, Dr. Tracey was a doctoral student and teaching assistant at Rutgers University.

Shelley B. Wepner is currently an associate dean of the School of Human Service Professions, director of the Center for Education, and a professor of education at Widener University in Chester, Pennsylvania. She received her doctorate from the University of Pennsylvania and has been a supervisor of curriculum and instruction and reading specialist in New Jersey. Her research interests include the use of technology for literacy development and teacher education, and the leadership qualities of reading specialists and education deans. Her previous publications include three award-winning software packages and five co-edited or co-authored books on literacy.

Junko Yokota is an associate professor in the Reading and Language Department of National-Louis University, Chicago. Her work focuses on issues related to children's literature, the literacy development of culturally diverse students, and early literacy. She works with school districts in the Chicago area in staff development and curriculum development.

Donna Yung-Chan, an early childhood teacher at Public School 1 in New York City, has taught prekindergarten for 13 years. In November 1998, she received the National Board for Professional Teaching Standards certification in Early Childhood (Generalist). She also was recently awarded the Title I Distinguished Educator award from the New York State Education Department and New York City Board of Education. Ms. Yung-Chan holds a master's degree in education from Brooklyn College.

INDEXES

Author Index

Subject Index

Index to Children's Literature

Index to Computer Software